The Irish Derby

AN ILLUSTRATED HISTORY

1962–1995

THE
Irish Derby
AN ILLUSTRATED HISTORY
—— 1962–1995 ——

DANIEL RODDY

GILL & MACMILLAN

Gill & Macmillan Ltd
Goldenbridge
Dublin 8
with associated companies throughout the world
© Daniel Roddy 1995
0 7171 2120 8

Index compiled by Gloria Greenwood
Print origination by Identikit Design Consultants, Dublin
Printed by ColourBooks Ltd, Dublin

A catalogue record is available for this book
from the British Library.

1 3 5 4 2

CONTENTS

FOR MY MOTHER

ACKNOWLEDGMENTS

I must extend my most profound thanks to the staff of the Gilbert Library, Pearse Street, Dublin, in particular Maura Kennedy and Jimmy McLoughlin, for their assistance and patience in dealing with me, which was greatly appreciated. Likewise, the staffs of the National Library, Dun Laoghaire and Deansgrange libraries, all of whom were unfailingly helpful. I owe a special debt of gratitude to Jim Marsh, recently retired Manager of the Curragh Racecourse, for extending the facilities of the Turf Club library to me, and indeed for lending me some priceless racecards.

Among others I must single out Barbara Durack of Radio Telefís Éireann for her generous assistance, and I would like to thank especially Dr Vincent O'Brien who despite ill health was most courteous and helpful. May I also extend my grateful thanks to the many racing journalists associated with the Irish newspapers, on whose original work through the decades I have shamelessly drawn in the course of the following pages.

The Timeform Ratings quoted — which are copyright — are taken from the 'Racehorses' series and appear by kind permission of Timeform.

I am greatly indebted to Christine Moore for providing me with back numbers of such valuable magazines as *Pacemaker International* and *The Blood-Horse*. My good friends Noel Murphy and David Grafton were a fund of useful ideas and suggestions.

Finally, I could not have got to the finishing line without tremendous work from Marie, who deciphered my handwriting and helped to put a coherent shape on what often seemed to me to be an unintelligible mess. Thank you, Marie.

D.R.
July 1995

ILLUSTRATIONS

The Author and Publishers wish to thank the following photographers and photographic agencies for permission to reproduce their work in this book.

Jim Connolly

Liam Healy

Caroline Norris

INPHO

Where appropriate, each photograph is identified by the photographer's initials.

INTRODUCTION

The Irish Derby had an inauspicious beginning. The inaugural running of the classic took place at the Curragh on Wednesday 27 June 1866 and English trainer James Cockin had the honour of saddling the first winner, Selim, in a race which attracted only three runners. Cockin was to go on to train three Irish Derby winners in all, but the race in those early years was not of high quality.

In fact for the first six years of its existence the Derby was run over a distance of an extended mile and six furlongs. Only in 1872 was the distance reduced to one and a half miles.

Other factors which prevented the Irish Derby from being spoken of in the same breath as its Epsom counterpart were the conditions which provided for a scale of weights and penalties. Accordingly, it was in no sense a true championship race and indeed it was not until as late as 1946 that the Irish Derby came into line with Epsom, with all colts carrying the same weight.

This is not to say that some famous horses did not win the Irish Derby in the ninety-six years prior to its transformation through sponsorship in 1962. The most illustrious name associated with the Irish Derby was of course Orby, who in 1907 became the first horse to complete the Epsom and Irish Derby double. A further fifty-seven years were to elapse before Orby's feat would be repeated.

Trained by the legendary Richard 'Boss' Croker, after his Epsom victory Orby was accorded a reception upon his return to Dublin which far surpassed in fervour that given to contemporaneous visits by members of the British royal family. Scarcely a surprise, that! The doubtless apocryphal greeting of an old woman to Croker after Orby's triumphant return — 'Thank God and you, sir, we have lived to see a Catholic horse win the Derby' — summed up the popular mood in Ireland and Croker, a bit of a scoundrel if truth be told, was made a Freeman of the City of Dublin.

There were other notable feats associated with the Irish Derby. The great Gallinule, commemorated annually in a race named after him at the Curragh, sired the winner of every Irish Derby but one between the years 1895 and 1901. Included in that number was the filly Gallinaria in the year 1900. It was to be another ninety years before another filly would triumph in the classic primarily the preserve of the colts. Gallinule also sired another famous filly, Pretty Polly, whose name will also be familiar to Curragh racegoers.

Between the two world wars Irish flat racing was in a state of stagnation. In the decade 1922–1932 every Irish Derby, with one exception, fell to an English-trained horse. The Irish Derby in fact became little more than a consolation prize for failed English classic contenders.

The Second World War, paradoxically, saw something of an improvement in the fortunes of Irish-trained horses. Among the Irish Derby winners during the war years was the late Joe McGrath's great unbeaten colt, Windsor Slipper, in the view of some respected judges the best horse ever to have been trained in Ireland.

Nathoo, a son of McGrath's outstanding stallion, Nasrullah, won the 1948 Irish Derby for the Aga Khan. Nasrullah was subsequently exported to the United States where he became one of the most influential sires of the century. Among his progeny were American 'horses of the year' Nashua and Bold Ruler, the Epsom Derby winner Never Say Die, and Never Bend, perhaps best known on this side of the Atlantic as the sire of Mill Reef.

The 1950s ushered in a period of sustained progress for Irish racing. In 1951, for instance, four of the five English classics fell to horses bred in Ireland. In the course of the decade two names came to prominence whose outstanding achievements were to help elevate the status of Irish flat racing on to an altogether higher plane. I refer of course to the late Paddy Prendergast and to the incomparable Vincent O'Brien.

Horses trained in Ireland enjoyed increasing success both at home and more importantly abroad. After a somewhat unlucky second in the Epsom Derby the Seamus McGrath-trained Panaslipper won the Irish Derby in 1955. Ballymoss followed a similar path two years later and in the following year, 1958, Vincent O'Brien's great champion dominated the European racing scene. The Coronation Cup, the Eclipse Stakes, the King George VI and Queen Elizabeth Stakes and finally the Prix de l'Arc de Triomphe all fell to owner Mr John McShain's marvellous colt. In the same year, 1958, young Michael Rogers saddled Hard Ridden to win the Epsom Derby, in the process bridging a gap of over fifty years since Orby had last registered an Irish success in the world's most prestigious classic.

In retrospect one can see that the Irish Sweeps Derby was an event waiting to happen. The brainchild of the aforementioned Joe McGrath, the inaugural running in 1962 of the newly sponsored race was a watershed in the history of Irish flat racing. As Fergus D'Arcy puts it in his erudite and entertaining account of the history of the Irish Turf Club: 'It would be difficult to overstate the impact of the Irish Sweeps Derby of 1962 in launching Irish racing into the forefront of the sport internationally.'

The following three decades represented in general a period of consolidation of the new and enhanced reputation of Ireland's premier classic race. True, there have been substandard renewals and occasional fallow periods in the course of the 1970s and 1980s when the race appeared to be in danger of decline. Any such fears, however, were laid to rest with the arrival in 1986 of the latest sponsors to be associated with the Irish Derby, Anheuser-Busch. A significant increase in the prize fund, together with improvements in both the marketing and staging of the Derby, have combined to ensure that the international standing of Ireland's premier classic is at its highest ever level.

Indeed, without being unduly chauvinistic, it is arguable that the Budweiser Irish Derby has in some respects made significant advances *vis-à-vis* its Epsom counterpart in recent years. In contrast to recent experience at Epsom, the Curragh has enjoyed increased attendances and in addition there has been a genuine championship feel about a number of recent Budweiser Irish Derby renewals. Certainly the list of recent winners of Ireland's most prestigious classic makes for impressive reading.

In this book I have set out primarily to give an account of the thirty-four races that have taken place since the first sponsored Irish Derby was run in 1962. In addition I have tried to place each Irish Derby firmly within the context of the classic year in Europe. In some years this has proved quite easy; in others rather more difficult. I believe, however, that it is important to view the race in this wider perspective rather than simply take it as an isolated event without significance beyond itself.

Approaching the end of the twentieth century there is now little doubt that the Budweiser Irish Derby stands comparison with the best Derbies run anywhere in the world. Great credit is due to all those down through the years who have helped to bring about this most commendable state of affairs, in itself a source of great pride to all involved in the Irish horse racing industry.

1962 IRISH SWEEPS DERBY

THE CURRAGH 30 JUNE 1962

No event in Irish racing history captured the public imagination in quite the same way as did the inaugural running in 1962 of the Irish Sweeps Derby. The brainchild of the late Joe McGrath, the Irish Hospitals Sweepstakes organisation had since 1930 been running sweeps on English horse racing. The first such sweep was on the 1930 Manchester November Handicap and in the following year a sweepstake was inaugurated on the Epsom Derby. A man with a keen interest and involvement in Irish racing as an owner, breeder and also Turf legislator, McGrath decided in 1960 to transfer the sweep on the Epsom Derby to its Irish equivalent. He believed that the international standing of the Hospitals Sweepstakes could be harnessed to upgrade the status of the hitherto down-market Curragh classic so that it could be spoken of in the same breath as the corresponding races at Epsom, Chantilly and Churchill Downs.

His proposal was enthusiastically taken up by the ruling bodies of Irish racing, the Turf Club and the Racing Board, and the detailed planning which was to lead to the inauguration in 1962 of the revamped Irish Derby began. It is beyond the scope of this present work to detail the exhaustive and exhausting work which culminated in the successful launch of the Irish Sweeps Derby in June 1962. Among the matters which had to be dealt with, however, were sheep-grazing rights at the Curragh (voluntarily surrendered by owners such as the Aga Khan, Paddy Prendergast and the McGrath family) and the passage through the Dáil of legislation providing for the fencing in of the entire area of the Curragh, a venture requiring six miles of fencing.

There followed a torrent of media publicity in the months preceding the 1962 Derby, most of it engineered by the late Captain Spencer Freeman's publicity machine. The efforts of the team involved in promoting and staging the upgraded Irish Derby proved to be an outstanding success. (Paddy Connolly, the then manager of the Curragh racecourse, should be mentioned particularly in this regard.) Entries for the 1962 Sweeps Derby poured in from all parts of the globe, resulting in a world record first entry of 627 for the prestige event.

The contribution of £30,000 (the sum was suggested by the late Captain Spencer Freeman) towards the prize fund for the Irish Derby by the Irish Hospitals Sweepstakes meant that not only was the Curragh classic elevated far beyond its previous status as a minor consolation prize for Epsom Derby also-rans, but in fact in those early years the Irish Sweeps Derby was able to lay claim to the proud boast that it was the richest race in Europe.

A simple illustration of the transformation effected can be demonstrated by comparing the pre-sponsorship prize money with that received by the connections of the first Sweeps winner. In 1961 the 33/1 chance, Your Highness, garnered for his owner the princely sum of £7,921 5s. as a reward for his being first past the judge. The 1962 winner, by contrast, earned for his fortunate owner the very handsome prize of £50,027 10s. From 1962 onwards the Irish Derby could justifiably claim to be one of the two or three supreme championship tests for three-year-old thoroughbreds.

30 June 1962 thus marked the beginning of a new era for flat racing in Ireland. The Irish sporting public, not unexpectedly, clasped the new race to its collective bosom. From the early hours on that last Saturday in June all roads led to the Curragh: as early as 10.00 a.m. there was a steady flow of traffic towards the great plain of the Curragh of Kildare. By noon thousands were arriving on special trains, two of which had come from Belfast, direct to the siding which had been specially provided by CIE for the occasion. By the time racing was due to commence at 2.00 p.m. with the Midsummer Scurry Stakes a vast crowd had congregated. Some estimates put the attendance which had foregathered at more than 70,000. This was almost certainly an over-enthusiastic assessment — none the less it is doubtful if a bigger crowd has ever assembled at the Curragh than that which attended on that 1962 June Saturday.

It is often the case that a major sporting occasion fails rather dismally to live up to the expensive advance publicity which precedes it. It is gratifying to be able to record that the first running of the Irish Sweeps Derby in fact surpassed the most optimistic expectations of its promoters. Apart from the glorious pageantry of the occasion, the truly memorable climax to the race will long be remembered by all those privileged to have been there as well as by the millions watching on television.

Through the various acceptance stages the colossal first entry for the race was whittled down so that a representative field of twenty-four lined up to face the starter. What a contrast with the very first running of the Irish Derby in 1866, when a mere three contestants went to post! (Incidentally, the size of the field in the 1962 race — twenty-four — remains the biggest number assembled to face the starter in the period since the inauguration of sponsorship.)

Of the two dozen runners, four came from England, two from France and the balance were home trained — thus it was that the international dimension of the Irish Sweeps Derby was established from the very outset.

If the 1962 race had needed any extra boost, it had received precisely that as a result of the events which had occurred at Epsom just over three weeks previously. In a sensational race the Epsom Derby was won by Vincent O'Brien's Larkspur, a 22/1 outsider, but only after seven horses including the favourite Hethersett had been brought down in a mass pile-up. As a consequence of this regrettable incident some contended that Larkspur had been a lucky winner of the English classic. Well, that opinion would most certainly be put to the test for Larkspur, owned by the American Ambassador Raymond Guest, was putting his reputation firmly on the line at the Curragh.

Larkspur, who was by the Epsom Derby winner Never Say Die, had run four times as a juvenile, winning once. Prior to his Epsom triumph Larkspur had served notice of his classic potential when beating Sicilian Prince and March Wind by one length and one and a quarter lengths at Leopardstown over a mile and a half, in the process breaking the track record.

Vincent O'Brien's colt was forecast to go off favourite at the Curragh, but rather surprisingly the Ballydoyle stable jockey T. P. Glennon was on board the stable's second runner, Sebring. Earlier in the season Glennon had elected to partner Sebring in all his three-year-old races and Sebring had indeed run quite well at Epsom, finishing fifth behind Larkspur.

There was a body of opinion which favoured Sebring to reverse placings with the Epsom Derby winner, and clearly that particular argument would be resolved on the racetrack.

Among the other home-trained contenders those with the best chances of success seemed to be Arctic Storm and St Denys. The pair had finished first and second, separated by one and a quarter lengths in the Irish 2,000 Guineas, and arguments raged as to which of the two would be best suited by the longer Derby trip.

Of the English challengers Cyrus, trained by Geoffrey Brooke and ridden by Bill Rickaby, was the best fancied. After a successful two-year-old campaign, he was a prime contender for the English 2,000 Guineas, but had collided with the 'dolls' in running and had finished last. There had been signs of a return to form with a third placing at Royal Ascot. An intriguing challenger from England was the Thomson Jones-trained London Gazette. This was the Panaslipper colt who as part of the Sweeps Derby publicity campaign had been raffled by Carlow Golf Club for the princely sum of 2s. 6d. per ticket. Bought by Mrs McCalmont from the lucky winner, London Gazette had proven to be a more than useful animal, finishing a good third in the Lingfield Derby Trial. He was a lively outsider.

The French sent two horses to contest the inaugural Sweeps Derby and both were well fancied. Arcor, trained by the legendary Marcel Boussac, had been an unfancied 40/1 chance when chasing home Larkspur at a distance of two lengths at Epsom. That represented a distinct improvement on his pre-Epsom form and it was certain that Arcor would start a lot shorter than 40/1 at the Curragh.

But Arcor was not the leading French fancy for the race. The preponderance of informed opinion tended to favour his compatriot, Tambourine II. Following two early season victories the American-owned and bred colt had finished a close-up fourth in the French Derby to Val de Loir. Some thought it significant that Roger Poincelet, who had ridden Arcor at Epsom, was now to partner trainer Etienne Pollet's colt. The fact, however, that Tambourine II wore blinkers was not regarded in many quarters as being a propitious omen.

Glancing down a list of the names of the jockeys who featured in the inaugural running of the Sweeps Derby is tantamount to stepping back into a different age. Besides those mentioned elsewhere in the text, names such as Neville Sellwood, Eddie Cracknell, Willie Robinson, Dougie Page, T. P. Burns, H. J. Greenaway, Eph Smith and Scobie Breasley recall to mind an era when the sport of horse racing was less streamlined, when ownership was not concentrated in the hands of the wealthy few, when perhaps in truth racing was just a little more fun than it is nowadays. One runs the risk of allowing sentiment to take over, so let's return to reality.

One name was missing from the line-up of top-class jockeys from far and wide who were engaged to take part in the Irish Sweeps Derby of 1962. Lester Piggott was at the stage of his career when he was running into frequent scrapes with Britain's racing authorities. His riding of trainer Bob Ward's

Ione in a selling race at Lincoln, won by the stable's other runner Polly Macaw, who had been backed down from 3/1 to evens favourite, had displeased the powers that be and had landed Piggott with a two-month suspension. And so Lester was not there. But everyone else was.

The stage was set. Before a distinguished gathering which included the President, Mr de Valera, and a former president, Seán T. O'Kelly, the runners made their way to post for the second race on the card, the Irish Sweeps Derby, timed for 3.00 p.m. Betting on the big race took a fairly wide range, but reflecting Irish confidence in a home-trained success Larkspur was installed as 9/4 favourite. Next in the betting and clearly illustrating divided Ballydoyle opinion was the favourite's stable companion Sebring at 6/1. At 15/2 and attracting good money were the Irish 2,000 Guineas winner Arctic Storm and the French colt Tambourine II. It was 10/1 the second French challenger, Arcor, 100/7 St Denys, 25/1 Cyrus, and 33/1 bar these seven.

Starting stalls were not yet in operation in 1962 (the first Irish Derby to be started from stalls was in 1968), and so a huge responsibility rested upon the starter, Major Hubie Tyrell. The major did not fail the vast throng looking on, including the millions watching live on TV both in Ireland and around the world. Insisting that the horses and riders stand well back from the barrier start (compare and contrast Aintree, 1993!) Major Tyrell got them to walk in steadily, in line, and lowering his flag, the bell sounded, the voice of Michael O'Hehir boomed out over the Tannoy, and the historic race was under way.

Phil Canty on the Michael Hurley-trained St Denys was first to show. He was quickly joined by the horse won in the Carlow Golf Club raffle, London Gazette. Greville Starkey's mount did not remain long at the head of affairs, and after half a mile the Seamus McGrath-trained Gail Star moved up to race alongside St Denys. The field behind was closely bunched and there was some scrimmaging, as was inevitable.

At the half-way stage it was still St Denys who led from Gail Star, with Ticonderoga next, and Running Rock, Atlantis and Tambourine II all improving. At this stage supporters of the fancied Irish contenders Larkspur, Sebring and Arctic Storm were beginning to feel a little concerned as their fancies lay some way off the pace. They had even greater cause for concern shortly afterwards, for on the turn into the straight Roger Poincelet on Tambourine II dashed his mount into the lead. Straightening up for home Tambourine II had a good lead over St Denys, Ticonderoga, Atlantis, Larkspur, who had made up ground, Running Rock, Sebring and Solpetre.

For all the world it looked as if Poincelet had stolen the race. With two furlongs to run Tambourine II had a clear lead and his nearest pursuers were St Denys, Larkspur and Sebring, none of whom looked likely to get to the blinkered French-trained colt. It was then that the real drama of the race began. From far back in the field Bill Williamson on the Irish 2,000 Guineas winner Arctic Storm had begun to weave his way through the pack. Somewhat surprisingly Williamson, whose mount had been drawn one from the outside of the field,

persisted in making his effort on the inside and as a result encountered some traffic problems on the way. Some idea of the ground made up by Arctic Storm was that on the turn-in he was only about tenth and on the inner, and yet with just over a furlong to run the John Oxx-trained colt had the leader firmly in his sights.

From the stands it was clear that Arctic Storm was gaining with every stride on Tambourine II. In a green shirt (how appropriate!) Williamson conjured up a dramatic surge from his game partner and it seemed that what had appeared impossible was about to be achieved. With the crowd in full voice throughout the last furlong, Arctic Storm gradually cut the deficit between himself and the French-trained colt from a length, to a half-length, to a neck, and so into the final desperate last strides. With both jockeys pushing for all they were worth, the two horses flashed past the post locked together. Arctic Storm was the leader a couple of strides beyond the post, but on the line had he got up? The judge of course called for the evidence of the camera.

There followed an agonising delay while the crowd, and particularly everyone connected with the two principals, awaited the outcome of the photo finish. Naturally the vast majority of the attendance were hoping to hear the judge give the verdict to the home-trained contender. Sadly, however, it was not to be. By the narrowest of margins, a short head, Tambourine II had held the dramatic late challenge of the Irish 2,000 Guineas winner. It was five lengths further back to Sebring in third place, and jockey T. P. Glennon at least had the satisfaction of having his judgment vindicated, for his mount was two and a half lengths in front of his stable companion, the Epsom Derby winner Larkspur, who was fourth. And so, coincidentally, the second, third and fourth, all Irish trained, were ridden by Australian jockeys, for Larkspur was partnered by Scobie Breasley.

Tambourine II's time of 2 minutes 28.8 seconds was a record, beating the previous best time set by Talgo when winning the Irish Derby in 1956. When one considers the many high-class colts who both ran in and won the Irish Derby in the succeeding decades, it is perhaps surprising that it took all of thirty years for Tambourine II's 1962 record to be broken. But that's another story.

Owned by Mrs Dorothy Jackson, whose husband Howell had been president of General Motors, Tambourine II's dam was La Mirambule. Acquired by the Jacksons from France, La Mirambule won seven races including the Prix Vermeille. She was also second in the Newmarket 1,000 Guineas, the Prix de Diane and the Prix de l'Arc de Triomphe. It is worth noting that Tambourine II's sire, Princequillo, also sired Milan Mill, who never won a race herself, but went on to make her name in racing history as the dam of Mill Reef.

The post-mortems following the race were more than usually interesting. It emerged that Poincelet had completely disobeyed trainer Etienne Pollet's instructions by taking Tambourine II to the front so soon. However, the jockey explained that his mount was running very freely and he felt that he had no choice other than to let him stride on. There was no doubting that Poincelet's tactics had been crucial in fashioning Tambourine II's victory, but many commentators felt that Arctic Storm had been a very unlucky loser.

Just how unlucky he was was made clear by the colt's trainer, the late John Oxx, in an interview broadcast by RTE Radio on the eve of the 1992 Derby. (The interview had been recorded some years earlier.) Speaking to Noel Reid, the trainer revealed that Arctic Storm had returned to the unsaddling area after the 1962 race with clay on his knees. Oxx explained that Arctic Storm had struck into Larkspur's heels at a vital stage of the race and was practically brought down. As a result of this mishap, at the top of the hill Arctic Storm had only two or three horses behind him and an all but impossible task ahead of him.

In connection with Larkspur, it should be noted that Vincent O'Brien regards his Curragh defeat as one of the two most disappointing suffered by any of his horses in the Irish Derby in the period since 1962. (The other defeat will be dealt with in a later chapter.) In O'Brien's view Larkspur was suffering from the after-effects of his Epsom victory and 'when it came to getting down to it at the Curragh he didn't really stretch'. Certainly the ground could scarcely have been a factor in Larkspur's below-par display, for it was firm at both Epsom and the Curragh.

The unbiased professional view of the inaugural Sweeps Derby was articulated by Roger Mortimer who in the *Sunday Times* of 1 July 1962 wrote that Arctic Storm could be rated the best of the staying three-year-olds in England and Ireland. This judgment was proved to be sound, for in the King George VI and Queen Elizabeth Stakes at Ascot later in the summer, Arctic Storm went on to finish a close-up third to the older horses Match III and Aurelius.

Following his Curragh triumph Tambourine II had one more race in France, but only finished second. He subsequently injured a tendon and was retired to stud. He stood initially in France, but was then sent to the USA. As a sire it has to be said that he was frankly disappointing.

When the dust had settled on the inaugural running of the Sweeps Derby, universal opinion was that it had been an unqualified success. Whilst there was understandable disappointment that an Irish-trained runner had failed to win, Tambourine II's success for France did much to foster the international stature of the race, and that surely was what the promoters of the Sweeps sponsorship desired above all else.

As the final curtain descended on the Curragh on the last day of June 1962, a final curtain of a different sort rang down on that very evening in Dublin's last remaining variety theatre, the Theatre Royal, in Hawkins Street. Thus it was that as June gave way to July in the summer of 1962, memories of Tom Mix and Gracie Fields, Danny Kaye and Diana Dors were intermingled in the public consciousness with the rather less glamorous names of Tambourine II and Arctic Storm, the two colts who had fought out such a memorable and heart-stopping finish to the inaugural running of the Irish Sweeps Derby.

1M 4F

SATURDAY 30 JUNE 1962

GOING: FIRM

WINNER: Mrs Howell E. Jackson's Tambourine II by
Princequillo out of La Mirambule
R. Poincelet

SECOND: Arctic Storm by Arctic Star out of Rabina
W. Williamson

THIRD: Sebring by Aureole out of Queen of Speed
T. P. Glennon

S.P. 15/2   15/2   6/1
Winner trained by E. Pollet

ALSO: Larkspur 4th, Atlantis 5th, St Denys 6th,
Cyrus 7th, Our Guile 8th, Solpetre 9th, Trade
Wind 10th, Snowbound 11th, Arcor 12th,
Running Rock 13th, London Gazette 14th,
Le Pirate 15th, March Wind 16th, T. V. 17th,
Ticonderoga 18th, Sir Pat 19th, Borghese
20th, Mumzowa 21st, Gail Star 22nd, Talgo
Abbess 23rd, Trimatic 24th & last
Larkspur 9/4 fav
Winner: joint 3rd favourite
Distances: sh. hd, 5 lengths
Value to winner: £50,027 10s.
Time: 2 m 28.8 s
Timeform rating of winner: 133.

1963

IRISH SWEEPS DERBY

For the Irish nation, 1963 was the year of President John F. Kennedy. During the last week of June 1963, the man of Irish descent who had raised the standing of Americans of Irish origin to new heights, visited Ireland and received a reception which was to be equalled only by that accorded to the present Pontiff during his visit to Ireland in 1979. President Kennedy's visit, so extensively covered in the newspapers and on television and radio, served to confirm in the national consciousness the depth of the contribution that the small island of Ireland had made through its emigrants to the growth of the United States of America. It was no doubt the proximity of that celebratory return home of the emigrant son to the tragic events of 22 November 1963 that was responsible for imprinting memories of that particular year and its bitter climax so indelibly on the minds of Irish men and women everywhere.

As President Kennedy was leaving Shannon on Saturday 29 June 1963, the focus of racegoers was shifting inevitably towards the Curragh where the second running of the Irish Sweeps Derby was due to take place. If the late John F. Kennedy bestrode the Irish stage like a colossus in that well-remembered period, he had his equine match, it appeared, among the cast of thoroughbreds assembled for the Curragh classic.

François Mathet's Relko seemed to dominate his rivals to such an extent that the previews of the race effectively concentrated on the question of who might be second to the great French champion. Tom McGinty's article in the *Irish Independent* on the morning of the race appeared under the headline, 'Win for Relko Inevitable', and the text which followed in no way contradicted the sub-editor's succinct summary. Tony Power's preview in the *Irish Press* was headed, 'None to Oppose Relko', with a sub-head, 'Victory Assured on Epsom Form'.

A three parts brother to Match III, winner of the King George VI and Queen Elizabeth Stakes and the Washington International, Relko had enjoyed a good, if not outstanding, juvenile campaign. He had run five times and had won two of those races, being second twice and fourth once. Relko reappeared as a three-year-old in the Prix de Guiche at Longchamp and starting at odds-on he won very easily by three lengths from Vesuve. The Tanerko colt next ran in the French 2,000 Guineas (the Poule d'Essai des Poulains) at Longchamp where he impressed in beating the previously undefeated Manderley by two and a half lengths.

Improving with every race, François Mathet aimed his progressive colt at the Epsom Derby and on the day Relko proved himself to be a three-year-old of the highest class. Cantering entering the straight, Relko mowed down the opposition with contemptuous ease and won in effortless style by six clear lengths. As usual at Epsom there were excuses made for some of the beaten horses, but in the light of Relko's hugely impressive victory the stories from the losers' camps had something of a hollow ring.

Despite the all too obvious claims of the favourite, no less than sixteen horses were declared to take on Relko at the Curragh. Although the task appeared hopeless, three of those who had finished behind the French champion at Epsom threw down the gauntlet again. Paddy Prendergast's Ragusa had been third at Epsom, but had been all of nine lengths adrift. In Ragusa's favour, though, was the fact that he was an improving colt and his form had a progressive look to it.

Ragusa was a son of Ribot and as a slow maturing animal he raced only once as a juvenile. He showed plenty of promise though in that solitary venture on a racecourse, winning a seven furlong maiden at the Curragh. Ragusa progressed well physically over the winter but, with Prendergast leaving plenty to work on, the Ribot colt was unplaced on his seasonal début in the Players Navy Cut Trial Stakes at the Phoenix Park behind Lock Hard.

Stepped up to ten furlongs, Ragusa next contested the Dee Stakes at Chester where he was beaten three-quarters of a length into second place by My Myosotis. Suitably encouraged, Paddy Prendergast sent Ragusa to Epsom and considering his colt's inexperience the Rossmore Lodge trainer must have been well satisfied with his charge's fine third placing. Ragusa was sure to improve further, but then, was Relko likely to stand still? There was only one possible answer to that question, surely!

At Epsom the surprise packet of the race was Seamus McGrath's Tarqogan, who had finished fourth only a neck behind Ragusa. His form prior to Epsom was not very inspiring and it was obvious that the better ground at Epsom had contributed substantially to his improved performance. The uncertain weather in Ireland in the days prior to the Derby, which suggested that the going at the Curragh would be on the soft side, was therefore unlikely to be to Tarqogan's advantage.

Michael Rogers's Final Move had been seventeenth of the twenty-six runners at Epsom and it was reported that he just could not act on the track. His earlier Irish

form had been quite good. He had been
second to Lock Hard at the Phoenix Park
over a mile (in the same race in which
Ragusa was unplaced). Subsequently Final
Move had been beaten a short head by the
older Gay Challenger over twelve furlongs
at Leopardstown. He was entitled to take
his chance.

Of those who had not competed at
Epsom, the best fancied was the other French
raider, the Aga Khan's filly, Cervinia. As
highly rated in France as Paddy Prendergast's
brilliant Epsom Oaks winner, Noblesse,
Cervinia had run only once as a two-year-old.
Narrowly beaten then at Longchamp in
October, she reappeared to win her maiden at
the same venue in early May.

Cervinia then won the valuable Prix
Saint Alary at Longchamp in which the
French 1,000 Guineas winner, Altissima, was
only fourth. Beaten by half a length by Belle
Feronnière in the French Oaks at Chantilly,
it was reported subsequently that Cervinia
was found to be amiss after the race. Alec
Head's filly, to be ridden by Roger Poincelet,
successful of course in the inaugural Sweeps
Derby on Tambourine II, represented a
serious threat to the favourite.

Of the two English challengers the
Tamerlane colt, Tiger, which was trained by
Sir Gordon Richards, looked by far the better
proposition. Tiger had won his last two races
at Sandown and Salisbury, and while he was
difficult to rate his connections were
reported to be quietly confident.

Among the remaining Irish contenders,
Christmas Island, one of three challengers
from the Paddy Prendergast stable, was
considered in some quarters to have at least

as good a chance as his better fancied stable
companion, Ragusa. A son of Court Harwell,
he had been somewhat inconsistent, but in
winning both the Chester Vase and the
Gladness Stakes he had demonstrated
undoubted ability. Also in his favour was a
proven ability to act on easy ground.

Vincent O'Brien saddled two and of the
pair Chamero seemed much the better.
However, there was understood to be
concern at Ballydoyle about his ability to act
on the rain-softened going. Trainer Michael
Hurley was also double handed with Lock
Hard and Vic Mo Chroi. On bits of form both
of them had a squeak, but realistically the
feeling on the day was that these two, like
the rest of the horses, were there solely to
fight for the right to be second.

The betting on the Derby reflected the
public perception that it was a one-horse
race. Relko was an 11/8 on favourite and,
remarkably, next in the betting was his
compatriot, the filly Cervinia, at 100/8. The
Epsom third, Ragusa, was best of the Irish at
100/7, with Vincent O'Brien's Chamero a
100/6 shot. English challenger Tiger was at
18/1 and two points longer was the Epsom
Derby fourth, Tarqogan. It was 22/1 and
upwards the others.

Reflecting on the odds from today's
perspective, it is certain that with the tight
control on starting prices exercised by the
big British multiples no comparable prices
for horses other than the favourite would be
available to present-day punters.
Unquestionably, though, if in 1963 one had
the courage (or the foolhardiness?) to
oppose the favourite, there was plenty of
value to be had.

On what Tom McGinty, in the *Irish Independent* of Monday 1 July 1963, described as 'a bleak, wet afternoon, not unlike the weather we usually experience in February', the seventeen runners made their way across the Curragh to the start opposite the stands. It was on the way to the start that the real drama of the race began to unfold. Evidently sound when leaving the paddock, when the favourite Relko got to the start it appeared that his jockey, Yves Saint-Martin, was unhappy with the horse's fitness.

Confusion reigned for a time. Yves Saint-Martin, competing for the first time for one of the major European classics to have eluded him, was understandably reluctant to make a decision about Relko without first consulting the trainer, François Mathet. For what seemed like an eternity, but what amounted in fact to some thirteen minutes during which Saint-Martin had dismounted from Relko, the other runners circled around at the start with no one sure as to what was to happen next. It is interesting to note that during this interlude, experienced TV commentator Michael O'Hehir expressed the view that there appeared to be nothing physically wrong with Relko. Eventually Saint-Martin succeeded in contacting Mathet by radio telephone and the result of their conversation was the withdrawal of Relko from the race.

An image, captured on television, which lingers from that time is of Saint-Martin throwing his jockey's cap to the ground in frustration and disgust following upon the decision to withdraw his mount. Further reflections on Relko's withdrawal will follow a little later.

As to the race itself, when the field was belatedly dispatched, Christmas Island and Peadar Matthews set out to make the running. He was closely attended by the outsiders Diritto and Vic Mo Chroi. Tarqogan too was well placed, together with Prado, Lock Hard and Partholon. With Relko out, all eyes were intent on picking out the other fancied runners. The principal Irish challenger, Ragusa, was settled nicely in the middle of the field, while the filly, Cervinia, was towards the rear, together with Gordon Richards's Tiger.

Christmas Island continued to lead until about half a mile out, where he began to back-pedal. Approaching the straight Partholon held a narrow lead over Vic Mo Chroi, with Tarqogan and Tiger well placed. Ragusa was just behind the leaders at this stage. Vic Mo Chroi, running a tremendous race for Peter Boothman, took over from Partholon early in the straight, but just behind the combination Ragusa and his Australian jockey, Garnet Bougoure, were poised to challenge.

For a time it looked as though a major shock was on the cards as the 28/1 outsider, Vic Mo Chroi, continued to gallop on most resolutely. But by now Ragusa was closing remorselessly, and taking the lead at the distance, the Ribot colt quickly asserted himself.

Though Vic Mo Chroi never gave up the fight, Ragusa was not in danger of losing the lead at any stage throughout the final furlong, and at the finish he won decisively by two and a half lengths. Michael Hurley's Vic Mo Chroi was a most gallant second, having been in the first three throughout.

Two lengths further back in third place came the English hope, Tiger, who had kept on really well in the straight. In fourth place, another two and a half lengths back, was Seamus McGrath's Tarqogan, who had run a fine race on going which did not suit him. In fact Tarqogan thus had the distinction of finishing in fourth place in both the English and Irish Derbies.

Ragusa's win, a home success after Tambourine II's win for France in the inaugural running of the Sweeps Derby, was tremendously popular with Irish racegoers. However, it is no disrespect to Ragusa to say that much of the post-race comment centred on the non-participation of Relko. The *Racing Calendar* drily recorded the salient facts surrounding the affair: 'The Stewards gave permission for the withdrawal of Relko, which was due to the fact that this horse was found to be lame when he arrived at the start.' The *Calendar* added: 'The Stewards ordered samples to be taken from Relko after the race. The report from the analyst was negative.'

Officially, that was the end of the story. In the light of subsequent events it is pertinent however to ask: was there a more sinister explanation? It is worth noting that in the press release some days after the Curragh race, Relko's trainer, François Mathet, stated that on the Saturday evening Relko, besides his lameness, displayed other unusual symptoms. (These were not specified.) On Sunday morning, Mathet continued, Relko was completely sound and no longer limped.

The question has to be asked: is it possible that some illegal substance, not then known to the authorities, was administered to Relko which produced his strange and quite temporary affliction? Those who posed such questions had further weight added to their suspicions in a quite extraordinary postscript to the Curragh race which occurred some two weeks after the Irish Sweeps Derby.

On 11 July an announcement was made by the Jockey Club in England to the effect that several horses had tested positive to routine dope tests at the Epsom Derby meeting. It soon became known that Relko was one of the horses concerned.

In due course an enquiry was held and to summarise the contents of a fairly lengthy statement in the *Racing Calendar* of 29 August 1963, it was found that a substance other than a normal nutrient was present in the horse after the Epsom Derby. There was uncertainty as to what the effect of the substance was on Relko's performance at Epsom.

A little over a month later a further notice appeared in the *Racing Calendar* of 3 October. In brief, the Stewards of the Jockey Club reported that they had found that neither the trainer of Relko nor any of his employees had any case to answer. As at the Curragh, the official explanations raised more questions than they answered and did little to allay public disquiet over the entire Relko afair.

Thirty years on, it falls outside the scope of this work to delve further into the strange case of Relko. Certainly, however, for historians of the turf, or indeed for amateur sleuths, there would appear to be a great deal to work on in attempting to get at the truth of the somewhat murky business.

One consequence of Relko's withdrawal was that those fortunate enough to have backed Ragusa at the Curragh at his generous starting prices of 100/7 suffered a ten shillings (50p in today's terms) in the pound deduction from winning bets. With the principal danger on all known form removed from the race, it was of course a cross that could stoically be borne.

In all the blaze of media attention on the Relko withdrawal, insufficient credit was accorded to the winner of the Sweeps Derby, Ragusa. His win was in fact all the more meritorious when it is considered that Paddy Prendergast's charge lost a shoe in the course of the race.

The next assignment for Ragusa after the Curragh was the King George VI and Queen Elizabeth Stakes. Perhaps because of the perception that Ragusa was a lucky winner of the Sweeps Derby, the Ribot colt did not start favourite for the Ascot feature. Instead, Noel Murless's Ascot Gold Cup winner, Twilight Alley, was sent off 7/2 favourite. Ragusa was a generous 4/1 chance in a field which was well up to the usual standard associated with a King George.

In the event Ragusa stamped his authority on the race, winning easily by four lengths and five lengths from the four-year-old Miralgo and the ever consistent Tarqogan. Two further victories in 1963 (in the Great Voltigeur at York and the St Leger at Doncaster) only served to confirm that Ragusa was a very worthy Irish Derby winner. Indeed, one would have to say that even if Relko had taken part at the Curragh, there is no guarantee

that he would have got the better of Paddy Prendergast's high-class colt.

Ragusa was kept in training as a four-year-old and after winning a minor race at Naas he added the Eclipse Stakes to his impressive list of top-class victories. After finishing unplaced in the Arc, Ragusa was retired to stud. He had been a great servant to the Paddy Prendergast stable and had become a real favourite with Irish racegoers.

His fame was such that he had a stud farm named after him, the Ragusa Stud, which is situated in picturesque countryside just outside Ballymore Eustace, on the borders of Counties Wicklow and Kildare, just a few short miles from the scene of his great triumph at the Curragh on the last Saturday of June 1963.

As a son of Ribot, the outstanding dual Prix de l'Arc winner, and a classic winner to boot, Ragusa proved very popular at stud and went on to sire a number of high-class racehorses. Among his progeny were Ragstone, winner of the Ascot Gold Cup in 1974, Caliban, the 1970 Coronation Cup winner, Ballymore, who triumphed first time out in the 1973 Irish 2,000 Guineas and, above all, Morston, the sensational winner of the 1973 Epsom Derby. Sadly Ragusa died in that same year, 1973.

It says much for Ragusa's qualities as a thoroughbred that he went on from his controversial Sweeps Derby victory to establish himself firmly as a top-class colt. The spectre of Relko will always hover over his Curragh triumph, but racing is so full of imponderables that in the end reason and experience dictate that it is invariably better to give precedence to racecourse form rather than indulge in sometimes idle speculation. Even so, whenever the Irish Sweeps Derby of 1963 is discussed, there is little doubt that the names of not one, but two, horses will always tend to share equal prominence.

IRISH SWEEPS DERBY

1M 4F

SATURDAY 29 JUNE 1963

GOING: YIELDING

WINNER: Mr J. R. Mullion's Ragusa by Ribot out of Fantan II
G. Bougoure

SECOND: Vic Mo Chroi by Chamier out of Vic Girl
P. Boothman

THIRD: Tiger by Tamerlane out of Desert Girl
A. Breasley

S.P. 100/7   28/1   18/1
Winner trained by P. J. Prendergast

ALSO: Tarqogan 4th, Christmas Island 5th, Partholon 6th, Lock Hard 7th, L'Homme Arme 8th, Cervinia 9th, Final Move 10th, Prado 11th, Philemon 12th, Diritto 13th, Gala Chief 14th, Paddy's Birthday 15th, Chamero 16th & last

Relko 8/11 fav
Winner: 3rd favourite
Distances: 2½ lengths, 2 lengths
Value to winner: £48,732 10s.
Time: 2 m 45.6 s

Relko was found to be lame at the start and was withdrawn by permission of the stewards.
Rule 4 applies
Timeform rating of winner: 137.

1964

IRISH SWEEPS DERBY

One question above all others was insistently raised in advance of the third running of the Irish Sweeps Derby in 1964. Sceptics everywhere questioned the wisdom of trainer Michael Rogers in putting up his travelling head-lad cum jockey Willie Burke on the Epsom Derby winner and hot favourite, Santa Claus. The popular view was that Rogers was unnecessarily risking the clear chance that the favourite had of becoming the first horse since Orby in 1907 to complete the Epsom-Curragh Derby double by entrusting the ride on Santa Claus to the inexperienced 29-year-old Naas-born jockey. Indeed, for many, the decision to give Burke the ride after Scobie Breasley had guided Santa Claus to success at Epsom smacked of utter foolhardiness.

Others took a different view. Associated with Santa Claus in his day-to-day work in the stable, they argued that Burke knew every facet of the favourite's temperament and was accordingly, without doubt, the best man to partner the top-class colt in his bid for the famous double. Burke had only had a handful of rides all season, but he had shown that he could handle the big occasion when guiding Santa Claus to a comfortable success in the Irish 2,000 Guineas. He had done it once, his supporters argued, and he could be relied upon to do it a second time around.

Another dimension to the debate that raged among horse racing fans in Ireland was the perceived inferiority complex of Irish trainers when it came to engaging Irish jockeys. Among Irish trainers at the time, Australian riders were the flavour of the decade and there was a feeling that it was somehow a slight on a generation of Irish riders that Michael Rogers's decision to put up his stable jockey provoked such a critical reaction.

Such was the intensity of the debate on the matter that it unquestionably added a considerable extra weight of pressure on to the shoulders of the shy and retiring County Kildare jockey. In addition, the controversy ensured that interest in the 1964 Sweeps Derby extended far beyond the circle of those who would ordinarily have been attracted to it.

Nineteen runners were declared to face the starter, but Mr John Ismay's Santa Claus stood head and shoulders above the opposition. A high-class two-year-old, the son of Chamossaire had won the important National Stakes in the most impressive fashion imaginable and had gone into winter quarters as the shortest-priced favourite for the Epsom Derby since Dante in 1945. He had run but twice as a three-year-old prior to the Curragh, but those races had brought him victory in both the Irish 2,000 Guineas and the Epsom Derby. At Epsom he had beaten Indiana and Dilettante II by one length and two lengths, but many observers felt that Santa Claus had not handled Epsom's undulations particularly well and contended that he would be much more at home on the flatter, more galloping Curragh track. Others too were of the opinion that Santa Claus had not been ridden to best advantage by Scobie Breasley at Epsom.

If Santa Claus stood out, where was the danger to come from? On paper the pick of the opposition had to be Paddy Prendergast's Dilettante II, to be ridden by Lester Piggott. Dilettante II was still a maiden. Indeed his Epsom run was only his second ever outing. His first racecourse appearance had been in the Irish 2,000 Guineas, where he had been a respectable ninth to Santa Claus, but given the improvement that the Sicambre colt had shown at Epsom, he had to be regarded as a serious threat to Santa Claus.

And yet, remarkably, Dilettante II was only his stable's second choice in the race. Australian stable jockey, Garnet Bougoure, with one Sweeps Derby already under his belt on Ragusa, had elected to ride the Mossborough colt, Crete. Lady Honor Svejdar's charge was also a maiden and, coincidentally, had also competed in the same two races as Dilettante II. After finishing third in the Irish 2,000 Guineas, Crete had been sixth to Santa Claus at Epsom, beaten about six lengths. The Curragh going was predicted to be faster than at Epsom and this was thought to be more in Crete's favour than that of his stable companion, hence Bougoure's choice. Making up the Prendergast stable's trio of runners was the rank outsider, Ominous, whose chance on all known form was not apparent.

The French challenge for the Derby was headed by Etienne Pollet's Neptunus, to be partnered by yet another Australian, T. P. Glennon. After winning the French 2,000 Guineas, Neptunus had been beaten three lengths when fourth of ten to the subsequent French Derby winner Le Fabuleux in the ten furlong Prix Lupin. As France's top two-year-old of 1963, Neptunus was entitled to the height of respect. In any event he looked some way ahead of the other French runner, Charlie Bartholomew's Red Vagabonde.

The English challenge was three pronged. Keith Piggott's Anselmo had run a surprisingly good race at Epsom, finishing fourth to Santa Claus, beaten only a little over three lengths. However, the softish ground at Epsom had suited Anselmo and on earlier form he was not thought likely to appreciate the better going at the Curragh. In any event, if Anselmo had been seriously fancied, surely Lester, the trainer's son, would have been on board? That at least was the conventional wisdom. It is interesting to note that Anselmo, who had been with Paddy Prendergast in the earlier part of the season, was purchased just before Epsom by rock singer Billy Fury. The teenage idol was not, however, expected to attend at the Curragh, much to the disappointment of his many fans.

The second English contender, Devastation, from the Sam Hall yard, had won minor races at Doncaster and Kempton, was sure to appreciate the ground and was quietly fancied by connections. However, the pick of the English runners was undoubtedly Cecil Boyd-Rochfort's Lionhearted, the mount of Harry Carr. An unusual feature of the 1964 Sweeps Derby was the number of fancied runners who were maidens, and Lionhearted was yet another. After a promising third in the Lingfield Derby Trial, he became a prime candidate for the Epsom Derby. However, Lionhearted hurt himself during the course of the race and was virtually pulled up. In view of the fact that at Lingfield Lionhearted had finished in front of Indiana, who went on to be second to Santa Claus at Epsom, there was certainly a case to be made for the well-named Never Say Die colt.

Vincent O'Brien, with two Irish Derby victories to his credit in the pre-sponsorship era, was two handed on this occasion. The lightly raced Sunseeker was the mount of Australian Bill Pyers, but on the balance of his form he was the stable's second string

behind Hovercraft, to be ridden by stable jockey Jack Purtell — another Australian, incidentally. Hovercraft had finished a staying third to Master Buck in the Gallinule Stakes and looked to be an improving sort.

If, however, Hovercraft was to be given a chance, then his Gallinule Stakes conqueror, Master Buck, from the Michael Hurley yard, the mount of yet another Australian, Buster Parnell, surely had to be considered. The stable had saddled Vic mo Chroi to be second to Ragusa in the previous year's race and a similarly bold showing was expected.

The only other contender worth noting was the filly, All Saved — like Lionhearted, sired by the Epsom Derby winner, Never Say Die — from the Seamus McGrath stable. A very consistent two-year-old, All Saved had a victory over Sunseeker to her credit and in addition she had been a good third in the Timeform Gold Cup. Fifth in the English Oaks behind Homeward Bound on unsuitably soft going, she would have underfoot conditions much more to her liking at the Curragh.

The betting on the Derby followed the pattern set in the preceding year. Santa Claus was a very warm odds-on favourite at 4/7, punters clearly believing that Burke's presence on board was not at all likely to prove a hindrance. Next in the betting were the French hope, Neptunus, and Lester Piggott's mount, Dilettante II, both bracketed at 100/8. It was 100/7 the other Paddy Prendergast runner, Crete, 100/6 the leading English fancy, Lionhearted, and 20/1 bar these five. If the betting were to be believed, it was a one-horse race.

In contrast to 1963, there were no last-minute sensations at the start and the nineteen-runner field got off to a good even break on ground that was officially described as good. Right from the outset Paddy Prendergast's outsider, Ominous, with Peader Matthews in the saddle, set a very strong gallop and after a furlong he was over six lengths clear. Santa Claus, drawn four, was settled by Burke towards the rear and, sensibly, was kept to the outside so as to avoid any possible trouble in running. Ominous continued to blaze the trail and in the early stages his closest pursuers were Master Barry, ridden by the amateur Jody McGrath, the two French challengers, Neptunus and Red Vagabonde, followed immediately by the two Paddy Prendergast runners, Crete and Dilettante II.

At the half-way stage Ominous still led from Liam Ward's mount, King Paddy, and at this point Santa Claus was about fourth last. However, the field was quite tightly bunched and the favourite was very much in touch. From the stands in fact it was difficult to pick out owner John Ismay's colours of black with a prominent gold star and green hooped sleeves, as Santa Claus was on the outside of the field and rather obscured from view. As the field, however, made the descent towards the home turn, it could be seen that Willie Burke on Santa Claus was making significant headway and had the leaders very much in his sights.

Ominous had weakened out of contention by now, and as the runners swept around the turn for home John Oxx's outsider, Biscayne, led Master Barry, with Crete and Neptunus closest of the rest. Santa Claus was perfectly placed a few lengths off the leaders, but Lionhearted too had moved into a challenging position. Biscayne led into the straight but his lead was short lived. The well-fancied Lionhearted took it up two and a half furlongs out and for just a few strides an English victory looked possible.

Burke, however, was sitting ominously still on the favourite, and with two furlongs to go he produced Santa Claus with a devastating run on the outside. In a matter of strides the Chamossaire colt had raced clear and quickly opened up a winning lead. Long before Santa Claus reached the winning post the cheers were ringing out for the favourite. Most newspaper reports of the race emphasise the sheer volume of the cheering that accompanied Santa Claus's triumphal surge throughout the final furlong. The ease of the favourite's victory, officially four lengths, is well captured in numerous photographs of the finish, with Willie Burke taking a long look around him at his struggling rivals as he and Santa Claus passed the winning post.

Burke had actually every reason to be interested in what was happening behind him, for there was an absolutely breathtaking struggle for the minor honours taking place. A little over half a length covered no less than five horses and the help of the camera was required to sort out the finishing order behind Santa Claus. Lionhearted just held on to second place by a short head from Vincent O'Brien's 66/1 outsider, Sunseeker. The Aureole colt was in turn just a short head clear of Crete, who was himself a neck in front of All Saved, with Dilettante II only a head back in sixth place.

It was a great race for the runner-up position, in other words, but there was only one winner. Santa Claus had demolished the opposition, and the reception that horse and jockey got on their return to the unsaddling enclosure in front of the stands was probably unsurpassed. Upon dismounting Willie Burke was surrounded by well-wishers and was showered with the warmest of congratulations. Whisked away by jeep from the milling throng, Burke had to fight his way through another immense crowd before he gained the sanctuary of the weigh room. There is no doubt that Santa Claus's victory and the success of the locally based jockey combined to make the occasion a very emotional one. The jockey appeared to be physically and mentally drained by his ordeal, but given the tremendous pressure that he was subjected to before the race, that was hardly surprising. More to the point, Willie Burke had carried out to perfection the race plan which he and trainer Michael Rogers had worked out in the days leading up to the big race.

There were, of course, several hard-luck stories from the losing jockeys afterwards, but absolutely no one went so far as to assert that the result would in any way have been affected. Indeed the French-based Australian jockey, Bill Pyers, who rode Sunseeker into third place, summed up the view of all when he said: 'I have seen the best of the French three-year-olds in action, but Santa Claus would pull a cart and beat them.'

For the record Santa Claus's sire was Chamossaire and the dual Derby winner was easily his best horse. Chamossaire himself won four races including the St Leger.

Chamossaire, coincidentally, died in the year of his son's great successes, 1964.

For trainer Michael Rogers the result was a triumph. Santa Claus became the first horse since Orby in 1907 to land the Epsom-Curragh Derby double and blazed the trail for others who were to follow in subsequent years. At 39 years of age, and with Hard Ridden's Epsom Derby also to his credit, the young trainer had confirmed his rapid ascent to the very pinnacle of his profession. Rogers, who retired from training in 1970, later played a prominent role both as a steward of the Turf Club and as a member of the Curragh Racecourse Committee. He died, aged 60, in 1985.

After his memorable Curragh victory Santa Claus was sent to Ascot to compete in the King George VI and Queen Elizabeth Stakes. With only three opponents lined up against him, Santa Claus, again ridden by Willie Burke, started the shortest-priced favourite at 2/13 in the history of the race. The ground was very firm, and even on his way to the start Santa Claus did not look at ease on it.

By contrast, the French-trained four-year-old Nasram II, by coincidence a half brother to Tambourine II, the inaugural Sweeps Derby winner, revelled on the rock-hard going. With Bill Pyers in the saddle, Nasram II made all the running and registered a shock two length victory over Santa Claus, who for whatever reason simply did not give his true running.

There were those who blamed jockey Burke for the favourite's defeat, claiming that he had allowed the front-running French colt too much leeway on a course where, with a shortish run-in, front runners are favoured. However, there is little doubt that Santa Claus was not suited by the going and indeed Michael Rogers was unable to do much work with his dual Derby winner after the King George, his colt having been jarred up at Ascot. Santa Claus was due to run in the Doncaster St Leger, but in somewhat controversial circumstances he was withdrawn on the day before the race.

The colt's only subsequent race was in the Prix de l'Arc de Triomphe, where he was partnered this time by English jockey, Jimmy Lindley. Among his rivals were Nasram II and the 1963 Sweeps Derby winner, Ragusa. Santa Claus ran a fine race at Longchamp and finished a three-quarter length runner up to the Ribot colt, Prince Royal II. Both Nasram II and Ragusa were well down the field.

As a sire Santa Claus did not make a great impression at stud. He did however sire Reindeer, who won the Irish St Leger in 1969. Santa Claus died at the comparatively youthful age of 10 in 1970.

It is not as a sire, however, that Santa Claus will be remembered by Irish racegoers.

At his 1964 mid-summer peak, when he annexed two Derbies after winning the Irish 2,000 Guineas, he was a supremely impressive racehorse who left an indelible impression on the minds and hearts of Irish racegoers.

In addition, Santa Claus's Curragh triumph and Willie Burke's success struck a major blow on behalf of the skill and ability of Irish jockeys, who prior to that had not been rated on a par with their foreign counterparts. Irish-born jockeys are now very much to the fore in the world of flat racing. Apart from the home-based duo of Michael Kinane and Christy Roche, others at the top of their profession include Pat Eddery, Walter Swinburn, John Reid and Ray Cochrane. All of these household names owe a great deal to Michael Rogers and his initially controversial decision to engage Willie Burke to ride Santa Claus, one of the most popular winners of the Irish Sweeps Derby.

A sad postscript to the above. Willie Burke, whose name will always be associated with Santa Claus, died in January 1995, at 60 years of age.

IRISH SWEEPS DERBY

1M 4F
SATURDAY 27 JUNE 1964
GOING: GOOD

WINNER: Mr J. Ismay's Santa Claus by Chamossaire
out of Aunt Clara
W. Burke

SECOND: Lionhearted by Never Say Die out of
Thunder
W. H. Carr

THIRD: Sunseeker by Aureole out of Sun Deck
W. Pyers

S.P. 4/7f   100/6   66/1
Winner trained by J. M. Rogers

ALSO: Crete 4th, All Saved 5th, Dilettante II 6th,
Hovercraft 7th, Neptunus 8th, French Star
9th, Biscayne 10th, Anselmo 11th, Red
Vagabonde 12th, Master Barry 13th,
Devastation 14th, Horse Power 15th,
Ominous 16th, King Paddy 17th, Caricklee
18th, Master Buck slipped up

Winner: favourite
Distances: 4 lengths, sh. hd
Value to winner: £53,725
Time: 2 m 35.6 s
Timeform rating of winner: 133.

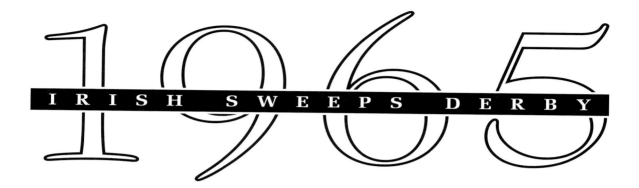

1965

IRISH SWEEPS DERBY

THE CURRAGH 26 JUNE 1965

The Sweeps Derby of 1965 was very much a case of Hamlet without the prince. In the Epsom equivalent a few weeks previously, the great Sea Bird II, eased down, had won comfortably by two lengths from Paddy Prendergast's Meadow Court. Put aside for an autumn campaign which duly yielded a supremely impressive six length victory in the Prix de l'Arc de Triomphe, Sea Bird II's absence at the Curragh at least ensured a far more competitive race than would otherwise have been the case.

At the start of the season Meadow Court was not included in Paddy Prendergast's plans for the major classics. Both Hardicanute and Carlemont were adjudged superior to their stable companion and were earmarked to do duty for the Rossmore Lodge stable. Fate, however, took a hand and both classic hopes, along with others in the stable, were struck down by a coughing epidemic which ruled them out of action.

Winner of a maiden race at Ascot as a two-year-old, Meadow Court made his seasonal début in the Gladness Stakes at the Curragh, where he was beaten two lengths by the Michael Dawson-trained Western Wind. Purely to test the strength of the English three-year-olds, Meadow Court was dispatched to contest the Dante Stakes at York. There, over the ten and a half furlong trip, Meadow Court finished an encouraging half-length second to the Ballymoss colt, Ballymarais, despite encountering some trouble in running.

At this stage Meadow Court was still rated behind his stable companion, Hardicanute, and the latter horse became the subject of considerable ante-post interest in the Epsom Derby market. However, it was then that the coughing epidemic struck Rossmore Lodge with the result that Meadow Court became the stable representative at Epsom where, as related above, he performed with great credit.

A total of twenty-one runners went to post for the fourth running of the Sweeps-sponsored race. Besides Meadow Court three others who had run at Epsom renewed rivalry and the connections of each of them had some grounds for optimism. The English 2,000 Guineas winner, Niksar, trained by Walter Nightingall, had been fourth at Epsom to Sea Bird II, some five and a half lengths behind Meadow Court. There was obviously a slight stamina doubt about the colt by Le Haar, but with Roger Poincelet, hero of the inaugural Sweeps Derby on board, clearly he could not be ruled out of contention.

Ron Smyth's Convamore had finished fifth at Epsom, only a neck behind Niksar. By Court Harwell, the same sire as Meadow Court, the Jimmy Lindley-partnered colt had advertised the Epsom form by going on to Royal Ascot where he had won the King Edward VII Stakes over a mile and a half by a neck from Bally Russe. Both the trip and the track were thought likely to suit Convamore. Meadow Court's York conqueror, Ballymarais, had been seventh behind Sea Bird II at Epsom, and clearly he would have to show improved form to get the better of the Paddy Prendergast-trained favourite.

Vincent O'Brien, bidding to win his first Irish Sweeps-sponsored Derby, saddled three runners. Scrapani had no realistic chance after finishing in the rear behind his stable companion Baljour in the Gallinule Stakes over ten furlongs at the Curragh. Baljour, however, by O'Brien's great champion, Ballymoss, was the choice of stable jockey Jack Purtell, and his judgment had to be respected. Prior to his

Gallinule Stakes victory Baljour had contested the Irish 2,000 Guineas, finishing sixth to Green Banner.

The other O'Brien runner was Donato, and this Alycidon colt was the mount of Scobie Breasley. Many felt that Donato was the pick of the O'Brien team despite Purtell's choice of Baljour. Donato had not run as a juvenile and on his first outing as a three-year-old had been second in a Curragh maiden. He evidently improved considerably from that run, for he next went on to Leopardstown where he impressed in beating another of his Derby rivals, Zend Avesta, by two lengths over the full Derby distance in the Wills Gold Flake Stakes. He was being stepped up again in class, but there was no telling how good he was.

A number of the other runners were worthy of consideration. Stuart Murless's Beddard, very cheaply bought, had won three on the trot including the Queen's Vase at Ascot. Certain to stay, he just didn't look quite good enough. John Oxx's Wedding Present had finished a staying fifth in the Irish 2,000 Guineas, a place in front of Baljour, and was fancied to run well. Oxx also saddled Jealous who had finished a moderate thirteenth in the Irish 2,000 Guineas.

Paddy Prendergast too was double handed, for besides Meadow Court he was also represented by Khalife, who had been favourite for the Gallinule Stakes, only to be outpointed by the aforementioned Baljour. He was expected to figure prominently.

As anticipated, Meadow Court was a warm favourite with the punters and at the off he was a tight 11/10 shot. Donato proved the stronger of Vincent O'Brien's twosome in the market and was second favourite at 6/1. His stable companion, Baljour, was at 10/1 alongside the Royal Ascot winner, Beddard. The Newmarket Guineas winner, Niksar, was next at 100/9. Western Wind who, after his early season victory over Meadow Court, failed in the English 2,000 Guineas was at 100/7, and it was 20/1 bar these six.

The going was officially described as yielding and as such the Curragh mile and a half would take some getting. The starter did his usual efficient job and the twenty-one-strong field was dispatched to a fairly level break. Among those prominent early on were the outsiders, Indian Snow, Scrapani and Solwezi, but Baljour and the Dante winner Ballymarais were also well placed.

The field remained quite tightly bunched and the gallop appeared to be a reasonable one. Ballymarais and Brian Connorton took the lead with about five furlongs to go, but even at this stage backers of the favourite were on good terms with themselves. The familiar sight of Lester Piggott, posterior aloft in the saddle and in close touch with the leaders as the horses neared the straight, sent a spasm of optimism through the veins of his backers. Meadow Court avoided some scrimmaging which occurred in the run down to the straight, and among those worst affected were Western Wind, Flaming Red and Kilcoran. Scrapani likewise encountered some trouble in running, while Niksar was hampered by some beaten horses as they dropped back.

All these unfortunate events probably had little or no bearing on the outcome of the race. Ballymarais continued to lead into the straight, but Piggott and Meadow Court were

sitting on his tail. Shortly afterwards Piggott asked Paddy Prendergast's charge to go about his business and the response was immediate. Meadow Court quickly asserted himself, opened up a sizeable lead, and long before the finish Lester Piggott was able to ease his mount down.

The Jimmy Lindley-partnered Convamore improved on his Epsom placing of fifth to finish a good second to Meadow Court, beaten two lengths. John Oxx's Wedding Present, appreciating the step-up in distance, ran a fine race to be third, three-quarters of a length further back. Ballymarais kept going to finish fourth and John Oxx's second string, Jealous, must have both surprised and delighted connections by finishing a highly meritorious fifth.

Among the disappointments of the race were Beddard who finished in sixteenth place, and Vincent O'Brien's pair, Donato who was seventeenth, and Baljour nineteenth of the twenty finishers, Kilcoran having been to all intents and purposes pulled up.

Meadow Court's victory was tremendously popular for a number of different reasons. As well as giving Paddy Prendergast his second Sweeps Derby success following upon Ragusa in 1963, Meadow Court provided Lester Piggott with his first Irish Derby. Usually expressionless, Piggott was clearly very moved by the tumultuous reception he received and the newspapers of the day carried numerous photographs of the legendary jockey wreathed in smiles. It is remarkable to reflect that thirty years later the irrepressible Piggott is still thrilling racegoers all over the world.

However, the triumph of Meadow Court is remembered in the public mind for one thing only — Bing Crosby's involvement in the post-race scenes. Piggott had worn the powder blue and scarlet hooped colours of Max Bell in powering Meadow Court to victory. On the night before the race, however, Bell and his partner, Frank McMahon, sold a one-third share in the colt to the world famous American crooner.

Clearly Crosby was elated with the victory of the favourite and in the unsaddling enclosure he treated onlookers to an impromptu few bars of that well-known ditty, 'When Irish Eyes are Smiling'. With the happy scenes beamed to millions of TV viewers throughout the world, the joyous aftermath of Meadow Court's victory probably did more to promote the international standing of the Irish Sweeps Derby than any other single event before or since.

Three further details are of note about the 1965 renewal. The time of the race — 2 minutes 46.8 seconds — is the slowest time yet recorded in all of the runnings of the Derby in the sponsorship era. Secondly, both first and second were the progeny of the same sire, Court Harwell, a record unequalled since. And, finally, for those who revel in quite useless bits of information, Meadow Court was originally known by the unflattering name of Harwell Fool.

Lester Piggott, by the way, rode a hat trick at the Curragh on Derby Day 1965. His victory aboard the somewhat reluctant Dandini in the final race on the card, the French Furze Stakes, drew unstinting praise from *The Irish Times* columnist, Terence De Vere White, clearly a beneficiary of the outcome. 'Men', the columnist reported with evident approval, 'have been given MBEs for less.'

Although not particularly well bred, Meadow Court proved that his Curragh success was no fluke when following up with a victory in the prestigious King George VI and Queen Elizabeth Stakes. In the absence yet again of Sea Bird II, the Irish-trained colt was 6/5 favourite to land the spoils. With his blinkered stablemate Khalife cutting out the running for Meadow Court, the race went very much according to plan.

Khalife performed his pacemaking duties splendidly and did not relinquish the lead until two and a half furlongs out. The Geoff Lewis-ridden Soderini briefly hit the front at this point, but Piggott pushed Meadow Court through a gap on the rails some two furlongs down and, quickly gaining the ascendency, he maintained a two length advantage all the way to the line.

Meadow Court provided Lester Piggott with his first King George success after numerous disappointments. The Court Harwell colt, though plainly not among the very best horses that Piggott had ever ridden, must surely none the less retain a special place in his heart.

After Ascot Meadow Court went to Doncaster where he was a virtually unbackable 4/11 favourite for the St Leger. However, the ground was very heavy and the colt just could not handle it. He finished a ten length second to Provoke, trained by Major Dick Hern. Meadow Court competed in the Arc and with the ground again soft he was not at his best, finishing ninth of the twenty runners behind the spectacular winner, Sea Bird II.

Officially rated 14 lb behind Sea Bird II in the Free Handicap at the end of the season, Meadow Court was not one of the better class Irish Derby winners. As a sire he enjoyed little success and was eventually exported to Canada in 1969.

Meadow Court, however, will be remembered as one of the stars of a great period of outstanding success for his trainer, Paddy 'Darkie' Prendergast. The Rossmore Lodge-based maestro topped the list of winning trainers in England in each of the years 1963, 1964 and 1965. A list of his big-race successes in that period alone makes for most impressive reading.

The principal winners were as follows:
- Ragusa (1963 Irish Derby, 1963 King George VI and Queen Elizabeth Stakes, 1963 St Leger, 1964 Eclipse Stakes);
- Noblesse (1963 Epsom Oaks);
- Khalkis (1963 Eclipse Stakes);
- Sixpence (1963 Cheveley Park Stakes);
- Pourparler (1964 1,000 Guineas);
- Hardicanute (1964 Champagne Stakes and Observer Gold Cup);
- Meadow Court (1965 Irish Derby, 1965 King George VI and Queen Elizabeth Stakes);
- Carlemont (1965 Sussex Stakes);
- Young Emperor (1965 Coventry and Gimcrack Stakes).

Initially Paddy Prendergast gained his reputation as a superlative handler of two-year-olds and indeed one of these flyers, Windy City, topped the two-year-old Free Handicap in 1951. However, after winning his first Irish Derby with Dark Warrior in 1950, Prendergast went on to prove himself with a string of successes in all the important classic and Group 1 races both at home and in England, with one notable exception.

Despite several placed efforts he never succeeded in winning the Epsom Derby and this was a source of great disappointment to him. He died in 1980, but not before he, along with Vincent O'Brien, had elevated the stature of Irish flat racing to a level previously unimagined.

With his successes with Ragusa and Meadow Court, Prendergast proved in the very early days of the Sweeps-sponsored Irish Derby that home-trained contenders could compete with the best in the world at the highest level. A self-made man, Paddy Prendergast's name will always be treasured among those who believe that Irish trainers, given the material, are the equal of any in the world.

IRISH SWEEPS DERBY

1M 4F

SATURDAY 26 JUNE 1965

GOING: YIELDING

WINNER: Mr G. M. Bell's Meadow Court by Court
Harwell out of Meadow Music
L. Piggott

SECOND: Convamore by Court Harwell out of
Absolution
J. Lindley

THIRD: Wedding Present by Macherio out of
Muscosa
W. Williamson

S.P. 11/10f 20/1 33/1
Winner trained by P. J. Prendergast

ALSO: Ballymarais 4th, Jealous 5th, Zend Avesta
6th, Khalife 7th, Western Wind 8th, Niksar
9th, Sierra de Mizas 10th, Scrapani 11th,
Ballyciptic 12th, Flaming Red 13th, Mabrouk
14th, Ga-Greine 15th, Beddard 16th, Donato
17th, Indian Snow 18th, Baljour 19th,
Solwezi 20th, Kilcoran 21st and last

Winner: favourite
Distances: 2 lengths, $^3/_4$ length
Value to winner: £56,180
Time: 2 m 46.8 s
Timeform rating of winner: 129.

The first winner of the Irish Sweeps Derby, in 1962, Tambourine II beats Arctic Storm by a short head. (JC)

Another view of Tambourine II's dramatic win in 1962. The winner is partially hidden on the rails. (JC)

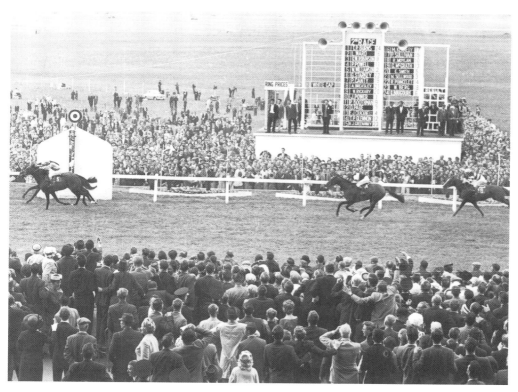

Tambourine II with the winning jockey Roger Poincelet, in 1962. (JC)

Ragusa was an easy winner in 1963. (JC)

Santa Claus and Willie Burke after their very popular victory in 1964. (JC)

The 1964 finish: A tremendous scrap for 2nd place, but Santa Claus is out on his own. (JC)

Joe McGrath presents the trophy to Mr and Mrs John Ismay, following Santa Claus's victory. (JC)

Santa Claus's victory was so complete that Willie Burke was able to look back at the battle for 2nd place. (JC)

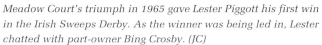

Meadow Court's triumph in 1965 gave Lester Piggott his first win in the Irish Sweeps Derby. As the winner was being led in, Lester chatted with part-owner Bing Crosby. (JC)

Sodium and Ribocco were the first English winners of the Sweeps Derby. (JC)

Derby day, 1967: Mrs Jacqueline Kennedy with the then Taoiseach, Jack Lynch. (JC)

The great Sir Ivor was sensationally beaten in 1968, having won a thrilling victory at Epsom a few weeks earlier.

The photograph on the left shows him at Ballydoyle with Vincent O'Brien. (JC)

Ribero was the winner at the Curragh in 1968, with Sir Ivor beaten by two lengths at the finish. A smiling Lester Piggott, who had piloted Sir Ivor to his Epsom victory, is pictured aboard the winner. (JC)

1966

THE CURRAGH 2 JULY 1966

Several astute judges were of the view that Charlottown, winner of the 1966 Epsom Derby, was one of the better Derby winners. Accordingly he was widely touted as a very likely winner of the Irish equivalent when his trainer Gordon Smyth confirmed his participation in the Irish Sweeps Derby. Charlottown, who was unbeaten as a two-year-old, was a most beautifully bred horse. By Charlottesville out of Meld, if ever a horse was bred to win a classic, Charlottown was.

His sire won the French Derby and the Grand Prix de Paris, while his dam, Meld, was one of the greatest of her sex. She carried off the fillies' equivalent of the triple crown in 1955, winning the 1,000 Guineas, the Oaks and the St Leger. As a juvenile Charlottown was trained by 'Towser' Gosden, father of present-day trainer, John, but after ill health caused him to retire, the stable was taken over by Gordon Smyth.

Charlottown had something of an idiosyncrasy. He had light, shelly feet and was always liable to tear a shoe off. At Epsom Charlottown had in fact shed a plate just before the big race, but luckily was able to be reshod in time to take his place in the line-up. As a result of Charlottown's mishap the start of the Epsom Derby was delayed by a quarter of an hour. Fortunately the delay had no effect on Charlottown's performance and although he won by only a neck from Pretendre, many considered that the Scobie Breasley-partnered colt had something in hand of his rivals.

Not wishing to risk a repeat of Charlottown's Epsom problem, connections looked to the United States for a solution. The treatment prescribed was to pump plastic into Charlottown's feet so as to provide a base for the nails. In the circumstances Charlottown's progress to the start of the Curragh would be viewed with understandable concern by both connections and punters alike.

The Epsom winner was bound to be sent off a hot favourite, but there was no shortage of runners prepared to challenge his supremacy. The principal rival on form was George Todd's Sodium, who had finished fourth at Epsom. A maiden after his two-year-old campaign although he had run well in both the Observer Gold Cup and the Royal Lodge Stakes, Sodium had won at Brighton before lining up at Epsom. Finishing just over seven lengths adrift of Charlottown at Epsom, Sodium had so disappointed George Todd that he decided to have a private dope test carried out at his own expense. Sodium had sweated up badly and was quite distressed before the Derby, but the test in any event proved negative.

A subsequent theory advanced for Sodium's below-par display was that he had eaten part of his bedding on the morning of the race. They say that it never pays to make excuses for horses, but at least this particular explanation had the value of novelty attached to it! For some, Sodium was the epitome of the kind of horse for whom everything had to go exactly right before he would consent to put his best foot forward. When beaten into third place in the White Rose Stakes at Ascot in April by the Vincent O'Brien-trained Right Noble — subsequently a big disappointment when joint favourite for the Epsom Derby — jockey Frankie Durr claimed that his mount had got into all sorts of trouble in running.

In addition to Charlottown and Sodium, no less than twenty-one other horses were declared to stake their claim for glory. Four of the also-rans at Epsom were among this number. Vincent O'Brien's Ambericos had been the best of these, finishing sixth, which followed a good fifth placing to Kashmir II in the English 2,000 Guineas. The maiden Khalekhan, trained by Paddy Prendergast, had been seventh at Epsom and was expected to improve. Michael Rogers's Ballymoss colt, Radbrook, had been eighth behind Charlottown and earlier in the season had won the stakes race named after his sire at the Curragh. Stuart Murless's Baylanx had been only twentieth at Epsom and didn't figure on many short lists.

The best fancied of the Irish challengers was Paveh, who was trained by David Ainsworth and was to be ridden by Paddy Powell, who had won the 1954 Irish Derby on Zarathustra. First time out as a three-year-old, Paveh surprised connections by winning the Players Navy Cut Trial Stakes in soft going over a mile at the Phoenix Park. In his subsequent appearance he had won the Irish 2,000 Guineas by three-quarters of a length from Ultimate II who, however, had let down the form subsequently. Paveh's form was difficult to evaluate and there were some stamina doubts about the Tropique colt whose sire was a Coronation Cup winner. If Paveh could stay the trip, there was every chance of him being concerned in the finish.

There were others, too, who attracted interest in the pre-race speculation. Chief among these was Peter Walwyn's Crozier who had finished second, beaten two and a half lengths by Pretendre at Royal Ascot. Given that Pretendre had previously been beaten by a neck when second to Charlottown in the Epsom Derby, clearly Crozier was held on form, but none the less with improvement he had to be in with a shout.

The dark horse of the race was Democrat, a stable companion of Radbrook. This Pinza colt had promised greatly when third to Reubens in the National Stakes as a juvenile, and although a disappointing fourth on his seasonal début in the Irish 2,000 Guineas, such was his early season reputation that he actually started an odds-on favourite for the first of the Irish classics. It was reported that Michael Rogers's colt was burning up the gallops at home, and if such stories were to be believed, then the losses incurred in the 2,000 Guineas might perhaps be recovered.

An Irish contender who was quietly fancied in some quarters was the Brud Featherstonhaugh-trained Busted. A promising second to Agogo at Naas was followed up by success in the Gallinule Stakes at the Curragh. The big bay son of Crepello looked a classy sort and connections were known to be hopeful.

Among the trainers who were doubly represented was Stuart Murless. While his Epsom failure Baylanx had little chance on the book, the same could not be said of stable companion Agogo. His Naas victory over Busted had been followed up by a rather unlucky fourth to Pretendre and Crozier at Royal Ascot, beaten six lengths.

The betting on the race followed a fairly predictable course. Epsom Derby winner, Charlottown, was favourite at slight odds-on, 10/11. Second favourite was Sodium at 13/2 and best of the Irish was Paveh at 100/8. A feature of the early years of the Irish Sweeps Derby was the special place betting on offer. Sodium was available at 4/6, while Paveh was a 5/2 shot. A forerunner of the now very prevalent 'without the favourite' mode of betting, it could scarcely be said that the odds on offer were over-generous.

The day was hot and the going officially good as the twenty-three runners were dispatched by the starter. The gallop, and it was a good one, was set to half a mile out by the outsider Not So Cold, the mount of Wally Swinburn, father of Walter. The field was well strung out in the first mile, with the favourite Charlottown held up by Scobie Breasley towards the rear. When Not So Cold weakened the Crepello colt, Busted, took up the running and led the field down towards the straight.

At this point neither Charlottown nor second favourite Sodium was particularly well placed. Turning into the straight the hopes of those who had speculated their cash on Busted were high, as Peter Boothman was making the best of his way home on the Irish hope. It was an Irish 1-2-3 at this point, for Busted was followed by Agogo, with Nicky Brennan up, and Paveh who was ridden by Paddy Powell. With two furlongs to go Paveh, the main Irish fancy, took over from Busted, but the real drama of the race was taking place just behind the leader. The jockeys on the two English principals had had to make decisions as to how to manoevre their charges into challenging positions.

While Frankie Durr on Sodium had picked his way through the pack to get near to the rails, Scobie Breasley on Charlottown, who had made up a lot of ground from the top of the hill, elected to make his move on the wide outside.

Meantime, as the two market leaders were poised to deliver their challenges,

Paddy Powell and Paveh continued at the head of affairs and for a few strides inside the final two furlongs it looked as if the Irish 2,000 Guineas winner was going to keep up the gallop to the line. Frankie Durr's mount got first run on the Epsom Derby winner, and as soon as Paveh was tackled by Sodium, David Ainsworth's colt gave way. By contrast, it took Charlottown some time to get into top gear, and it was not until inside the final furlong that the Charlottesville colt was able to mount a sustained challenge. Despite Charlottown's best efforts, Sodium was always holding the Epsom Derby winner and at the finishing line there was a length between the two horses.

Paveh kept on gamely to finish third, two and a half lengths further back. The surprise packet of the race was the 100/1 outsider, Baylanx, who finished fourth, two lengths further back, and according to jockey Bobby Elliott might have been even closer but for encountering trouble in running early in the straight. Stuart Murless, trainer of Baylanx, also saddled the fifth home, Agogo, while Paddy Prendergast's Khalekan improved on his Epsom placing by one place, finishing sixth.

Some supporters of Charlottown were critical of Scobie Breasley's handling of the favourite, feeling that he had given the Epsom Derby winner too much to do. Breasley had been forced to take the wide route when making his challenge and a gap did not immediately present itself when he first made his move. The jockey, however, was adamant that Charlottown had had every chance and that Sodium had beaten him fair and square.

Sodium's win in any event was a vindication of Frankie Durr's pre-race opinion that the Epsom form would be reversed. Trainer George Todd was not present to see his colt win as he had a phobia about travelling and hadn't been outside England for almost fifty years. If Ireland could not claim the winner as of right, there was some consolation in that Sodium was bred at the Kilcarn Stud near Navan by Major E. O'Kelly. Sodium was sired by the 1961 Epsom Derby winner, Psidium, whose best horse he was by far.

After his Curragh success Sodium went on to Ascot where he was 6/4 favourite in a field of five to add the King George VI and Queen Elizabeth Stakes to his Irish Derby spoils. However, he was outgunned by the four-year-old filly, Aunt Edith, trained by Noel Murless and ridden by Lester Piggott. Beaten half a length by the older horse, Sodium was by no means disgraced, and it was announced subsequently that his next major assignment would be the Doncaster St Leger.

Before that, however, he had yet another joust with his old rival, Charlottown, in the Oxfordshire Stakes at Newbury. Punters this time plumped for Sodium who was sent off 11/8 on favourite, with Charlottown returned at 11/8 against. Lester Piggott was on board Sodium, while Jimmy Lindley substituted for Scobie Breasley on Charlottown, the popular Australian having been injured in a fall earlier in the day. In the event Sodium ran a very disappointing race, finishing a thirteen length third of four to the Epsom Derby winner.

There seemed to be no good reason for the Curragh winner's poor effort and George Todd's colt's erratic and unpredictable performances were proving to be a real puzzle for students of the formbook. The only inference that could be taken from a study of the comparative form of the two Derby winners was that Charlottown was the superior and that Sodium's victory at the Curragh owed a lot to a combination of Frankie Durr's enterprise and a troubled run for the Epsom Derby winner.

Back in 1966 the spirit of competition, or to put it another way, the influence of commercial bloodstock considerations had not yet assumed pre-eminence over all other factors in the sport of horse racing. As a consequence, a further clash between the two great rivals was served up for racegoers in September. The Doncaster St Leger, then run on a Wednesday, was the contest chosen and punters, not unnaturally, made Charlottown 11/10 favourite to confirm finally his superior standing *vis-à-vis* Sodium. The Sweeps Derby winner was virtually friendless in the market at 7/1.

In racing, the imp of the perverse tends to make his presence felt on too many occasions for the punters' comfort, and the Doncaster St Leger of 1966 was the setting for another of his appearances. In a desperate finish to the oldest of the English classics, Sodium got the better of Charlottown by a head. A stewards' enquiry was announced to give fresh hope to backers of the favourite, but Sodium kept the race and once again students of the formbook were left to ponder the less compelling aspects of the horse racing game. Perhaps the only lesson that could reasonably be drawn from an examination of the season's encounters between the two Derby winners is that

betting on horse racing is something less than an exact science.

The ebullient owner of Sodium, Mr R. J. Sigtia, made the brave decision to keep his Irish Derby winner in training as a four-year-old. It was a courageous move, but regrettably it didn't pay off. A half-length defeat by the Harry Wragg-trained Salvo in the Hardwicke Stakes at Royal Ascot didn't presage a bad season for George Todd's colt, but sadly Sodium then had the misfortune to run up against a much improved four-year-old. It was doubly ironic that the horse in question had been so comprehensively beaten by Sodium at the Curragh a year earlier.

Trained for Stanhope Joel by Brud Featherstonhaugh as a three-year-old, Busted, who had finished twelfth behind Sodium in the Irish Sweeps Derby, was transferred at the end of the season to Noel Murless at Newmarket. Under Murless's guidance Busted blossomed into a high-class colt. After winning the Coronation Stakes at Sandown by an impressive three lengths, Busted went on to thrash a top-class field in the Eclipse, beating Great Nephew by two and a half lengths without coming off the bit. Sodium, the 15/8 favourite, was a severe disappointment in the same race, finishing out of the money.

Busted and Sodium next met in the King George VI and Queen Elizabeth Stakes at Ascot one week later. Busted again showed what an improved colt he had become, with an authoritative three length win from Salvo. Sodium by contrast was a modest sixth of nine and it was clear that he was no longer the force he had been as a three-year-old.

Busted went on to remain undefeated in 1967, proving that some horses take longer to mature than others and that patience is perhaps the greatest single virtue for anyone involved with thoroughbreds. The Crepello colt was later to make his mark as a sire and was responsible for, among others, the 1974 St Leger winner Bustino, and Mtoto, who won the King George in 1988 as well as finishing a most unlucky second in the Arc that same year.

Enough of Busted. His conqueror in the 1966 Sweeps Derby, Sodium, will perhaps be regarded as one of the more perplexing of his breed. He was certainly no friend of the punters, but his unpredictable exploits in his classic year have earned him a somewhat quixotic place in racing's hall of fame.

IRISH SWEEPS DERBY

1M 4F
SATURDAY 2 JULY 1966
GOING: GOOD

WINNER: Mr R. J. Sigtia's Sodium by Psidium out of Gambade
F. Durr

SECOND: Charlottown by Charlottesville out of Meld
A. Breasley

THIRD: Paveh by Tropique out of Persian Shoe
P. Powell

S.P. 13/2   10/11f   100/8
Winner trained by G. E. Todd

ALSO: Baylanx 4th, Agogo 5th, Khalekan 6th, Algicide 7th, Reubens 8th, Al Alawi 9th, Polemic 10th, Crozier 11th, Busted 12th, Not So Cold 13th, Petit Jean 14th, Radbrook 15th, Beau Chapeau 16th, Ambericos 17th, Democrat 18th, Ascot 19th, White Gloves 20th, Milesvena 21st, Ripping Time 22nd, Drumlane 23rd & last

Winner: 2nd favourite
Distances: 1 length, 2$\frac{1}{2}$ lengths
Value to winner: £52,157 10s.
Time: 2 m 31.5 s
Timeform rating of winner: 128.

1967

IRISH SWEEPS DERBY

THE CURRAGH 1 JULY 1967

Twenty-three runners contested the sixth sponsored running of the Irish Derby. The fact that such a large field lined up would tend to suggest that the race had an open look about it, and that indeed was the case. Even so, nominating the favourite was a fairly simple task. The Epsom Derby runner-up, Ribocco, to be partnered by Lester Piggott, was the clear form choice, but no less than six of those who had finished behind Ribocco at Epsom were declared to take him on again.

A good-class two-year-old, Ribocco, trained by 27-year-old Fulke Johnson Houghton, had triumphed in the important end of season juvenile test, the Observer Gold Cup at Doncaster. Ribocco's three-year-old campaign, however, did not get off to a distinguished start. A moderate run in the Craven Stakes at Newmarket was followed by another disappointing display when Ribocco was beaten two lengths by French Vine in the Dee Stakes over ten furlongs at Chester. Worse was to follow when the Ribot colt finished a poor fifth of ten to Heave Ho in the Lingfield Derby Trial over the full Derby distance.

Ribocco's subsequent two and a half length second to the Jim Joel-owned and Noel Murless-trained Royal Palace at Epsom suggested that the Ribot colt was at last going the right way, but there still remained a serious question mark about him. Ribocco had displayed unmistakable signs of temperament on a number of his racecourse appearances.

He had exhibited a marked reluctance to entering the stalls and while that would not trouble him at the Curragh in that the tapes/barrier style of dispatch still operated there, it wasn't the colt's only idiosyncrasy. Ribocco didn't like to race too close to other horses and at Epsom Piggott had deliberately brought him wide of the other runners to deliver his challenge. It had worked out satisfactorily at Epsom, but could Piggott repeat the performance at the Curragh? With twenty-two opponents it would not be plain sailing by any means.

The third and fourth horses home at Epsom were also in the Curragh line-up. Sir Gordon Richards's Dart Board had been two lengths behind Ribocco at Epsom, but there were good grounds for believing that he could improve on his running there. Upset in the preliminaries at Epsom, Dart Board had been dripping with sweat on his way to the start. In the circumstances he had performed creditably. Dart Board's previous form was not outstanding — he had won a fairly moderate race at Brighton over twelve furlongs — but he was obviously improving and seemed sure to run well. Certainly there was some confidence that he could improve on the stable's third placing with Tiger in the 1963 Sweeps Derby behind Ragusa.

Royal Sword from the Michael Rogers stable had been fourth at Epsom, four lengths adrift of Ribocco. The Right Royal V colt had previously won the Gold Flake Stakes at Leopardstown over ten furlongs from Dominion Day and My Kuda, and prior to that had been third over the same distance at the Curragh to White Gloves and My Kuda. He was improving, as his running with My Kuda suggested, and had realistic prospects of supplementing his trainer's 1964 success with Santa Claus.

As regards the other also-rans at Epsom, it was difficult to fancy any of them. Dancing Moss had been tenth to Royal Palace, El Mighty seventeenth, Kiss of Life eighteenth and Tapis Rose last but one of the twenty-two runners. Their connections

were to be commended for their fortitude and spirit of adventure, but success did not appear to beckon.

Dangers to the three prime contenders from the Epsom race however abounded. The Irish 2,000 Guineas winner, Atherstone Wood, was one such. Awarded the Irish classic on the disqualification of Kingfisher, Buster Parnell's mount had subsequently won the Gallinule Stakes at the Curragh and his credentials were therefore impressive. The ground at the Curragh for the Gallinule Stakes was firm and on the better ground forecast for the Derby, Atherstone Wood was considered to have every chance of annexing the big prize for the Stephen Quirke stable.

Seamus McGrath mounted a two-pronged challenge for the race so closely associated with his father. Signa Infesta was the more fancied of the two runners. After an initial win in a seven furlong event at Naas, the imposing St Crespin colt, standing seventeen hands, won the Players Navy Cut Stakes over a mile at the Phoenix Park. The doubt about him was that he had suffered from a bout of coughing after his Phoenix Park victory, and while the stable was happy that he was over the worst, an interrupted preparation is never ideal for a major classic. The other McGrath challenger was Heave Ho, early season conqueror of Ribocco in the Lingfield Derby Trial. Without a run since, Heave Ho was not particularly well fancied, but he was certain to stay the trip and obviously could not be ignored.

Among the other Irish contenders, Brud Featherstonhaugh, trainer of Epsom also-ran Dancing Moss, had a more likely string to his bow in the well-regarded Fortino II colt,

Fortissimo. Twice a winner at Naas and Leopardstown, over twelve furlongs on each occasion, his stamina was guaranteed, and if there was to be a surprise Fortissimo was just the sort to produce it.

Besides Dart Board there was as usual a strong overseas challenge. The French, attempting to win their second Sweeps Derby, dispatched Steady II, the mount of Roger Poincelet, who had of course already tasted victory in a Sweeps Derby. Successful in three of his four races as a three-year-old, Steady II had won over twelve furlongs at Chantilly. However, French three-year-old form was difficult to evaluate and to that extent Steady II was something of a dark horse.

The Dante Stakes winner Gay Garland, from the Harry Wragg stable, was another invader to be feared. The mount of Ron Hutchinson, Gay Garland had disappointed at Royal Ascot after his York success but, reported back to his best, he was a lively outsider.

The most interesting of the overseas runners however was Noel Murless's Sucaryl, the trainer's first ever runner in Ireland. Without an outing as a three-year-old, as a juvenile Sucaryl had won at Chester over an extended seven furlongs. The St Paddy colt had been an intended runner at Royal Ascot, but had been unable to compete as it was discovered that he was not qualified under the conditions of entry.

Previously withdrawn from the French Derby, Sucaryl had been a galloping companion of the Epsom Derby winner, Royal Palace, and whilst reputedly inferior to that horse, he had none the less impressed

work watchers as a colt of considerable potential. His trainer was adept at producing horses fit enough to win first time out, and indeed his prowess in that regard had been amply demonstrated earlier in the season when both Royal Palace and Fleet had triumphed in their respective Newmarket Guineas classics without the benefit of a prior run.

But perhaps of greater public interest than Noel Murless's undoubted abilities as a trainer was the fact that George Moore rode Lady Sassoon's colt. The Australian Moore had replaced Lester Piggott as Murless's first jockey after the much-publicised split between the master of Warren Place and his long-time number one jockey. To add salt to the wound, Murless and Moore had annexed three English classics in the first year of their association, while Lester Piggott had struggled as a freelance with both quantity and quality of winners, well down on his usual strike rate.

The underlying tension of this occasion created a heightened sense of anticipation at the Curragh in the pre-race preliminaries. Lester Piggott was on the favourite, sure enough; but would his former ally combine with Moore to deprive the ever colourful Piggott of his much sought after first classic winner as a freelance?

The going at the Curragh on Sweeps Derby day was good, and added lustre was accorded Irish racing's big day by the presence in the attendance of Mrs Jacqueline Kennedy, widow of the former US President. The charismatic lady, who had so impressed the watching world with her dignified bearing in the wake of her husband's assassination, was for many among the attendance the principal focus of attention on the day.

For those, however, who preferred to concentrate on the racing, there was some fairly hectic betting on the big race. Whatever the doubts about Ribocco's temperament, the magic of Piggott's name exercised an irresistible fascination for Irish punters and the Ribot colt was a heavily backed favourite, closing at 5/2. The principal challenger, Royal Sword, was very strong in the market and wound up a solid 11/2 second favourite. George Moore's mount, Sucaryl, and the French hope, Steady II, were both bracketed at 8/1. The Epsom Derby third, Dart Board, was one point longer at 9/1. After these, Signa Infesta was a 100/9 chance, it was 18/1 both Fortissimo and Gay Garland, and 22/1 bar those mentioned.

Not for the first time and certainly not for the last, there was an unanticipated delay before the big race got under way. One of the 150/1 outsiders, Rare Jewel, spread a plate at the start and having to be reshod, the race was held up for approximately ten minutes. For a nervous temperamental colt such as Ribocco, this was scarcely a welcome development. Charles Engelhard's colt was fortunate, however, in one respect — the 1967 Irish Sweeps Derby was the last one to be started without the benefit of stalls, to which Ribocco had a distinct aversion.

When at length the field got away the 100/1 shot, Skamander, with John Roe up, led the way. With twenty-three runners there was a fair amount of scrimmaging in the early stages, but all the principal hopes escaped any serious buffeting. The runners had only gone about five furlongs, however, when a dramatic incident occurred. The second favourite, Royal Sword, ridden by Michael Kennedy, appeared to lose his footing and fell. It was a nasty fall and for a short while it seemed as if the jockey had suffered a serious injury. Fortunately, Kennedy recovered quickly and was indeed pronounced fit to resume riding later in the afternoon.

Sadly, Royal Sword was not so lucky. It transpired that the well-fancied Right Royal V colt had broken a leg in running and tragically had to be put down. Several horses were impeded by the fall of the second favourite, most notably Dart Board, whose jockey, Scobie Breasley, reported later that his mount had lost several lengths when colliding with the falling Royal Sword.

While all this was happening the outsider Dan Kano, with Paddy Powell on board, had taken up the running. Dan Kano led until six furlongs out, where he was passed by Sovereign Slipper, the mount of Des Lake. Soon after the McGrath colt, Signa Infesta, made a significant move and led the field into the straight. For a few strides a famous victory for the Glencairn team looked on the cards, but significantly in behind Signa Infesta it could be seen that both Sucaryl and Ribocco were poised to unleash their challenges.

Failing to stay, Signa Infesta faded early in the straight, where George Moore pushed his mount, Sucaryl, into the lead. Had the script been written in advance? Was the Murless-Moore combination set to deny Piggott the classic victory he so craved? Supporters of the favourite (and there were many) held their collective breath. Ribocco looked to be travelling smoothly just in behind the leader, but would he answer the call when asked?

Piggott waited and waited, as only he can, whilst his rival continued to make the best of his way home. It was not until inside the final furlong that Lester popped the question. Produced on the outside, the Ribot colt quickened immediately and passed Sucaryl with a nice turn of foot. Without doing a whole lot more than was necessary, Piggott eased his mount home by three-quarters of a length, with the gallant Sucaryl a very game second. It was three lengths back to Dart Board, who overcame his collision with Royal Sword to reproduce his Epsom placing.

Gay Garland was fourth, a further half a length adrift, while the 150/1 outsider, Dan Kano, belied his odds finishing in fifth place, with the Irish 2,000 Guineas winner Atherstone Wood a good sixth. Disappointment of the race was the French-trained Steady II who was a moderate thirteenth of the twenty-two finishers.

The winning favourite received a tremendous reception from the Irish crowd. The cheering, of course, was primarily for the incomparable Lester Piggott. Riding his second Irish Sweeps Derby winner, following upon Meadow Court in 1965, it is certain that Ribocco's triumph was one of the most satisfying classic victories in the legendary jockey's long and eventful career. Proving that he could deliver the goods at the highest level as a freelance, the taste of victory must have been all the sweeter in that his immediate victim at the Curragh was a Noel Murless-trained runner.

Piggott was obviously beginning to develop a soft spot for the premier Irish classic. For the second time in the space of two years the post-race photographs reprinted in the various newspapers gave the lie to those who claimed that racing's ultimate professional never smiled. Rarely in his career, indeed, can Lester's grin have been quite so broad as it was after the sleek Ribocco's convincing victory.

Ribocco cost his wealthy owner Charles Engelhard $35,000 as a yearling. The owner was to figure prominently in the story of the Irish Derby over the following few years, as will be set out in the succeeding chapters. His Ribocco went on from his Curragh success to prove himself a very good-class three-year-old.

He was made favourite for the King George VI and Queen Elizabeth Stakes and was a fast-finishing third to Busted and Salvo, beaten three lengths and a neck. Busted, it will be recalled, competed in the previous year's Sweeps Derby without success, but really thrived as a four-year-old. After disappointing when only third to Dart Board at Goodwood, Ribocco next ran in the Doncaster St Leger and, emulating Ragusa and Sodium, added the final English classic to his Irish Derby success. Joint favourite at Doncaster, Ribocco beat the other joint favourite, Queen Elizabeth's Hopeful Venture, by one and a half lengths in a very fast time.

For a horse who had an early season reputation as an unreliable sort, Ribocco's temperament had improved with racing. His career ended with a very gallant third placing in the Prix de l'Arc de Triomphe behind Topyo and old rival, Salvo, beaten only a neck and a short head in a most exciting finish. Lester Piggott made no excuse for Fulke Johnson Houghton's colt. He didn't need to.

Ribocco had proved himself a splendid advertisement for his great sire and indeed for his young trainer. When he won at the Curragh Ribocco was Johnson Houghton's first ever runner in Ireland, and Ribocco gave him his first classic victory. The trainer will doubtless always remember the occasion with pleasure and pride. So also will his very famous jockey, for whom Ribocco's Curragh triumph represented confirmation that his decision to go freelance was one that would propel Lester Piggott's already successful career on to an even more exalted plane of excellence.

IRISH SWEEPS DERBY

1M 4F
SATURDAY 1 JULY 1967
GOING: GOOD

WINNER: Mr C. W. Engelhard's Ribocco by Ribot out of Libra
L. Piggott

SECOND: Sucaryl by St Paddy out of Sweet Angel
G. Moore

THIRD: Dart Board by Darius out of Shrubswood
A. Breasley

S.P. 5/2f 8/1 9/1
Winner trained by R. F. Johnson Houghton

ALSO: Gay Garland 4th, Dan Kano 5th, Atherstone Wood 6th, Dancing Moss 7th, El Mighty 8th, Tapis Rose 9th, Fortissimo 10th, Signa Infesta 11th, Crepe Clover 12th, Steady II 13th, Rugged Man 14th, Skamander 15th, Sovereign Slipper 16th, Kiss of Life 17th, Rare Jewel 18th, Heave Ho 19th, Zaracarn 20th, Palmas 21st, Mark Scott 22nd, Royal Sword fell

Winner: favourite
Distances: $^3/_4$ length, 3 lengths
Value to winner: £57,590
Time: 2 m 30.4 s
Timeform rating of winner: 129.

IRISH SWEEPS DERBY

N ot for many years had the racing public looked forward with such keen anticipation to any race as they did to the annual renewal of the Irish Derby on the final Saturday of June 1968. Exactly one month beforehand, in one of the most exhilarating displays ever witnessed at Epsom, the Irish-trained, American-bred colt, Sir Ivor had produced a blinding surge of acceleration to power past the high-class Connaught and win the Epsom Derby in breathtaking style. The 4/5 favourite, Sir Ivor had won by only one and a half lengths, but it was not the winning distance but rather the sheer brilliance of the colt's performance that had observers immediately elevating the Vincent O'Brien-trained three-year-old into the company of the great names of the turf.

Owned by Raymond Guest, the American Ambassador to Ireland, Sir Ivor, besides the £58,525 prize money at Epsom, had landed for his sporting owner one of the most audacious gambles in the history of horse racing. Before the horse had taken on quality opposition as a two-year-old, Guest had struck a bet of £500 each way at 100/1 for the following year's Epsom Derby with the leading British bookmaker, William Hill. The successful ante-post bet realised £62,500 for Sir Ivor's owner — a phenomenal sum, and in present-day values worth more than £500,000.

Sir Ivor's first outing as a two-year-old on 1 July 1967 was not especially promising. He was only fourth in the Tyros Stakes at the Curragh, but none the less in the parade ring after the race his jockey Liam Ward confidently predicted to trainer Vincent O'Brien that Sir Ivor would never again be beaten by any of the horses that had finished in front of him that day. How right Ward was! Sir Ivor proceeded to reel off three straight wins before the end of his juvenile season, culminating in a most impressive victory in France's premier test for two-year-olds, the Grand Criterium at Longchamp.

Ever the innovator, Vincent O'Brien took Sir Ivor away from Ireland for the winter of 1967/68 and stabled his star in the milder climate of Pisa in Italy. The bid to beat the frost was a master stroke. Benefiting from his sojourn in warmer climes, Sir Ivor returned to action as a superbly honed three-year-old and immediately took up where he had left off the previous season. He triumphed in his comeback race, the 2,000 Guineas Trial Stakes at Ascot, and went on to add the first two colts' classics, the 2,000 Guineas and the Epsom Derby to his winning record. The next step on the road to racing immortality was the Curragh and the Irish Derby.

With six straight wins behind him, it was no surprise that Sir Ivor's presence among the entries for the premier Irish classic frightened off most of the potential opposition. Thirteen owners none the less were prepared to pit their charges against the peerless champion. Of the fourteen runners, ten were Irish trained. Although the majority of the home-trained contenders appeared to have no realistic chance, there were those who thought that Giolla Mear, owned by the President of Ireland Éamon de Valera and winner of his two trial races, might perhaps shake up the favourite.

However, it was the only French-trained runner, Val d'Aoste, who was generally regarded as the principal challenger to Sir Ivor. Third in the French Derby (the Prix du Jockey-Club), Val d'Aoste had finished some two lengths behind a horse called Timmy My Boy, whom Sir Ivor had readily defeated in the Grand Criterium. Best on form of the three English challengers was Lucky Finish who had beaten another of the English

contenders, Ribero, by a head and a short head into third place in a desperate finish to the Dante Stakes at York. However, since Ribero had gone on to Ascot where he had been beaten by twelve lengths by Connaught, Sir Ivor's immediate victim at Epsom, the formbook made a cast iron case for Vincent O'Brien's colt.

The newspapers of the day reflected the prevailing mood of confidence in the dual classic winner's chance at the Curragh. The *Irish Press* banner headline on the morning of the race proclaimed: 'No Danger to Sir Ivor'. Previewing the race in *The Irish Times*, Michael O'Farrell pronounced that 'only the most unforeseeable accident in the Devon Loch category can prevent Sir Ivor [from winning] . . .' Devon Loch, a gelding owned by the Queen Mother, had stumbled unaccountably some fifty yards from the winning post when well clear in the 1956 Grand National.

The bookmakers evidently shared the belief of the professional pundits that only an act of God could intervene to prevent Sir Ivor from fulfilling his destiny. In his newspaper advertisement on the morning of the race, flamboyant Dublin bookmaker Terry Rogers, all but throwing in the towel, invited his clients to 'back their fancy to finish second to the "horse of the century", Sir Ivor'.

At Epsom Sir Ivor had been ridden in never-to-be-forgotten style by Lester Piggott. The horse was to be the first of Piggott's four Epsom Derby winners for Vincent O'Brien (Nijinsky, Roberto and The Minstrel were the others). At that time Liam Ward was contracted to ride all O'Brien's horses in

Ireland, and so it was he and not Piggott who partnered Sir Ivor at the Curragh. Piggott had to be content with the ride on the 100/6 shot, Ribero, trained by Fulke Johnson Houghton who had sent out Ribocco to win the previous year's race. Ribero, like Ribocco, was owned by wealthy businessman Charles Engelhard, and even though Piggott again donned the Engelhard colours, only coincidence backers could have fancied the combination to strike for a second year in succession.

Many of the racegoers who thronged the Curragh on that pleasant midsummer Saturday had come not to wager on the Derby, but for the sheer pleasure of watching a great champion. In any event, it would have been difficult to make a great deal of profit from a horse starting at the prohibitive odds of 1/3! The extent to which Sir Ivor was perceived to tower over the opposition was well illustrated by the 10/1 price quoted against the second favourite, the popular each-way fancy, Giolla Mear.

The going on the day was good, as it had been at Epsom; Sir Ivor was known not to like firm going, so conditions were in his favour. The Derby was the second race on the Curragh's six-race card. An unfancied 10/1 shot, French Serenade, ridden by T. P. Burns (later to be associated for many years with the Vincent O'Brien stable), won the first race by a short head from the joint favourite Sorrentina. Barely was the six furlong sprint over before the crowds began to hasten towards the parade ring to get a close-up view of the wonder horse, Sir Ivor.

The big handsome bay colt looked a picture of strength and agility as he was led around the ring. Physically he seemed to dwarf his opponents. As the jockeys mounted and set out to guide their charges across the Curragh to the starting point, the atmosphere was strangely devoid of the tension that usually precedes a major classic. The result, after all, appeared to be a formality for surely, as the experts had pointed out, the formbook could not lie. Or could it?

No unexpected alarms or excursions intervened to delay the start. The horses were loaded readily, Sir Ivor being last but one into the stalls. Was it just then, as the starter released the field, that a rather disconcerting question drifted into the consciousness of all those who up to that moment had not contemplated the possibility of defeat? How many horses had achieved the Derby double? Only Santa Claus in 1964 and Orby back in 1907 had been successful. Statistics were against Sir Ivor, then, but that consideration was summarily dismissed as the race got under way.

When the field had sorted itself out Seamus McGrath's Stitch, ridden by Peadar Matthews, and the Irish President's Giolla Mear, in the hands of T. P. Burns, made the early running. At this early stage Sir Ivor was settled towards the rear of the field. The pace appeared to be a good one, although afterwards the clock did not bear this out. With a mile to go, Ward, on Sir Ivor, began to thread his way through the field and, as expected, the hot favourite was travelling very smoothly.

At the half-way stage Giolla Mear and Stitch were still in front, with the English challenger Ribero and Paddy Prendergast's

New Member taking closer order. Sir Ivor was positioned behind the leading group and as the field swung right towards the home straight nothing seemed to be going easier than the Epsom Derby winner.

Sweeping into the straight, with just over three furlongs to run, both Stitch and Giolla Mear dropped away, and now it was Lester Piggott on Ribero who hit the front. However, even though Charles Engelhard's green colours with chocolate sash were to the fore, the eyes of the crowd were as one trained on the even more famous chocolate and blue hoops carried by the favourite.

Sir Ivor was tracking Ribero like a cat waiting to pounce. Two furlongs out a murmur of anticipation rose from the spectators as Sir Ivor ranged up to Ribero's quarters, for all the world looking an assured winner. This was it then — the moment that the expectant audience, including the millions watching on television, had waited for. That blistering burst of acceleration that had so ruthlessly cut down the opposition at Epsom would surely sweep aside the English-trained pretender.

The crowd in the grandstands waited for the moment, and waited, and waited. Piggott and Ribero continued to gallop on strongly, but, incredibly, it was Ward on Sir Ivor who was seen to be pushing and scrubbing in a desperate attempt to propel his mount past his resolute rival. Inch by inch, as the two courageous animals strained every muscle through those punishing two furlongs, with the rest of the field well beaten, it was Ribero who now appeared to be the master.

Was this possible? The gap between the two colts widened, at first to a neck, then to half a length, and soon there was a length between them. Surely there had to be a final effort from Sir Ivor? Liam Ward must have kept something up his sleeve. Astonishingly, the answer to these unspoken questions was to be in the negative.

In the final 150 yards, Ribero stretched his advantage over his hapless rival to two lengths at the line. With the exception of some isolated pockets of cheering, doubtless from those who had profited from the result, the outcome was greeted with a shocked silence. The wonder horse, the 'horse of the century', had been upstaged sensationally by a rival who, on any reading of the formbook, was palpably inferior to him.

What had gone wrong? The post-mortems commenced immediately; and to this day the eclipse of Sir Ivor remains a contentious subject in racing circles. One theory, strongly canvassed by those who had so unhesitatingly plumped for the O'Brien horse, was that only some veterinary excuse could possibly account for the upset. In the newspaper reports of the race there was considerable speculation that Sir Ivor was perhaps sickening for the cough, a malady that had been reported among some of the beaten favourite's stable companions. However, Sir Ivor was back on the racetrack within a week of his Curragh defeat, so this could not have been the reason.

What was beyond question was that the formbook had been torn to shreds. The change of jockey between Epsom and the Curragh was singled out by some as a possible explanation for the favourite's defeat. At Epsom Sir Ivor was held back by Piggott until very late in the race. Had what

Julian Wilson has described as Liam Ward's 'orthodox' riding at the Curragh contributed to Sir Ivor's defeat? The matter remains controversial. It is noteworthy that in Raymond Smith's otherwise comprehensive account of the amazing career of Vincent O'Brien, there are no references to Sir Ivor's sensational defeat in the 1968 Irish Derby. Perhaps the subject is too sensitive.

The details of Sir Ivor's subsequent career probably give the greatest clues to his Curragh failure. Beaten into third place in the Eclipse Stakes on unsuitably firm ground, Sir Ivor then triumphed in the Champion Stakes at Newmarket over what perhaps was his ideal distance of ten furlongs. In the Prix de l'Arc de Triomphe he was beaten into second place by that great racehorse, Vaguely Noble.

For most thoroughbreds eight races in a season, particularly bearing in mind the class of the opposition, is more than enough, but Sir Ivor was nothing if not tough. In November O'Brien brought his champion back to the land of his birth and, underlining his trainer's masterly skills, Sir Ivor gained a superb victory in the Washington International at Laurel Park. Run over one and a half miles, and on very testing ground, Sir Ivor's (and Lester Piggott's) success did much to foster the growth of horse racing on an international scale.

How does one rate Sir Ivor? Should one say that he was a truly great horse, but one who was not quite at his best over a mile and a half; that it was the genius of Lester Piggott alone that propelled him to his extraordinary victory in the Epsom Derby? And yet, how does that conclusion square with Piggott's widely publicised assertion that Sir Ivor was superior to the magnificent Nijinsky, the last horse to win the triple crown of racing (2,000 Guineas, Derby and St Leger)? Yet another top jockey, Sandy Barclay, who rode Connaught and who finished second in the 1968 Epsom Derby, was even more forthright in his assessment of Sir Ivor: 'the most brilliant horse . . . I have ever seen'.

The truth is that Sir Ivor's Curragh defeat will remain a subject for heated debate as long as people continue to be fascinated by the sport of horse racing. Ribero's triumph must take its place at the pinnacle of those upsets in the sport that have given rise to that most repeated of epigrams, 'the glorious uncertainty of racing'.

What of the winner, Ribero? A second successive winner of the Irish Sweeps Derby for his lucky owner Charles Engelhard, Ribero, like Ribocco, was bought at the Keeneland sales. A full brother to Ribocco, he was sired by the outstanding dual Prix de l'Arc de Triomphe winner Ribot and was out of the Epsom Derby winner Hyperion's fine brood mare Libra. As his breeding suggests, stamina was Ribero's strong suit, and over the fair but demanding Curragh circuit it was his undoubted stamina which helped him to record his greatest victory.

It is doubtless an unfair reflection on the achievements of a most gallant thoroughbred and his successful trainer, Fulke Johnson Houghton, but for historians of the turf the 1968 Irish Derby will forever be recalled, not for Ribero's creditable victory, but rather for Sir Ivor's entirely unexpected defeat.

IRISH SWEEPS DERBY

1M 4F

SATURDAY 29 JUNE 1968

GOING: GOOD

WINNER: Mr C. W. Engelhard's Ribero by Ribot out of
Libra
L. Piggott

SECOND: Sir Ivor by Sir Gaylord out of Attica
L. Ward

THIRD: Val d'Aoste by Val de Loir out of Nounouche
J. Deforge

S.P. 100/6   1/3f   100/6
Winner trained by R. F. Johnson Houghton

ALSO: Laudamus 4th, Lucky Finish 5th, New
Member 6th, Alaric 7th, Stitch 8th, Giolla
Mear 9th, Panco 10th, Saragan 11th,
Meadsville 12th, Sunset Glory 13th,
Home Farm 14th & last

Winner: joint 3rd favourite
Distances: 2 lengths, same
Value to winner: £55,340
Time: 2 m 33.9 s
Timeform rating of winner: 126.

1969

IRISH SWEEPS DERBY

After successive Sweeps Derby victories with Ribocco and Ribero, the Fulke Johnson Houghton-Lester Piggott-Charles Engelhard team came to the Curragh on the last Saturday in June 1969 with very high hopes of completing a historic treble. The vehicle carrying the weight of their expectations was Ribofilio, who, like the 1967 and 1968 winners, was a son of the great Italian horse, Ribot.

Ribofilio had enjoyed a successful juvenile campaign and, unusually for a colt by Ribot, he had come to hand early. In June he registered a convincing victory in the Chesham Stakes over six furlongs at Royal Ascot. In August Ribofilio travelled to Deauville, but was a disappointing sixth to Princeline in the Prix Morny on heavy going, which apparently did not suit him. Interestingly, one of his Curragh opponents, Prince Regent, finished third in that Deauville race some four and a half lengths ahead of Ribofilio.

The Johnson Houghton-trained colt, however, recovered his form and ended his two-year-old season with two excellent victories. Firstly, he triumphed in the Champagne Stakes over seven furlongs at Doncaster, beating Tudor Music and Hotfoot by two lengths and the same. Subsequently he was an authoritative winner of the Dewhurst Stakes at Newmarket, beating the Irish challengers, Deep Run and Murrayfield by three lengths and two and a half lengths.

Crowned the two-year-old champion, Ribofilio was confidently expected, as a son of Ribot, to improve with age and to stamp his authority on his generation. His first race as a three-year-old was in the Ascot 2,000 Guineas Trial, where he accomplished all that was expected of him with a comfortable two length and five length victory over Harasser and Tugwood. Favourite for the 2,000 Guineas at Newmarket, Ribofilio, with Piggott up, shocked and dismayed his supporters with a dismal display. Tailed off and eventually pulled up behind Right Tack, exhaustive tests were subsequently carried out on the colt without producing any explanation for his disastrous flop.

Ribofilio next contested the Epsom Derby and, despite his Guineas reverse, punters again entrusted him with their cash and the Lester Piggott-partnered colt was once again sent off favourite. Again however Ribofilio disappointed, finishing fifth to Blakeney, beaten a little over three lengths. In third place at Epsom, incidentally, was the aforementioned Prince Regent, two lengths behind Blakeney, with Vincent O'Brien's Moon Mountain fourth, only a short head behind the French-trained colt.

The above three horses — Blakeney, Prince Regent and Moon Mountain — all of whom had finished in front of Ribofilio at Epsom, were in opposition again at the Curragh, and yet much of the pre-race speculation centred on Ribofilio. The word from the gallops was that Ribofilio had recaptured his best two-year-old form and it was reported, furthermore, that Lester Piggott was confident that his mount would reverse placings with those who had finished in front of him at Epsom.

Needless to remark, connections of the animals in question didn't see things in quite the same light. In particular Arthur Budgett's Derby winner, Blakeney, had to be given every chance of confirming the Epsom form. A lightly raced son of the unlucky 1962 Epsom Derby favourite, Hethersett, Blakeney had run twice only as a juvenile. After running a promising fourth first time out, four lengths behind Caliban, Blakeney won his only other race as a two-year-old, a seven

furlong maiden at Newmarket in October, and he retired to winter quarters as a colt of definite potential.

That potential came close to being realised on Blakeney's first outing as a three-year-old. In the Lingfield Derby Trial Blakeney finished a three-quarter length second to The Elk and in the closing stages Arthur Budgett's colt was rapidly catching the winner. Blakeney's success at Epsom was therefore not entirely unexpected and the combination of speed, stamina and resolution shown there by the relatively inexperienced colt suggested that he could improve yet further.

If Blakeney was fancied, so too was Etienne Pollet's Prince Regent, who had two lengths to make up on Blakeney as compared with Epsom. A top juvenile in France, where it will be remembered he had been some way in front of Ribofilio in the Prix Morny, Prince Regent had run three times as a three-year-old. Two victories at Longchamp in the Prix Greffulhe and the Prix Lupin preceded his Epsom run. There, ridden by Jean Deforge, he was in the opinion of many critics a very unlucky loser in that his pilot had yet again exhibited that seeming inability of French jockeys to negotiate a successful path around the tricky Epsom switchback. With Geoff Lewis replacing Deforge in the saddle, Prince Regent was entitled to the most serious consideration for this, the eighth running of the Irish Sweeps Derby.

Of the fifteen runners no less than five were saddled by Vincent O'Brien. After Sir Ivor's shock defeat in 1968, it is perhaps possible that the Ballydoyle maestro was beginning to think that the Sweeps Derby was an unlucky race for him. Undaunted, however, his team contained at least two runners whose chances had to be respected. Stable jockey Liam Ward's pick was Onandaga, yet another son of Ribot and owned by the American J. W. Galbreath. Onandaga had improved steadily as a three-year-old. After winning the Ballysax Maiden over ten furlongs at the Curragh, Onandaga had become bogged down in the soft ground and was only a moderate third in the Royal Whip behind Candy Cane over the full Derby distance at the Curragh. On his subsequent run, however, Onandaga had won the Gallinule Stakes over ten furlongs at the Curragh, beating Deep Run by two lengths. The line was a tenuous one, but it will be recalled that Ribofilio as a juvenile had beaten Deep Run by three lengths in the Dewhurst Stakes, and if the form line through Deep Run could be believed, Onandaga's chance was there for all to see.

In any event, it was surely significant that Ward had chosen Onandaga in preference to the Epsom Derby fourth, Moon Mountain. Yves Saint-Martin had ridden Moon Mountain at Epsom and was not adjudged to have ridden a distinguished race on the Comtesse de la Valdene's colt.

The French jockey attempted to make all the running on Moon Mountain at Epsom and in addition he was unable to keep his mount on a true course in the straight. In the circumstances, to be beaten a little over two lengths was no disgrace and Moon Mountain had an undeniable chance on the evidence of the formbook. Incidentally, it is worth noting that the Comtesse de la Valdene had a particularly strong hand in the Derby for,

besides Moon Mountain, her colours were also being carried by Prince Regent as well as by one of the O'Brien outsiders, the Ballymoss colt, Ballantine.

Although only third choice of the Ballydoyle quintet, many shrewd judges considered that Reindeer, from the first crop of 1964 Sweeps Derby hero, Santa Claus, was a lively outsider. Ridden by the experienced T. P. Burns, who had won the 1957 Irish Derby and English St Leger for O'Brien on the great Ballymoss, Reindeer was lightly raced, but had registered successive victories over ten furlongs at both the Phoenix Park and Leopardstown.

The only other contender who merited serious consideration was the second French raider, Beaugency, representing the team of Alec and Freddie Head. Beaten only a short head in the Prix du Jockey-Club (the French Derby), Beaugency was held on previous French form by Prince Regent, but was evidently improving and was expected to run well.

The betting on the race underlined the competitive nature of the contest. Pre-race confidence in Ribofilio was reflected in the fact that Lester Piggott's mount was a firm 2/1 favourite at the off. This was no one-horse market, however, for both Blakeney and Prince Regent were strongly supported and wound up joint second favourites at 7/2. The layers were not giving too much away in this instance. French challenger Beaugency was next in the betting at 9/1, with Vincent O'Brien's trio proving best of the rest. Onandaga at 100/8 was marginally preferred to both Moon Mountain and Reindeer who were priced at 100/7. If you fancied any of the rest, you could get 33/1 and upwards on your money.

As the stalls opened, one wonders what the former Taoiseach Seán Lemass, a keen racing fan, must have been thinking. Newspapers of the day had reported that the politician, widely regarded as the most influential Irishman of his generation, had drawn a horse, Vivadari, in the sweep on the race. Seamus McGrath's colt was a 150/1 outsider, so the ex-Taoiseach's chances of collecting a major dividend seemed a trifle remote.

Right from the outset Vincent Rossiter on the Ballydoyle long shot, Ballantine, made the running. The early pace was fast and most of the field were content to keep Ballantine in their sights at this point. When Ballantine cracked in what was obviously a well orchestrated plan of campaign, both Onandaga and Reindeer, also from the Ballydoyle yard, took up the running.

At this juncture Ribofilio was nicely placed, just off the leading group, while Prince Regent, who had been last early on, was tracking Piggott's mount. Supporters of the Epsom Derby winner, Blakeney, must however have been a little apprehensive as it could be seen that Ernie Johnson was having to work quite hard to maintain a challenging position.

The order remained pretty much unchanged as the field came down the hill and turned into the straight. Those who had speculated a little on Reindeer were on good terms with themselves when the 100/7 shot struck the front early in the straight, by all appearances going well. However, just behind T. P. Burns's mount the familiar sight of the erect Piggott bottom on Ribofilio presaged an imminent challenge for the lead. Asking Ribofilio for his effort on the outside of Reindeer, Fulke Johnson Houghton's colt immediately got the better of his inexperienced rival. An unprecedented and perhaps unbeatable third successive Irish Derby triumph for trainer, owner and jockey loomed as a distinct possibility as the stoutly bred Ribofilio set sail for home.

But the race was far from over. All the while, as Piggott had guided Ribofilio into the lead, he had been tracked by Geoff Lewis on Prince Regent. The green colours and yellow sleeves of Ribofilio's pilot were now ominously threatened by the yellow with green-hooped sleeves worn by Prince Regent's jockey. Coming wide of Ribofilio, Lewis got a tremendous response from his mount and the combination surged past Piggott's charge, showing a superb burst of acceleration.

Lewis had timed his challenge to perfection. Ribofilio had nothing left to offer. At the line Prince Regent had a length to spare over the unfortunate Ribofilio, who had set an unenviable record in having been a beaten favourite in three successive classics. The pair dominated the final stages to such an extent that it was five lengths back to the best of the Vincent O'Brien quintet, Reindeer, who just held Blakeney out of third place by a short head. The Ballydoyle trainer also saddled the fifth and sixth horses home, Onandaga and outsider Selko.

For the veteran French trainer Etienne Pollet the result was a triumph and vindicated his view that Prince Regent was a most unfortunate Epsom loser. Saddling his second winner of the Sweeps Derby, following upon Tambourine II's success in the inaugural running, Prince Regent brought to an end a decade of outstanding achievement for his highly respected trainer. As well as his Irish successes, Pollet had the distinction of handling two of the greatest colts of the 1960s, indeed of the century, Sea Bird II and Vaguely Noble, both of whom numbered the Prix de l'Arc de Triomphe among their successes. For many astute racegoers, Sea Bird II was the outstanding horse of the century, and whilst great racehorses make great trainers, Pollet's record speaks for itself.

In addition to the horses already mentioned, other top-class animals trained by Pollet included Thunderhead II (English 2,000 Guineas, 1952), Never Too Late II (English 1,000 Guineas and Oaks, 1960), Hula Dancer (English 1,000 Guineas and Champion Stakes, 1963) and Right Royal V, about whom I will write further.

A couple of incidental details are worth mentioning about the 1969 Irish Derby, both bearing on the national hunt side of horse racing. Some Irish racing fans were unhappy about the actual name of the Derby winner. The wartime chaser Prince Regent, trained by the great Tom Dreaper, was in many experts' opinion the equal of Arkle, and it seemed somehow regrettable that his name did not preserve its unique status however worthy his namesake. Secondly, although among the overnight declarations, Deep Run did not in fact take part due to a bout of coughing. It is of interest to note, however, that the Pampered King colt who, as noted earlier, had shown flashes of quite

excellent form, went on to become the most prolific high-class national hunt sire of the post-war era. Among his progeny was that great mare, Dawn Run, the only horse ever to complete the Champion Hurdle-Cheltenham Gold Cup double.

The subsequent careers of the principals in the Irish Derby of 1969 are of interest. Ribofilio was an unfortunate colt, but his hard-pressed supporters probably had other adjectives in mind when they thought about him. After completing the formality of winning a two-runner race at Goodwood, Ribofilio next contested the St Leger at Doncaster. He was opposed by *inter alia* his old rivals, Blakeney and Reindeer.

Sent off 11/10 favourite, Ribofilio duly finished in front of both Blakeney, who was fifth, and Reindeer, who was sixth. However, he could not master Harry Wragg's 7/1 shot, Intermezzo, and was second, beaten one and a half lengths. This completed a unique four-timer for Ribofilio — beaten favourite in the four classics in which he had competed — a record unlikely ever to be equalled, never mind surpassed! There was no doubt as to who was clear favourite for the title of Bookmakers' Horse of the Year 1969!

Prince Regent meantime was put by to contest the Prix de l'Arc de Triomphe. With his trainer's outstanding record in the Arc, Prince Regent was made favourite for the race. Proving that the three-year-olds of 1969 were not perhaps the best ever to represent their generation, Prince Regent finished only fifth at Longchamp.

The race is remembered chiefly for the fairy-tale success of Seamus McGrath's Ascot Gold Cup winner, Levmoss, who held off the high-class mare, Park Top, by three-quarters of a length. It should be pointed out, however, that Prince Regent was by no means disgraced and in fact finished ahead of the other three-year-olds who contested the October championship race. Among those who finished behind him at Longchamp were those durable sorts Blakeney and (yes!) Ribofilio.

Prince Regent was a son of the aforementioned Right Royal V who had been trained by Etienne Pollet to win a string of top-class races. These included the Grand Criterium, the French 2,000 Guineas, the Prix Lupin and the French Derby. In England Right Royal V won the King George VI and Queen Elizabeth Stakes in which he outclassed the Derby and St Leger winner, St Paddy. Right Royal V was also second to Molvedo in the Prix de l'Arc de Triomphe.

In view of his breeding and record, great things were expected of Prince Regent when he was retired to stud after an unsuccessful four-year-old campaign. He went on to sire the winners of well over four hundred races, but he never got a horse as good as himself. In fact he became best known as a sire of national hunt horses, including such useful sorts as Cybrandian and Tinryland, and the top-class Remittance Man, winner of the Arkle and Queen Mother Champion Chases at Cheltenham in successive years. Prince Regent died at the Collinstown Stud in County Kildare in May 1993 at the venerable age of 27 years.

The 1969 Sweeps Derby hero was a long way from being the best ever winner of the premier Irish classic. He was, however, almost certainly the best horse of his generation. Certainly his tremendous turn of foot, displayed at its most potent in the Irish Sweeps Derby of 1969, will long be remembered by those who were there to see it.

IRISH SWEEPS DERBY

1M 4F

SATURDAY 28 JUNE 1969

GOING: GOOD

WINNER: Comtesse de la Valdene's Prince Regent by
Right Royal V out of Noduleuse
G. Lewis

SECOND: Ribofilio by Ribot out of Island Creek
L. Piggott

THIRD: Reindeer by Santa Claus out of Reine des Bois
T. P. Burns

S.P. 7/2   2/1f   100/7
Winner trained by E. Pollet

ALSO: Blakeney 4th, Onandaga 5th, Selko 6th,
Northern Mist 7th, Augustus 8th, Beaugency
9th, Moon Mountain 10th, Ballantine 11th,
Santamoss 12th, Vivadari 13th, Bunkered
14th, Tanzara 15th & last

Winner: joint 2nd favourite
Distances: 1 length, 5 lengths
Value to winner: £53,390
Time: 2 m 36.1 s
Timeform rating of winner: 129.

1970

IRISH SWEEPS DERBY

With eight straight wins behind him the great Nijinsky dominated the field for the 1970 Irish Derby as no horse before him had done. Despite Nijinsky's record Vincent O'Brien, however, must have harboured secret fears that the Curragh classic, very much as two years previously in the case of Sir Ivor, might prove one step too far for his magnificent Northern Dancer colt.

On paper there was nothing to test the Charles Engelhard-owned colt. Undefeated, his juvenile campaign is easily summarised: five outings, five wins. Included in this tally were Group victories at the Curragh in the Railway, Anglesey and Beresford Stakes respectively, together with a most impressive win in the end of season juvenile champion-ship, the Dewhurst Stakes at Newmarket. Nijinsky of course topped the Free Handicap for juveniles in 1969.

Prior to the Sweeps Derby Nijinsky had raced three times as a three-year-old. He won his preparatory race, the Gladness Stakes,

easily at the Curragh and followed up with a very smooth two and a half length victory over Yellow God in the 2,000 Guineas at Newmarket. On fast ground at Epsom, Nijinsky had dispelled whatever doubts existed about his stamina with a comfortable two and a half length win over Gyr, with Stintino three lengths back in third place.

Up to that point Nijinsky's Derby was the fastest recorded since electronic timing had been introduced in 1964. In winning at Epsom, Nijinsky also became the first colt since Bois Roussel in 1938 to defend successfully an undefeated record in the Derby.

With such credentials, was there a horse that could possibly beat Nijinsky at the Curragh? There were fourteen aspirants to Nijinsky's crown, but none of them seemed to possess the requisite class. Of those that had finished behind Nijinsky at Epsom, only Meadowville (fifth) and Approval (seventh), both English trained, were dispatched to renew rivalry with Vincent O'Brien's champion colt. The French challenged with Chantilly winner, Master Guy, a stable companion of Gyr (beaten into second place at Epsom) and trainer Etienne Pollet was rumoured to have postponed his pending retirement because of his faith in the Relko colt. Among the Irish outsiders Charlie Weld's Ringsend, to be ridden by Irish champion jockey Ryan 'Buster' Parnell, was written up in some quarters as an each-way prospect.

But, in truth, reason suggested that only Nijinsky could beat Nijinsky. A highly strung colt, he had exhibited signs of temperament at both Newmarket and Epsom, and in particular his tendency to sweat before races was somewhat off-putting. Would a suspect temperament betray the majestic thoroughbred?

For the average punter Nijinsky was not a serious betting proposition. However, the presence of a great horse is always guaranteed to bring out Irish racegoers, and a splendid crowd foregathered at racing's headquarters for the annual renewal of the Sweeps Derby.

In those days a train trip to the Curragh was the favourite mode of travel for many racegoers. It is quaint now to read the CIE advertisement for their travel arrangements for Derby day. You could travel to the Curragh from Dublin for twelve shillings standard return and the combined cost of travel and admission to the Grand Stand was 24/6d! (in today's currency approximately £1.22). First-class passengers could travel return for eighteen shillings and the combined cost of a first-class return and

admission to the reserved enclosure was fifty-eight shillings. Oddly, the CIE advertisement expressed its prices in the lesser denomination of shillings, as opposed to the pound. Curious!

Whatever the mode of travel, all eyes that day at the Curragh were for the champion 'wonder horse' Nijinsky. The colt, named after the legendary Russian dancer, Vaslav Nijinsky, who had enchanted ballet audiences in Paris and London before the First World War, looked every inch a champion as he paraded before the race. However, it was noticeable that as race time drew near Nijinsky became more and more agitated. There must have been some considerable anxiety among both connections and indeed Nijinsky's admirers as the prized colt began to sweat profusely in the preliminaries. An even more disconcerting sign was that on his way to the start Nijinsky's tail was swishing about ominously. Invariably a sign of temperament, often indicative of a mulish attitude, owner Charles Engelhard who had enjoyed such a marvellous record in the Curragh classic must have entertained dark doubts that his long-cherished ambition to see Nijinsky retire as an undefeated champion was to be ruthlessly shattered in this, his colt's ninth race.

Only four thoroughbreds previously during the twentieth century had ended their careers undefeated — Colin, in the early years of the century, Bahram and Nearco (the latter the grandsire of Nijinsky) in the 1930s, and the legendary Ribot in the 1950s. Would Nijinsky join this illustrious quartet?

Despite the worrying show of temperament from the Canadian-bred colt,

Nijinsky started a hot 4/11 favourite. The Epsom Derby also-rans Approval and Meadowville were joint second favourites at 10/1, with the French challenger Master Guy at 100/7. Ringsend was available at 33/1 and it was 66/1 bar five. Not too many, it must be said, were prepared to risk serious money or any money at all indeed on the longer-priced candidates.

It was a humid afternoon, with rain about, but fortunately conditions stayed fine for the main event. The thirteen runners were loaded up, the concentration of all present focused on the starting point across the Curragh plain, and soon the race was under way. The early pace was surprisingly moderate. Expectations were that at least one of the challengers would ensure a strong pace with a view to stretching Nijinsky's stamina to the limit, but it didn't work out that way. As Double Dick, with John Roe up, made the running, Liam Ward, who, as in 1968 replaced Lester Piggott on the Epsom Derby winner, realising that he could conserve Nijinsky's finishing burst, dropped his mount back to the tail of the field.

As Double Dick continued to show the way to Dubrava and Nor, Ward was content to allow Nijinsky to remain among the last three. Four and a half furlongs out Double Dick started to weaken and half a furlong later George McGrath raced clear on Illa Laudo, with Nor close up and Nijinsky still nearer last than first.

Illa Laudo was first into the straight, with Nor next, followed by Lester Piggott on Meadowville. Nijinsky was still towards the rear and the French colt Master Guy was stone last. Just as Nijinsky's supporters were becoming a trifle anxious, Ward made his challenge on the inside. It was here that a problem arose. Ward had kept Nijinsky on the rails throughout, and for a few strides after the field had turned into the straight, there looked to be some possibility that the combination might get trapped on the rails. But favourite backers were quickly able to breathe again. Neatly side-stepping Illa Laudo, Nijinsky skipped to the outside of George McGrath's mount and the way ahead was clear. Meantime the nose-banded Meadowville on the extreme stand side was coming with his run, while simultaneously Master Guy was improving into a challenging position. The three horses raced together to the furlong pole, where Ward asked Nijinsky to quicken. The response was immediate. Without having to be put under any discernible pressure, the Northern Dancer colt accelerated smoothly to make winning look oh so easy.

For the record, Meadowville, with Piggott aboard, was second, while Master Guy, partnered by J. Taillard, ran on to be third. Nor was a gallant fourth, Illa Laudo a respectable fifth and Dubrava sixth. The official distances were three lengths and the same, but it could have been doubled or trebled had Ward so desired. The simple truth was that it was Nijinsky first and the rest nowhere.

Afterwards Ward explained that as soon as the race started Nijinsky relaxed in his hands, concentrated on the job in hand and never gave him a moment's anxiety. It was perhaps an exaggeration to conclude, as Ward did after the race: 'My own grandmother could have ridden him.'

From the stands it certainly looked that way. For owner Charles Engelhard, Nijinsky's victory meant that he had owned the winners of three Irish Derbies in four years, as well as the second in the other one — a truly remarkable record.

Nijinsky's Irish Derby victory was tremendously popular with the Curragh racegoers and he received a warm reception on his return to the unsaddling arena. A classic horse with a classic name, he embodied in his powerful athletic frame all of that indefinable quality of greatness that marks out the true champion. Nijinsky in his classic year, 1970, did much more though than simply dominate his contemporaries. For the European racing public, Nijinsky's triumphs brought the name of his previously unknown sire to the forefront of attention. Vincent O'Brien's superb colt was a son of the great Canadian racehorse, Northern Dancer, whose influence today is worldwide and whose bloodlines are in constant demand wherever thoroughbreds are marketed.

Northern Dancer was bred by the Canadian E. P. Taylor at Windfields Farm, Toronto. The best possible endorsement of Colonel Bradley's famous maxim, 'If you want the best, you breed the best to the best and hope for the best', Northern Dancer was by Nearctic out of Natalma and in his pedigree he brought together a truly international combination of the world's leading lines. As mentioned previously, Nijinsky was a grandson of the great unbeaten Nearco, one of the most influential stallions of the century. Italian bred, Nearco won fourteen races in all, including the Grand Prix de

Paris in which he trounced the Epsom Derby winner Bois Roussel.

For a horse that was to prove such an important breeding influence for succeeding generations, in physical appearance Northern Dancer was not especially prepossessing. He was small, 15.2 hands high, and he had three white feet, not usually regarded as a good sign, but as a racehorse Northern Dancer was something else. In a career which due to injury spanned less than a year, between August 1963 and June 1964 he ran no less than eighteen times, winning fourteen races and being placed in the other four. In these bare statistics alone, one can perhaps appreciate how toughness was imbued into all of Northern Dancer's stock. The colt's principal victory in this short but dynamic career was the 1964 Kentucky Derby in which besides becoming the first Canadian-bred to win the race he shattered the course record!

It was on Vincent O'Brien's advice that platinum magnate Charles Engelhard purchased Northern Dancer's son, Nijinsky, at the 1968 Canadian Thoroughbred Horse Society's sale for what turned out to be the bargain basement price of $84,000. Nijinsky was from Northern Dancer's second crop and was out of the Canadian Oaks winner, Flaming Page. It is no exaggeration to say that no yearling purchase before or since has so unalterably changed the course of the breeding industry in Europe.

With the Irish Sweeps Derby under his belt, his ninth straight win, it seemed inevitable that Nijinsky would remain undefeated for the balance of his racing career. This certainly was the dream both of

Vincent O'Brien and of Charles Engelhard. The immediate plan mapped out for Nijinsky after his Curragh triumph was to prove his superiority over all comers in the two principal all-aged Group 1 races — the King George at Ascot and the Prix de l'Arc at Longchamp.

The first part of the plan went off to perfection. Opposed by five top-class older horses at Ascot, Nijinsky put up perhaps the most impressive winning performance of his career. He won the King George VI and Queen Elizabeth Stakes hard held by two lengths, in the process dismissing the 1969 Epsom Derby winner, Blakeney, as if he were a selling plater. After this effortless success against older horses, it appeared to be just a formality for Nijinsky to complete his racing career undefeated. Within a week of his Ascot triumph, however, disaster struck. Nijinsky contracted a virulent form of the skin disease, ringworm, and Vincent O'Brien had to give his colt a complete rest from training.

After suffering such a debilitating illness, many commentators were surprised when it was announced subsequently that Nijinsky was to be put back into training with the St Leger as his objective. The owner, Charles Engelhard, was alone responsible for this decision. No horse since Bahram in 1935 had completed the triple crown of 2,000 Guineas, Epsom Derby and St Leger, and the platinum magnate who had battled for years against a weight problem, and realising that he was unlikely to live long enough to ever have a thoroughbred as good as Nijinsky, was determined to see his great colt complete the historic treble.

After a rushed preparation, therefore, Nijinsky ran in the St Leger at Doncaster on 12 September 1970. The colt's rivals were determined to test Nijinsky's stamina to the limit and the race was run at a furious pace. If Nijinsky had a weak link, then the tactics employed were sure to expose it. It was not to be, however. Nijinsky's sheer class saw him through. With Piggott apparently full of confidence, Nijinsky cruised up to the leaders a furlong and a half from home and won easing up by one length from Meadowville. It was a remarkable performance over a trip — one mile six and a half furlongs — almost certainly beyond Nijinsky's best. There were great scenes of rejoicing after Nijinsky's fabulous Doncaster win, and for owner Charles Engelhard a lifetime's ambition had been realised but, as was to be demonstrated later, there was a price to be paid.

Upon returning home after his eleventh successive victory and with claims ringing around the equine world that Nijinsky was the greatest racehorse of all time, Vincent O'Brien was perturbed to discover that his champion had lost over two stone in weight as a result of his exertions at Doncaster. It was by far the greatest weight loss that Nijinsky had sustained during his career. With the Arc as Nijinsky's objective, the Ballydoyle maestro had but three weeks to restore Nijinsky to peak form. It was to prove a task that defeated the legendary skills of probably the greatest flat race trainer of the century.

For many, Nijinsky's Arc defeat at the hands of Sassafras remains the single most controverisal race in Lester Piggott's long and distinguished career in the saddle. Many observers blamed Piggott for Nijinsky's defeat, contending that the jockey for once had erred in giving his mount too much to do. Lester himself refutes this view. As recounted in both Julian Wilson's biography and in Raymond Smyth's book on Vincent O'Brien, Piggott maintains that Nijinsky was not at his best on Arc day. He never gave him the same 'feel' as in races earlier in the season. Accordingly, Piggott decided to let the horse settle nearer the back than he would ideally have wished. In doing so he was going against the specific instructions given to him by Vincent O'Brien.

Turning into the short Longchamp straight Piggott was, as he admits, further behind that he would have wanted to be. Even so, once given the office, Nijinsky quickened and closed remorselessly on the leaders. With 150 yards to go the combination had drawn level with Sassafras, partnered by Yves Saint-Martin, and shortly afterwards Nijinsky actually poked his nose in front. The old Nijinsky would have gone on from there and put the issue beyond doubt, but on this occasion it just didn't happen.

Debate continues as to how precisely Nijinsky came to be beaten at Longchamp. The simple fact is that with about thirty yards to go Nijinsky swerved to his left. Was it because he resented the whip, which for the first time in his life Piggott had used on him? Piggott has claimed that the use of the whip did not bring about the swerve. It is a debatable point. No satisfactory alternative explanation for Nijinsky's swerve has ever been put forward. Piggott contends, and doubtless he is correct, that had Nijinsky kept a straight line he would have won.

Be that as it may, to the disbelief of the thousands in the stands and the millions watching on TV, Sassafras got up in the last two strides to beat the mighty Nijinsky by a head. The dream of Charles Engelhard, and indeed of Vincent O'Brien, to see their champion retire from racing undefeated was shattered unalterably in those dramatic last few strides at Longchamp.

Worse was to follow. In a decision which Vincent O'Brien must surely with hindsight regret, it was decided to attempt to restore wounded pride by running Nijinsky in the Champion Stakes at Newmarket just thirteen days after the Arc. It was to prove a sad mistake. Nijinsky had lost his unbeaten record and little could have been gained even if he had won at Newmarket.

He did not win the Champion Stakes. The signs of temperament that had always bubbled close to the surface of the majestic Nijinsky boiled over at Newmarket. On edge, noticeably trembling during the parade and at one point actually rearing up, Nijinsky was not himself at any stage and went down ingloriously to defeat at the hands of the inferior Lorenzaccio.

It was a sad end to a glorious chapter in racing's ever changing history. The post-mortems on Nijinsky's final two defeats continue to exercise the minds of students of the turf. The conventional wisdom is that the hard race that Nijinsky had in the St Leger told against him in his final two races. Lester Piggott, and I for one agree with him, does not subscribe to this theory. In his view, the bout of ringworm suffered by Nijinsky after his King George success was principally responsible for his decline afterwards.

Masked by Piggott's skilful handling at Doncaster, the lingering effects of the debilitating illness were sadly manifest for all to see at Longchamp and Newmarket. One sad corollary of the controversial end to Nijinsky's career was to hasten the decline in status of the oldest of the English classics, the St Leger. Ever since his participation in the St Leger was held to be responsible for Nijinsky's final two defeats, owners since 1970 have tended to bypass the race, and as a result the once prestigious triple crown of racing is rarely if ever attempted. A continuing argument still rages as to whether the growing emphasis on speed as opposed to stamina, as reflected by the deterioration in the standing of the St Leger, is to the long-term advantage of the sport, but such matters are beyond the scope of this present work. Suffice to say that in the eyes of many, a great champion should excel over his peers over a range of distances, and that Nijinsky most certainly did.

A great classic horse ideally should transmit his greatness to his progeny.

Nijinsky, not surprisingly, did just that. Included among the top-class horses sired by Nijinsky were Golden Fleece, Shahrastani, Caerleon and Ile de Bourbon. Further reference to each of these horses will follow in later chapters.

His career may have ended in controversy, but it is in victory that the great Nijinsky will be remembered. Was Nijinsky the best of all the champions that have passed through the hands of his peerless trainer? In the course of a recent interview with me, Vincent O'Brien made the following revelatory comment about Nijinsky: 'For a horse who stayed one and a half miles, he had such speed that I believe he would have won the July Cup had he been trained for it.'

Probably the classiest horse of the post-war era, and the greatest son of a great sire, Nijinsky cut a swathe through his classic generation very much in the manner in which the legendary dancer after whom he was named thrilled and delighted ballet audiences in the early years of this century.

IRISH SWEEPS DERBY

1M 4F

SATURDAY 27 JUNE 1970

GOING: GOOD

WINNER: Mr C. W. Engelhard's Nijinsky by Northern
Dancer out of Flaming Page
L. Ward

SECOND: Meadowville by Charlottesville out of
Meadow Pipit
L. Piggott

THIRD: Master Guy by Relko out of Musical
J. Taillard

S.P. 4/11f   10/1   100/7
Winner trained by M. V. O'Brien

ALSO: Nor 4th, Illa Laudo 5th, Dubrava 6th,
Approval 7th, Noble Life 8th, Ringsend 9th,
Honest Crook 10th, Nip and Tuck 11th,
Double Dick 12th, Oh Brother 13th & last

Winner: favourite
Distances: 3 lengths, same
Value to winner: £56,992 10s.
Time: 2 m 33.6 s
Timeform rating of winner: 138.

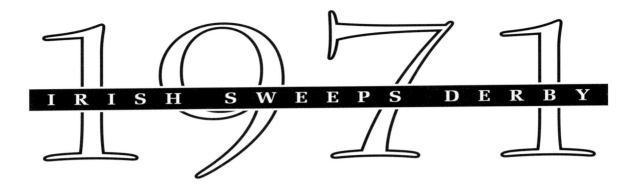

1971 IRISH SWEEPS DERBY

In the opinion of several respected judges Mill Reef, the winner of the 1971 Epsom Derby, was the best English-trained winner of that classic in the post-war era. In the absence of Ian Balding's star performer, the 1971 renewal of the Irish Sweeps Derby was somewhat reduced in stature, although a competitive field was none the less assembled for the centre-piece of the Irish flat racing calendar. As events were to transpire, however, it was not the result of the 1971 race but an incident of a rather less predictable nature that was to be forever associated with the Irish Derby of that year.

Epsom placed form was more than adequately represented at the Curragh, with the horses that had finished second, third and fourth to Mill Reef in the line-up. Linden Tree, trained by Peter Walwyn and the mount of Duncan Keith, had been beaten two lengths into second place by Mill Reef. After looking a winner early in the straight at Epsom, Linden Tree was made to look positively pedestrian by Mill Reef's turn of foot. Incidentally, Peter Walwyn's colt was blinkered at Epsom in an effort to make him concentrate better.

A talented colt, Linden Tree, by the Epsom Derby winner Crepello, had enjoyed a successful juvenile campaign, culminating in a victory in the prestigious Observer Gold Cup. A 25/1 chance at Doncaster, Linden Tree made the running and fought back courageously to beat Nijinsky's half brother Minsky by a head. Prior to his Epsom run, Linden Tree had won the Chester Vase, but only by a short head from Frascati, and his Epsom performance represented a step up on that form. In the run-up to the Curragh classic there was talk of his connections purchasing another horse to ensure a strong pace for Linden Tree, but nothing came of that and Duncan Keith's mount was obliged to make do without the benefit of a pacemaker.

At Epsom Linden Tree had two and a half lengths to spare over the third placed Irish Ball. There was a body of opinion which held that the French-trained Irish Ball had a good chance of reversing Epsom placings with Peter Walwyn's colt. Like many a compatriot before and since, Irish Ball had been quite unable to handle the hill down to Tattenham Corner and as a result had got himself into a hopeless position. Under pressure, Irish Ball made up a lot of ground in the straight at Epsom, giving his supporters hope of a more rewarding run at the Curragh.

Prior to Epsom, Irish Ball was third on heavy going at Longchamp, beaten just over five lengths over an extended ten furlongs. Lester Piggott was in the saddle on that occasion and it seemed significant that the maestro had deserted the grey colt by Baldric II, although perhaps the story wasn't quite that simple.

The 'long fellow' was associated at the Curragh with Lombardo, the more fancied of the two runners from the Rossmore Lodge stable of Paddy Prendergast. Previously successful for the stable in the Sweeps Derby with Meadow Court in 1965, Piggott's mount had finished fourth to Mill Reef at Epsom, one and a half lengths adrift of Irish Ball and four lengths in all behind Linden Tree. By Ragusa, who of course had won the 1963 Sweeps Derby, Paddy Prendergast believed that Lombardo had not been ridden to best effect at Epsom and the intention was to ride him with more restraint this time. A winner over ten furlongs at Leopardstown by four lengths from Ortis (who was later to finish second to Mill Reef in the King George),

Lombardo carried most Irish hopes of success in the country's premier classic.

Paddy Prendergast also saddled Guillemot, and this Sea Bird II colt was the mount of Liam Ward. Disqualified on his previous run after finishing second to Grenfall, beaten half a length in the Gallinule Stakes, Guillemot had no more than an outsider's chance. Vincent O'Brien trained Grenfall and stable jockey John Roe had picked this one in preference to the other Ballydoyle representative, Tantoul. The latter, however, had at least shown his ability to get the trip, having beaten Galileo-Galilei over course and distance on his previous run.

Probably the most intriguing of the Irish runners was Stephen Quirke's Parnell, a chestnut colt by St Paddy. This three parts brother to Miralgo had run up a string of victories, culminating in an easy win in the Queen's Vase at Royal Ascot over two miles. Clearly he would stay. The question was: was he good enough?

Bidding to win the great race for his owner Mrs Howell E. Jackson for the second time, the French-trained Music Man was a son of Mrs Jackson's inaugural winner of the Sweeps Derby, Tambourine II, and his victory over the distance at Chantilly at least showed that he would get the trip. His overall form, however, appeared inferior to the other French challenger, Irish Ball.

None of the remainder — there were fifteen runners in total — could realistically entertain any hope of winning, but doubtless expectations were harboured for them all. The betting market reflected the belief that Epsom Derby form would be upheld. Linden

Tree headed affairs at 7/4, followed by Irish Ball at 7/2, with Lombardo third favourite at 13/2. Parnell and Grenfall were bracketed together at 7/1. It was 16/1 Guillemot and Music Man, 22/1 Tantoul and 100/1 bar these eight.

Backers of the favourite must have been a little perturbed to notice that Linden Tree showed a degree of reluctance to go down to the start. Given a lead he eventually consented to do so, but arrived at the start last of the fifteen runners. It subsequently emerged that Linden Tree's jockey, Duncan Keith, requested the starter, Hubie Tyrell, to put his horse into the stalls last, and this the starter agreed to do.

There followed one of the most contro-versial incidents in the history of the Irish Derby. With all fifteen runners installed — Linden Tree, it should be noted, was drawn No. 1 on the wide outside — the starter operated the device which opened the stalls and the horses set out on their twelve furlong trek around the Curragh. Well, fourteen of them did. Linden Tree took but one stride before whipping around to his left and stopping in his tracks.

After the field had gone quite some distance Linden Tree did in fact gallop off after them, as a photograph by Jack Murphy in the *Sunday Independent* of 27 June 1971 clearly shows. His chance though was gone. John Comyn, reporting in the same edition of the *Sunday Independent*, vividly describes the utter confusion that followed the start of the race. For some reason the course commentary system failed at the critical moment and so racegoers were not alerted by the familiar shout of 'They're off!' As a result,

many in the crowd were unaware that the favourite had been hopelessly left. The first six furlongs of the Derby were run off in an unreal silence. It was as though a phantom race were taking place.

The early running was in fact made by the Kevin Prendergast-trained outsider Wacoso, with Charlie Weld's Turbulent Eddy and English challenger Bayons Manor close up. The second favourite Irish Ball was also prominent early on. Irish Ball was steadied in fifth or sixth place as his fellow Gallic raider, Music Man, joined the leading group. There was very little change in the order until running down the hill towards the straight.

By this stage the course commentary had been restored, but regrettably this only succeeded in adding to the considerable confusion by identifying one of the leading group as none other that Linden Tree! Knowledgeable racegoers (i.e. those with binoculars) could, however, quite clearly see that Linden Tree, carrying the cherry colours with black sleeves and cap of Mrs McCalmont, was trailing the field! The confusion, indeed bafflement, among many of the Curragh spectators is easy to imagine.

Music Man had by now taken up the running, with Guillemot and Irish Ball making up ground as the field entered the straight. The course commentator, meantime, was having one of those days because with three furlongs to go he had Linden Tree in third place (presumably going like a winner!). The reality was a little different, however, for early in the straight Alfred Gilbert asked Irish Ball to go on and the response was immediate. Irish Ball sailed into the lead and the outcome was never thereafter in doubt. Guillemot could only keep going at one pace and in the final strides it was Piggott on Lombardo who snatched second place on the line. Irish Ball won easily by three lengths, and a short head only separated the stable companions Lombardo and Guillemot, with the 100/1 outsider Lucky Drake, emulating his half brother Nor (who had been fourth to Nijinsky in 1970), taking the fourth spot.

The truth was that the race was easy pickings for Irish Ball. Lombardo, despite being given every chance to get the trip by Piggott, didn't really see it out. Grenfall too failed to stay while Parnell was just not good enough. The proximity of Lucky Drake in fourth place tended to suggest that the race was lacking in its usual quality. On his previous outing Lucky Drake had been beaten in a Navan handicap.

The winner Irish Ball was sired by Baldric II, who won the 1964 Newmarket 2,000 Guineas and Champion Stakes for trainer Ernie Fellows. Baldric II, who like Tambourine II raced in the colours of Mrs Howell Jackson, also sired the Irish 1,000 Guineas winner Favoletta. Irish Ball was out of a mare called Irish Lass, who was a sister of the brilliant mare Lynchris. Trained by Pierre Lallie, Irish Ball was owned by the English theatrical impresario, Emile Littler, who in his time had directed such stars as Julie Andrews and Greer Garson. In passing, mention should be made of Paddy Prendergast's splendid achievement in saddling both the second and third horses behind Irish Ball.

But of course the result of the race was entirely overshadowed by Linden Tree's antics at the start. Whilst the incident brought back to mind Relko's withdrawal in the 1963 Sweeps Derby, there was one significant difference on this occasion. Relko had been withdrawn without coming under starter's orders, and thus those who had backed the French colt at least recovered their stake. The unfortunate punters who had supported Linden Tree were not quite so lucky. Having been installed and having come under starter's orders, all bets on Linden Tree were lost, despite the fact that his backers could scarcely be said to have got a run for their money.

Several stories gained currency in the wake of the Linden Tree affair. The most popular one was that Linden Tree's tail had somehow got caught in the stalls. A spokesman for the Peter Walwyn stable on the morning after the race seemed to lend credence to this 'tale'. Perhaps it is true that Linden Tree may have become upset in the stalls (probably not liking the hurly-burly of the preliminaries), but it is scarcely conceivable that the colt's tail was actually entrapped in the stalls mechanism as the stalls were opened.

In any event the stewards held an enquiry into the incident. Having heard evidence from the acting steward at the start, Captain R. P. H. Elwes, from Mr J. H. Tyrell, starter, and from Duncan Keith, they concluded that 'the stalls had opened perfectly, but that having taken one stride the colt [Linden Tree] whipped around to the left'. That was all there was to the official statement; it didn't answer too many questions.

Cutting through a morass of speculation, the simplest explanation for what happened is that Linden Tree, who had exhibited signs of temperament before in his racing career and who had been reluctant to go down to the start, was simply in no mood to race. Drawn on the wide outside and with no horse outside him, the rogue was presented with a simple opportunity to duck the issue and he duly seized his chance. Over twenty years later it is probably permissible to say this. A persuasive corroborative circumstance is that Linden Tree never ran again after his Curragh escapade. The strong suspicion must be that the temperamental colt became impossible to train.

In view of the favourite's effective non-participation in the race, questions were raised as to the value of the Sweeps Derby form. Its merits were soon to be tested. Irish Ball was prepared for the King George VI and Queen Elizabeth Stakes, where he met up again with Mill Reef who started 8/13 favourite. Irish Ball was second favourite at 9/2, with Ortis, who had been well beaten earlier in the season by Lombardo at Leopardstown, third favourite at 11/1. The Irish Derby third, Guillemot, was also in the field, but at 35/1 he was not fancied to trouble the judge.

In the event Mill Reef demolished the field in spectacular style, winning by no less than six lengths from Ortis. It was the widest winning margin up to that point since the race was introduced in 1951. Irish Ball was a major disappointment, finishing a moderate fifth, all of fifteen lengths adrift, with Guillemot two places further back. Mill Reef went on to prove himself a class above

his contemporaries with an emphatic three length victory over Pistol Packer in the Prix de l'Arc de Triomphe in a new course record time at Longchamp. Irish Ball was again well in arrears and on all the evidence had to be placed at least a stone behind Mill Reef, who had defeated him easily on their racecourse clashes.

There is little doubt that the 1971 renewal of the Irish Derby was a substandard affair. As stated at the outset, the race is remembered more for the antics of Linden Tree at the start than for the winning performance of Irish Ball. Some years ago a Dublin street poet used to sell his poetry, which he had collected in broadsheet form, around the public houses of Ireland's capital city. Centring almost exclusively on sporting themes, with horse racing very much to the fore, one of his ditties, reflecting the rueful experiences of a philosophical punter, mulled over Linden Tree's performance (or rather non-performance) at the Curragh on 26 June 1971. Although I bought a copy of the broadsheet I cannot now locate it. I do, however, remember the opening lines which perhaps sum up better than I could the feelings of disgruntled punters on that June Saturday:

'What was he thinking, that Linden Tree
On his way to the start of the Irish Derby . . ?'

The balladeer, whose name escapes me, reproduced in his broadsheet the text of correspondence which had passed between himself and the Revenue Commissioners in relation to an application for artistic exemption under the provisions introduced in 1969 by former Taoiseach, Charles J. Haughey, when he served as Minister for Finance. I am not sure if the poet's claim for exemption was granted by my friends in Dublin Castle, but whatever about the artistic merits of his work, he most certainly had his finger on the pulse of sporting Ireland.

What was he thinking, that Linden Tree On his way to the start of the Irish Derby . . ?

IRISH SWEEPS DERBY

1M 4F
SATURDAY 26 JUNE 1971
GOING: GOOD

WINNER: Mr E. Littler's Irish Ball by Baldric II out of Irish Lass
A. Gilbert

SECOND: Lombardo by Ragusa out of Midnight Chimes
L. Piggott

THIRD: Guillemot by Sea Bird II out of Belle Jeep
L. Ward

S.P. 7/2   13/2   16/1
Winner trained by P. Lallie

ALSO: Lucky Drake 4th, Music Man 5th, St Ives 6th, Tantoul 7th, Grenfall 8th, Parnell 9th, Turbulent Eddy 10th, Merry Slipper 11th, Bayons Manor 12th, Wacoso 13th, All Tan 14th, Linden Tree slowly away

Linden Tree 7/4 fav
Winner: 2nd favourite
Distances: 3 lengths, sh. hd
Value to winner: £62,100
Time: 2 m 36.6 s
Timeform rating of winner: 127.

1972

IRISH SWEEPS DERBY

1972 was to be the year of Roberto, or was it? As a two-year-old Roberto had won both the National and Anglesey Stakes, clearly signalling a bright three-year-old career. After a slight hiccup things appeared to be going very much according to plan. By the American sire, Hail To Reason, Roberto prevailed in a desperate finish to the Epsom Derby by a short head from Rheingold. There are many who believe fervently that it was Lester Piggott's strength alone that was the essential difference between success and failure at Epsom. Be that as it may, in winning at Epsom Roberto made amends for a narrow defeat by High Top in the Newmarket 2,000 Guineas. But that particular setback was the prelude to a major controversy which erupted in the run-up to the premier English classic.

The veteran Australian jockey Bill Williamson had partnered Roberto in his Newmarket defeat. Beaten by half a length, some critics felt that Williamson had perhaps given his mount too much to do. None the less the clear understanding on all sides after Newmarket seemed to be that Williamson would retain the ride on Roberto for the Epsom Derby. There followed one of those strange quirks of fate that occasionally occur and whose effect is to alter the course of racing history.

Williamson injured his shoulder in a race at Kempton on 27 May (the Epsom Derby was due to be run on 7 June). Although it wasn't a serious injury and the jockey assured Vincent O'Brien that he would be fit to ride at Epsom, Roberto's owner, the American sports impresario John W. Galbreath, owner of the Pittsburgh Pirates baseball team, was not happy with the situation. (Incidentally, Galbreath named Roberto after Roberto Clemente, one of the all-time greats of baseball.) Galbreath believed that the 49-year-old Williamson couldn't possibly be fit enough to do his horse justice and unilaterally engaged

Lester Piggott to take the ride on Roberto. Vincent O'Brien ultimately supported his owner's decision.

In replacing Williamson with Piggott, Galbreath promised the Australian jockey that he would receive a percentage of the prize money equal to what Piggott would receive, should Roberto win. This was a generous offer, but of course it did little to assuage hurt pride.

The late jockey switch was unpopular with the racing press and indeed with sections of the racing public who felt that the likeable Williamson had been unfairly treated. As a result there was a distinctly unfriendly pre-race reception at Epsom for Piggott when he took Roberto down to the start for the Derby.

Roberto's dramatic short head victory undoubtedly mollified many of those who had been most vociferous in their condemnation of Piggott beforehand, and certainly for those who backed Roberto down to 3/1 favourite there could have been few if any grounds for complaint. None the less a rather sour taste lingered after the affair.

It is said indeed that the decision to 'jock' him off Roberto was one that Williamson felt very keenly. The veteran jockey retired from the saddle in the following year, 1973, and died a few years later from cancer, still harbouring within the hurt over what he perceived to be his humiliating treatment over Roberto. Sentiment, however, has never been very much to the fore in the pursuit of sporting excellence. For owner John W. Galbreath Roberto's Epsom triumph meant that he had achieved a notable double in that he became the first owner ever to win both the Kentucky and Epsom Derbies. (Paul Mellon later emulated this feat.)

After Epsom Roberto moved on to the Curragh in his bid for a Derby double and in keeping with Vincent O'Brien's practice at the time it was his stable jockey, John Roe, who took over from Piggott in the plate. Destined to be favourite, Roberto was one of three runners from the Vincent O'Brien stable and neither of the other two could be entirely dismissed from calculations. Manitoulin, owned by Mrs J. W. Galbreath, had been only eleventh at Epsom, but on his previous run he had won the Royal Whip over course and distance and had an outsider's chance.

The other O'Brien runner was Buckstopper, by Buckpasser, who was owned by E. P. Taylor, breeder of the legendary Northern Dancer. Unbeaten in two runs as a juvenile, Buckstopper had been fourth to Bog Road, Ballymore and Star Lark — all of whom took their place in the Derby line-up — in the Gallinule Stakes over ten furlongs at the Curragh on his only three-year-old outing. Difficult to rate, the Derby would tell just how good he was.

Besides Manitoulin three of those who had finished behind Roberto at Epsom renewed rivalry at the Curragh. They were the English challengers Scottish Rifle and Steel Pulse, and the lone French invader, Alec Head's Lyphard. John Dunlop's Scottish Rifle, the mount of Ron Hutchinson, had fared best of the trio at Epsom in finishing sixth to Roberto, beaten just over eight lengths. On his previous run Scottish Rifle had beaten Pentland Firth by half a length in the Predominate Stakes at Goodwood over the full Derby distance. Pentland Firth had gone on to finish third, beaten a short head and five lengths by Roberto at Epsom, so quite clearly on all known form Scottish Rifle had to improve to trouble the favourite. In Scottish Rifle's favour, however, was the fact that his Goodwood victory had been achieved on good to soft going and similar conditions were forecast for the Curragh. The Epsom Derby, by contrast, had been run on firm ground.

Steel Pulse was trained by Scobie Breasley who as a jockey had never actually won the Sweeps Derby, his best efforts being when placed on Tiger (1963), Charlottown (1966) and Dart Board (1967). Bill Williamson's mount, Steel Pulse, had been only ninth at Epsom, but had put up a much better performance at Royal Ascot subsequently.

In the Prince of Wales Stakes over ten furlongs Steel Pulse had been anything but disgraced in finishing second, beaten five lengths to the great Brigadier Gerard in a race run in record time. As a juvenile Steel Pulse had also run particularly well in the Grand Criterium at Longchamp, finishing a close second to Hard to Beat, with Roberto a disappointing fourth. On his best form Steel Pulse seemed certain to be involved in the final shake-up.

The French horse Lyphard was a popular fancy, but his Epsom run was frankly disappointing. Well fancied for the Blue Riband of English racing, for which he started joint second favourite, Lyphard and Freddie Head had failed spectacularly to handle the track at Epsom and finished a poor fifteenth of the twenty-two runners.

Prior to his Epsom misadventure, Lyphard had been a close fourth to Hard to Beat in the Prix Lupin at Longchamp and although he had chalked up two victories before that, there seemed to be something of a question mark over the temperament of the well-bred Northern Dancer colt. On the credit side it was likely that Lyphard would appreciate the going, his best form having been shown with give in the ground.

Besides Roberto the Irish challenge was not without substance. In the pre-race prognostications there was considerable debate as to which was the better of the two horses who had finished first and second in the Gallinule Stakes over ten furlongs, a recognised trial for the premier Irish classic. In that race Bog Road from the McGrath yard had finished four lengths in front of Ballymore, but the latter horse, on only his second ever racecourse appearance, was giving his conqueror 7 lb. On his only other outing Ballymore, by the 1963 Sweeps Derby hero, Ragusa, had sprung a major surprise when landing the Irish 2,000 Guineas by three lengths from Martinmas, with Bog Road only fifth. Trained by the great Paddy Prendergast for Mrs Meg Mullion, Ballymore, with the forecast give in the ground, was well fancied to emulate his sire and credit the Rossmore Lodge maestro with his third Sweeps Derby success.

Fourteen runners went to post in all on ground described officially as good to yielding. The month of June had been the second coldest on record and with the weather remaining unsettled the first day of July (which was the date for the 1972 Derby) was a little on the cool side. There was a brief hiccup as the parade ended when Ron Hutchinson was dislodged from his mount, Scottish Rifle, but the partnership was quickly reunited. The betting exchanges concentrated largely on just three horses. Roberto, not surprisingly, was sent off favourite at 15/8, Ballymore was a solid second best at 3/1, with the French challenger Lyphard very well supported at 7/2. It was 10/1 the two English challengers, Scottish Rifle and Steel Pulse, and 33/1 bar these five.

From the outset Extension, with Christy Roche up, set the pace, presumably for the benefit of his stable companion, Ballymore. Extension continued to make the running and at the half-way mark he had opened up a lead of some half a dozen lengths. The 100/1 outsider Star Lark, from the Michael Hurley stable and partnered by Tommy Murphy, took it up from Extension running around towards the straight.

Even before the field turned into the straight, supporters of the favourite were already in a disconsolate frame of mind. Roberto never promised at any stage to be involved in the finish and he was a beaten horse long before the field entered the home straight. Turning in, a number of horses seemed to have a chance, including the second favourite, Ballymore. He, however, despite having the assistance of Lester Piggott, ran all over the place in the straight and was not a factor at the business end of the race.

From over two furlongs out in fact only two horses counted. Scottish Rifle and Steel Pulse pulled clear of the remainder and settled down to a hard-fought duel. Partnered by the two Australians,

Hutchinson and Williamson, it was impossible to tell which of the two colts would emerge victorious as they matched stride for stride down the straight. Scottish Rifle had the rails while Steel Pulse was on his outside. Both horses were giving their all and as they entered the final furlong it was still all to play for.

Inside the final furlong, however, Steel Pulse just began to look the stronger. He didn't pull away from his close rival; he just edged that bit ahead as the two horses galloped on towards the finish. Slowly the gap between the two of them increased: first it was a neck, then a half-length, and by the time Steel Pulse reached the winning post he was a length clear of the gallant runner-up, Scottish Rifle. In a typical low-key post-race comment, Williamson said: 'I was not running away at the finish, just gained a length in the last furlong and that's about it.'

Both first and second had given of their very best and in so doing had pulled clear of the rest of the field. Ballymore was a long-looking six lengths back in third place, while the 100/1 outsider Star Lark belied his odds by finishing fourth, a further length back. In fifth place came the somewhat disappointing French challenger, Lyphard, whose jockey Freddie Head was subsequently interviewed by the stewards for failing to keep a true course in the straight (shades of his Epsom aberrations). In sixth place was Manitoulin who was best placed of the O'Brien trio. Stable companion and favourite, Roberto, was a bitterly disappointing twelfth of the fourteen runners.

Much of the post-race inquest focused on the lamentable display by the Epsom Derby winner. According to John Roe, Roberto simply didn't like the softish going. In his view Roberto was not suffering from the after-effects of his hard race at Epsom. Some observers thought otherwise; but be that as it may, Roberto was never going well at any stage and his performance was a sad let-down to his supporters.

In any event it was Steel Pulse who had won and his Indian owner, Mr Ravi Tikkoo, had picked up his colt at the Newmarket sales for a mere 4,000 guineas. By the French sire Diatome, who was unlucky enough to be foaled in the same year as Sea Bird II, but who did win the Washington International, Steel Pulse was out of a mare called Rachel. She was the winner of four races including Goodwood's Nassau Stakes. By the spectacular Newmarket 2,000 Guineas winner Tudor Minstrel, Rachel's dam was the Queen Mary Stakes winner Par Avion. By any standards Steel Pulse was a well-bought yearling!

Steel Pulse's Irish Derby victory was a very popular one. Fate is a quixotic thing and there was something just a little ironic in Bill Williamson's success at the Curragh on Steel Pulse, with the Epsom Derby winner, Roberto, from whom he had been jocked off, well in arrears. The Curragh crowd gave Williamson a warm ovation as he returned to the unsaddling area and the veteran Australian jockey was clearly appreciative. 'I was . . . deeply moved with the reception which the crowd gave me after the race', he told Tony Power of the *Sunday Press*.

The paths of Steel Pulse and Roberto were to cross a little later in the season, but before that Roberto was to take part in a memorable race for the Benson and Hedges Gold Cup at York. In the ever changing game of musical chairs that marked the riding arrangements for 1972, Lester Piggott deserted Roberto in favour of Barry Hills' Rheingold at York and the redoubtable Galbreath was not best pleased. The American-based Panamanian rider, Braulio Baeza, was flown in for the ride on Roberto and he proceeded to engineer one of the greatest racing upsets of the post-war era.

The unbeaten four-year-old colt, Brigadier Gerard, was going for his sixteenth successive victory at York, a win which would have equalled the great Ribot's long-standing record. Prior to York, Brigadier Gerard had in fact come up against Steel Pulse in the King George VI and Queen Elizabeth Stakes at Ascot. Steel Pulse had disappointed, finishing an eight and a half length fourth to the Brigadier and all the lines of form suggested that Dick Hern's champion would brush aside the opposition at York. Racing, however, is an unpredictable sport and that particular truth was about to be demonstrated yet again.

Making every yard of the running, Roberto and his new pilot Baeza were never going to be caught and the partnership finished three lengths clear of Brigadier Gerard, with Piggott's Rheingold a further twelve lengths back in fourth. The racing world was staggered, but then there is nothing new about that.

Roberto was then aimed at the Prix de l'Arc de Triomphe and among the opposition was his Curragh conqueror, Steel Pulse. The going at Longchamp was fast and Roberto's connections were understandably hopeful that with underfoot conditions favourable, Roberto would end his three-year-old career on a winning note and incidentally reverse the Curragh form with Steel Pulse. This latter ambition was achieved but the former was not, for Roberto was only seventh at Longchamp behind the French filly San San, with Steel Pulse further back.

If Galbreath and O'Brien were happy about Baeza's riding of Roberto at York, they were significantly less enthused about his performance at Longchamp. Completely ignoring pre-race instructions, the Panamanian rode Roberto exactly as he had done at York and the tactics proved suicidal with Roberto, who over a mile and a half needed to be held up, running out of steam in the straight.

What then is the final verdict on the classic generation of 1972? While it is a little unfair to call future generations into account in answering this question, certainly as a sire Roberto was far more successful than Steel Pulse. Among the many top-class horses sired by Roberto were Touching Wood, Lear Fan, Critique, Al Talaq, Tralos and Zalazal.

Roberto was also the brood mare sire of the brilliant miler Warning. Interestingly, indeed, one of the failures at the Curragh, Lyphard, was also to go on to establish himself as a high-class sire, his most notable son being that magnificent racehorse, Dancing Brave. Steel Pulse, by contrast, has left no such impression on the stud book.

On an overall evaluation of the class of 1972 it is fair to say that Roberto was a superior colt to his Curragh conqueror, Steel Pulse. Scobie Breasley's colt was a narrow compact sort who peaked for the Curragh classic, his one true moment of glory, but lacking scope, was unable to add to his laurels. As for Roberto, one can accord him the accolade of champion three-year-old of 1972, despite the fact that his overall record was patchy and his ability to stay a mile and a half on anything other than firm ground questionable. One of his poorest days, and by contrast his rival Steel Pulse's best, was on the first day of July 1972 at the Curragh, when trainer Scobie Breasley and jockey Bill Williamson combined to enjoy one of the sweetest pay days of their respective careers.

IRISH SWEEPS DERBY

1M 4F

SATURDAY 1 JULY 1972

GOING: GOOD TO YIELDING

WINNER: Mr R. N. Tikkoo's Steel Pulse by Diatome out of Rachel
W. Williamson

SECOND: Scottish Rifle by Sunny Way out of Radiopye
R. Hutchinson

THIRD: Ballymore by Ragusa out of Paddy's Sister
L. Piggott

S.P. 10/1   10/1   3/1
Winner trained by A. Breasley

ALSO: Star Lark 4th, Lyphard 5th, Manitoulin 6th, Pardner 7th, Bold Bid 8th, King Charles 9th, Falaise 10th, Buckstopper 11th, Roberto 12th, Extension 13th, Bog Road 14th & last

Roberto 15/8 fav
Winner: joint 4th favourite
Distances: 1 length, 6 lengths
Value to winner: £58,905
Time: 2 m 39.8 s
Timeform rating of winner: 125.

1973

IRISH SWEEPS DERBY

THE CURRAGH 30 JUNE 1973

Symptomatic of the changing times in the former island of saints and scholars the Department of Social Welfare took out a prominent advertisement in all the national newspapers on Saturday 30 June 1973 to announce details of a new and revolutionary piece of social legislation. Under the heading, 'New Social Welfare Benefit for Unmarried Mothers', the advertisement advised the public that henceforth unmarried mothers with one child were to be the beneficiaries of a new allowance of £8.15 per week, increasing by £2.00 per week for each extra child. Some would have it that this official recognition of the one-parent family marked the beginning of the end for the stability of the traditional social unit within Irish society.

Be that as it may, on that same day a rather less momentous event, the twelfth running of the Irish Sweeps Derby, took place. For the first time since the race had undergone a transformation with the injection of sponsorship money from the Irish Hospital Sweepstakes, in 1973 neither the first nor second at Epsom was among the line-up of fifteen thoroughbreds declared to face the starter at the Curragh. There was as a consequence a widespread perception that the 1973 renewal was some way below the usual high standard. With the benefit of hindsight, it has to be accepted that such a view was well justified.

A few weeks earlier the Epsom Derby had produced a major shock when the previously unraced colt, Morston, got the better of Lester Piggott's mount, Cavo Doro, with the maiden Freefoot in third place, Bernard Van Cutsem's Ksar fourth, and Kevin Prendergast's Ragapan fifth. The third, fourth and fifth home at Epsom all renewed rivalry at the Curragh and given that only two and a half lengths separated the threesome at Epsom, supporters of each were entitled to argue the merits of their chosen fancy.

Spice was added to the mixture by the presence of Vincent O'Brien's Hail The Pirates, who was to be ridden by Lester Piggott. In the unavoidable absence through injury of Cavo Doro, whom Piggott had bred himself, and who if he had competed would undoubtedly have started favourite, the American-bred Hail To Reason colt was well fancied to compensate his jockey for Cavo Doro's misfortune.

The form horse was of course Harry Wragg's Freefoot, the mount of Jimmy Lindley. He had been beaten three lengths in all by Morston at Epsom and had acted well on the firm ground. He had previously been beaten a short head by Proverb over the full Derby distance at Chester and the Relko colt quite clearly was a sound staying type. However, the fact that he was still a maiden after no less than eight outings in total didn't inspire confidence. Despite the fact that history was against him, in that no maiden had ever won the Irish Derby, Freefoot most certainly had to be respected.

Ksar was the problem horse in the field. Favourite at 5/1 for the Epsom Derby, he had looked all over a winner when he made his dash for the line just over two furlongs out. But his effort petered out and in the end he had finished a disappointing fourth, beaten a total of four lengths. The most logical interpretation of Ksar's Epsom performance was that he simply did not get the trip, and yet on his previous run he had won the Lingfield Derby Trial over the full Derby distance. Lingfield is perhaps the racetrack that is the closest in its conformation to Epsom, and so connections were understandably somewhat puzzled by

Ksar's fade-out at Epsom. After due consideration they had evidently come to the conclusion that Ksar had been unsuited to the course at Epsom and so decided to give the Kalydon colt another chance to prove himself at the Curragh.

Despite the undoubted claims of both Freefoot and Ksar, ante-post interest in the classic had centred on Ragapan, who had finished behind both of these rivals at Epsom. Beaten a total of five and a half lengths at Epsom, Ragapan had run the best race of his career on that occasion and it was widely believed he was a rapidly improving colt.

By the 1963 Irish Derby winner Ragusa, Ragapan was a June foal who had been slow to reach maturity. At Epsom his jockey Bill Williamson was adamant that with a trouble-free run Ragapan would have shaken up the top two. Impeccably bred, out of the dam of the Irish 1,000 Guineas winners Front Row and Black Satin, Ragapan had prior to Epsom finished unplaced behind Mon Fils in the English 2,000 Guineas and was bidding to provide his recently defunct sire with a posthumous Derby double, Morston also being a son of Ragusa.

The only other Epsom runner to renew rivalry with those who had finished in front of him was the Barry Hills-trained Natsun, who had been eleventh to Morston and whose chances on paper appeared fairly remote. Two other English challengers, however, were worthy of closer attention. Lightly raced, Dick Hern's Aureole colt Buoy had won two of his three races. Unraced as a juvenile, he had won in good style over twelve furlongs at Newmarket in May before following up with a facile victory again over a mile and a half in the Predominate Stakes at Goodwood, winning by four lengths from Funny Fellow. Joe Mercer's mount would obviously love the trip. The question was would he have enough speed at the business end of the race.

The American-bred Laurentian Hills, the mount of Greville Starkey, had also won his last two races, the first over ten furlongs at Epsom, and subsequently over the full Derby distance at Royal Ascot. Like Buoy, it was difficult to rate him, but in a year in which no horse stood out his chances could not be dismissed lightly.

Vincent O'Brien's Hail The Pirates had been campaigned exclusively in Ireland in his five three-year-old races. He had performed poorly in soft ground in the Irish 2,000 Guineas — and thus the forecast fast going would favour him — but otherwise had won his four remaining races. After his 2,000 Guineas flop, Hail The Pirates had run at Leopardstown where in the Player-Wills Stakes over ten furlongs he had comfortably beaten Weaver's Hall and Hurry Harriet by two lengths and two and a half lengths. From the Seamus McGrath stable Weaver's Hall threw down the gauntlet again at the Curragh, but on paper didn't seem to have much chance of reversing placings with the O'Brien horse.

After Leopardstown Hail The Pirates subsequently took the Gallinule Stakes, again over ten furlongs, at the Curragh by three lengths and the same from Decimo and Star Appeal, both of whom opposed him again in the Derby. The Hail To Reason colt had not taken on opposition of the highest class, but he had won his races with considerable ease,

and with Lester Piggott on board he was bound to come in for considerable support.

Fifteen runners in all went to post on ground that was officially firm. The remainder of the field, besides those referred to earlier, were Irish-trained outsiders. Seamus McGrath's Weaver's Hall has already been mentioned and the stable also ran Park Lawn, who had been a moderate fifth to Hail The Pirates at Leopardstown. Another handler who was doubly represented was Kevin Prendergast. His Tekoah, who had tuned up for the Curragh with a narrow victory in an extended seven furlong handicap at Dundalk, was very much the second string to his better fancied stable companion, Ragapan.

Mick O'Toole saddled North Wall, but a seventh of eight placing to Ballymore at Leopardstown was scarcely an encouraging preliminary. The Christy Grassick-trained Alchopal was by the 1966 Sweeps Derby third, Paveh, but his victory at Limerick Junction (now Tipperary) hardly looked good enough. Last but not least was Ted Curtin's maiden, Tall Noble, a nicely bred Vaguely Noble colt, whose best run was a creditable third placing to Hail The Pirates, but for whom both the ground and indeed the calibre of the opposition was likely to prove a somewhat daunting combination.

Although betting forecasts had suggested that Ragapan would be favourite for the Derby, on the day the punters on the course latched on to Lester Piggott's mount, Hail The Pirates, and he was sent off the 11/4 favourite. It was an open market, however, and close up in the betting were Ragapan at 7/2, Buoy at 4/1 and Ksar at 5/1. Freefoot was returned at 13/2, it was 16/1 both Laurentian Hills and Natsun, and 33/1 and upwards the rest.

The early gallop was set by the 200/1 outsider Park Lawn, ridden by Buster Parnell. The lesser fancied of Seamus McGrath's two runners, Park Lawn set a blistering pace and these tactics, as it turned out, were to have a decisive bearing on the final outcome of the race.

Joe Mercer on Buoy was the first to start cutting back the leader's advantage. Weaver's Hall and George McGrath kept his stable companion in his sights throughout the race and was well placed when Park Lawn not unexpectedly, shot his bolt. Coming down the hill towards the straight Hail The Pirates and Ragapan also began to make ground. Buoy went on to lead rounding the bend towards the straight, but he was quickly pressed by Weaver's Hall.

As the horses turned into the straight Weaver's Hall had Buoy on his inside, and with less than three furlongs to go the McGrath horse struck the front. Hail The Pirates was soon flat to the boards and making no impression, and for a few strides Ragapan flattered briefly. Buoy too was unable to respond and it was soon clear that Weaver's Hall had them all in trouble.

Although both Ragapan and Buoy kept going gamely all the way up the straight, with the latter running on best to take second place, Weaver's Hall was never in danger of defeat. At the line George McGrath's mount had two and a half lengths to spare over Ragapan, with Buoy another one and a half lengths back in third place. Two lengths further back Hail The Pirates,

who patently failed to stay, just kept Ksar out of fourth place by a short head.

The result was a huge shock, the winner being returned at 33/1, making Weaver's Hall the longest-priced winner of the race since the inauguration of the Sweeps sponsorship. The outcome, however, fitted into the 1973 pattern of classic upsets, following upon Mon Fils's 50/1 triumph in the English 2,000 Guineas and Morston's success at 25/1 in the Epsom Derby. Despite the fact that very few punters could possibly have backed Weaver's Hall, the result was an extremely popular one.

Winning trainer Seamus McGrath, besides being a director of the Hospitals' Trust, is a son of the late Joe McGrath, the man whose vision and initiative had been largely responsible for selling the idea of the Sweeps Derby to the Irish racing authorities. Besides training the winner, Seamus McGrath also had the unique distinction of owning Weaver's Hall. In the pre-sponsorship era McGrath had trained Panaslipper to win the 1955 Irish Derby for his father. His name, however, will always be most closely associated with Levmoss, the colt he trained to win both the Ascot Gold Cup and the Prix de l'Arc de Triomphe in 1969.

For stable jockey George McGrath too — despite the surname, no relation of the trainer — the victory was a fitting reward for his years of service to the McGrath stable. The jockey in fact was only the third Irish-born rider to win the Sweeps Derby, his predecessors being Willie Burke (1964) and Liam Ward (1970).

After the race there was a deal of comment on the remarkable turn-around in form between the winner and Hail The

Pirates, as compared with their Leopardstown running four weeks earlier. Weaver's Hall had finished two lengths behind Hail The Pirates at Leopardstown, whereas at the Curragh he had finished six lengths in front of Vincent O'Brien's colt. Quite clearly the key to the apparent form discrepancy lay in the distance of the respective races. The Leopardstown race was run over ten furlongs and it seemed clear that the favourite had simply failed to stay the extra two furlongs at the Curragh. Weaver's Hall's stable companion Park Lawn's part in drawing the finish out of the suspect stayers in the race should not be underestimated. It should also be mentioned that those who looked far enough back also discovered that Weaver's Hall had finished in front of Hail The Pirates as a two-year-old.

Weaver's Hall may have been comparatively unfancied, but his pedigree had plenty of quality about it. Bred by the McGrath Trust, his sire was Busted, about whom I have written in the chapter on the 1966 race. A half brother to the Irish Lincolnshire winner All In All, Weaver's Hall was the second foal of his dam Marians. The granddam Damiens was bought for a then record price of 12,000 guineas at Ballsbridge and bred numerous winners, including Sixpence and Continuation. Marians had won as a two-year-old over five furlongs and was good enough to finish fourth in the Irish Oaks. She herself was by the top-class Italian stayer Macherio. Looking at Weaver's Hall's pedigree, it is easy to see how the Sweeps

Derby winner possessed all the stamina required to burn off the opposition on that summer's day in 1973.

As a postscript to the Irish Derby of 1973, it is interesting to note that Star Appeal, who finished seventh behind Weaver's Hall, went on subsequently to land the Prix de l'Arc de Triomphe as a five-year-old.

After his Curragh victory, Weaver's Hall next ran in the King George VI and Queen Elizabeth Stakes at Ascot. The field was a strong one, including Rheingold who had won four on the trot (and was subsequently to be successful in the Arc), Roberto, the 1972 Epsom Derby winner, Scottish Rifle, second in the 1972 Sweeps Derby, and the French filly Dahlia, who only seven days earlier had won the Irish Guinness Oaks. As things turned out Weaver's Hall was by no means disgraced in finishing fourth to Dahlia and Rheingold, although beaten just over eight lengths.

The result, however, demonstrated that the 1973 crop of three-year-old colts was not a vintage lot and later performances by Ragapan and Buoy only served to underline that point. However, in the nature of things such considerations are relative. For the winner's connections 30 June 1973 was a day to be savoured, the day when Joe McGrath's inestimable contribution to Irish racing was appropriately marked by his son's success in saddling the winner of the race which his father had done so much to make into one of the most significant on the world classic scene.

1M 4F

SATURDAY 30 JUNE 1973

GOING: GOOD TO FIRM

WINNER: Mr S. McGrath's Weaver's Hall by Busted out of Marians

G. McGrath

SECOND: Ragapan by Ragusa out of Panaview

W. Williamson

THIRD: Buoy by Aureole out of Ripeck

J. Mercer

S.P. 33/1   7/2   4/1

Winner trained by owner

ALSO: Hail The Pirates 4th, Ksar 5th, Natsun 6th, Star Appeal 7th, North Wall 8th, Laurentian Hills 9th, Decimo 10th, Freefoot 11th, Tall Noble 12th, Alchopal 13th, Tekoah 14th, Park Lawn 15th & last

Hail The Pirates 11/4 fav

Distances: 2½ lengths, 1½ lengths

Value to winner: £62,495

Time: 2 m 32 s

Timeform rating of winner: 122.

THE CURRAGH 29 JUNE 1974

At the beginning of the 1974 flat season the names of two horses were on everyone's lips when the upcoming classics were being discussed. Apalachee and Cellini, two names with a classic sounding ring to them, both in the charge of the great Vincent O'Brien, seemed to have the racing world at their feet. As juveniles both had exhibited racecourse potential of the highest order. Cellini had triumphed in the Dewhurst Stakes at Newmarket, while his stable companion Apalachee had annexed the other principal end of season juvenile championship race, the Observer Gold Cup.

Hopes built up over many months can crumble in a thrice. The three-year-old careers of both Apalachee and Cellini followed similar paths towards ultimate disappointment. On his seasonal reappearance Apalachee struggled home by a neck at 6/1 on at the Curragh. He went on to finish third at 4/9 in the Newmarket 2,000 Guineas and never raced again. Cellini

meantime scraped home in two preliminary races, before starting favourite for the Irish 2,000 Guineas. He too finished third and after another unsuccessful outing at Royal Ascot connections called it a day. The two choicely bred thoroughbreds were more valuable off the racecourse than on it.

With the pretenders unmasked, the search was on to discover the rightful heir to racing's annually vacated throne. The formbook was in tatters, so it was no surprise at all when an unconsidered 50/1 outsider, Snow Knight, romped home in the Epsom Derby on the first Wednesday in June. Second at Epsom was Imperial Prince, beaten two lengths, and trainer Noel Murless dispatched his charge to the Curragh with realistic hopes of gaining due compensation for his good Epsom run.

Imperial Prince was a half brother by Sir Ivor to the Newmarket 1,000 Guineas, Epsom Oaks and Irish Oaks winner Altesse Royale. Although he had been in training as a two-year-old the Sir Ivor colt had been slow to mature, and as a result did not see a racecourse until he was three. He began his racing career in the Wood Ditton Stakes at Newmarket — a race for unraced three-year-olds — which is often targeted by trainers who have colts with possible classic potential.

Clearly the word was out about Imperial Prince for he started favourite and he duly obliged, beating Regular Guy by a short head, despite showing distinct and understandable signs of greenness. Stepped up in class, Imperial Prince next ran in the Chester Vase and was an encouraging second, giving 4 lb and beaten two lengths by the more experienced Jupiter Pluvius. It is of relevance to note that behind Imperial Prince at Chester were both Straight As A Die (fourth) and Sir Penfro (fifth) respectively four and seven lengths behind Noel Murless's charge. All carried the same weight. Clearly Imperial Prince was a horse of some ability and his starting price of 20/1 for the Epsom Derby was a fair reflection of his chance. His second placing at Epsom strongly suggested that the son of Sir Ivor was going the right way and he appeared to hold excellent prospects of stepping up a place at the Curragh.

Owned by her husband Roger and bred by Mrs Vera Hue-Williams, Imperial Prince was one of two Hue-Williams-owned colts in the thirteen-runner line-up at the Curragh. The other, trained by Peter Walwyn, was English Prince, who ran in the colours of Mrs Hue-Williams and was a more than useful second string. Unraced as a two-year-old (he had weak hocks), English Prince first announced his arrival as a colt of considerable ability with an emphatic six length victory over Live Arrow in the Predominate Stakes, a recognised classic trial, at Goodwood over a mile and a half.

A son of Petingo, who had been second to Sir Ivor in the 1968 Newmarket 2,000 Guineas, English Prince next contested the King George VI Stakes at Ascot, again over a mile and a half. He duly won the race by one and a half lengths from the aforementioned Straight As A Die, who received 4 lb, but the manner of English Prince's victory did not impress race readers as the colt seemed to take a long time to get the better of opposition that was short of top class. Although the line through Straight As A Die suggested that there was little between them, it was Imperial Prince who was by far the more fancied of the two Hue-Williams contenders. Because of suspension incurred at Royal Ascot, Peter Walwyn's stable jockey, Pat Eddery, was unable to take the mount on English Prince at the Curragh and the experienced French pilot, Yves Saint-Martin, was engaged to take over in the saddle.

Of course the Irish Sweeps Derby of 1974 was not simply a two-horse race. The home challenge looked a trifle weak, but the French had dispatched a determined three-horse raid. G. Delloye's Gorfou, a colt by Sea Bird II, was the outsider of the trio and would have to show improved form to figure at the business end of the race. Worthy of closer inspection, however, were the two other French challengers, Caracolero and Mississipian. The former was owned by Madame Maria Felix Berger, who had also owned Nonoalco, winner earlier in the season of the Newmarket 2,000 Guineas, and

1975

IRISH SWEEPS DERBY

THE CURRAGH 28 JUNE 1975

French hopes that Green Dancer might prove himself an outstanding champion led to a widespread belief that the Gallic challenger would spreadeagle the opposition in the Epsom Derby of 1975. In the event, Dr Carlo Vittadini's blue and gold colours, sported by Pat Eddery on the prosaically named Grundy, swept to an impressive three length victory. The filly, Nobiliary, was in fact best of the French invaders, finishing second, with the non-staying Green Dancer — favourite at 6/4 — a very disappointing sixth.

Grundy was a flashy chestnut colt who had carried all before him as a juvenile. Unbeaten in his four races, success in the Champagne Stakes at Doncaster had preceded an unchallenged six length triumph in the prestigious Dewhurst Stakes. The Great Nephew colt went into winter quarters as hot favourite for the English 2,000 Guineas.

As often occurs in racing, the unexpected happened and the fates conspired to interrupt Grundy's preparation for his assault on the principal three-year-old prizes. A kick in the face from a stable companion was an unwelcome complication in Peter Walwyn's plans to get his top colt ready for his three-year-old campaign. Grundy's seasonal début was in the Greenham Stakes at Newbury, where he suffered a surprise defeat at the hands of Mark Anthony. Although disappointing to some commentators, connections were not too dissatisfied in that they believed that Grundy had not enjoyed the softish ground which had prevailed at Newbury.

During the summer of 1975 English stable lads were in militant mood. A strike was called in pursuit of better conditions and action was planned to coincide with the first colts' classic at Newmarket. As a result of the stable lads' actions in attempting to disrupt the start of the 2,000 Guineas, the race had to be started by flag. In the opinion of Pat Eddery, this unexpected development cost Grundy his chance of victory in the race.

In Eddery's view the race was run over a trip thirty yards short of the standard mile and even though Grundy ran on very well late, he could not get to the 33/1 shot, Bolkonski, and he was beaten by a diminishing half-length. After a second successive setback, it was beginning to look as if the fates had turned their back on the champion two-year-old of 1974.

The flashy chestnut with the three white feet and the distinctive white flashes on his head was next sent to the Curragh for the Irish 2,000 Guineas. The Great Nephew colt, purchased for a modest 11,000 guineas at the 1973 Newmarket October sales, silenced his detractors in impressive style. Without coming off the bridle, Grundy powered to a comfortable one and a half length victory over Monsanto. In doing so Grundy became the first horse to be placed in the Newmarket Guineas to go on subsequently and win the Irish equivalent. His reputation firmly restored, Grundy proceeded to his most authoritative win in the Epsom Derby.

Grundy's fifth race of a busy campaign was the Irish Sweeps Derby. Bidding to complete a double in the premier Irish classic in successive years for Peter Walwyn, the Pat Eddery-partnered colt seemed to tower over his opponents, at least on paper. Of his Epsom victims, the one with the best chance of causing a possible upset was Anne's Pretender from the Ryan Price stable. The chestnut colt by Pretense, however, had been well beaten at Epsom, finishing over seven lengths adrift of Grundy, and his chances of reversing the placings did not appear especially bright.

Hobnob, from the Harry Wragg stable, had been one of the big disappointments at Epsom finishing a remote sixteenth, but on earlier running he had to be given a chance. He had won the important Derby trial, the Dante Stakes at York, and on that bit of form alone he could not be left out of calculations.

The general feeling, however, was that the principal dangers to Grundy would come from colts who had not competed at Epsom. Chief among these was Vincent O'Brien's American-bred colt, King Pellinore. Purchased at the 1973 Keeneland sales for $230,000, King Pellinore was by Round Table out of Thong and as such was a half brother to O'Brien's Thatch, the champion miler of 1973. The American Horse of the Year in 1958, Round Table was himself a son of the Irish stayer, Princequillo, who coincidentally had sired the inaugural Sweeps Derby winner, Tambourine II, and as such it was expected that King Pellinore would be well suited to the mile and a half trip.

Given plenty of time as a two-year-old, King Pellinore had contested two fairly modest events towards the back end of the season, winning one and being placed second in the other. He was not especially highly rated going into winter quarters, but his form improved as a three-year-old. After missing his intended seasonal début at the Curragh owing to a freak rainstorm, King Pellinore easily won the Lunville Stakes over a mile. Upped in distance, he won the Gallinule Stakes over ten furlongs by six lengths from Phoenix Hall. The form of itself was nothing exceptional, but King Pellinore had won with a ton in hand and in a very fast time. He was a very worthy opponent to the Epsom Derby winner.

Two other colts who it was felt would provide worthwhile opposition to Grundy were Sea Anchor and Maitland. Major Dick Hern's Sea Anchor had been progressing quietly during his three-year-old career, and after winning a maiden at Sandown he went on to register a comfortable two and a half length victory over Libra's Rib in the King Edward VII Stakes at Royal Ascot. It is said that lightning rarely strikes in the same place, but even if the metaphor is a little strained the 1974 Sweeps Derby winner, English Prince, had preceded his Curragh triumph with success in the selfsame Royal Ascot feature.

The French challenger Maitland was hard to assess. Unbeaten in three races, he had done all that had been asked of him, and it seemed a fair assumption that he wasn't being sent to the Curragh without good reason. Representing the formidable team of Angel Penna and Daniel Wildenstein, Maitland was bidding to give Yves Saint-Martin a second successive victory in the Curragh classic.

Of the others, Derby Court, from the Seamus McGrath stable, was touted as a likely outsider, while John Oxx's second runner, Irish Star, had won over course and distance. None of the remainder excited a great deal of interest, either in the race previews or in the betting exchanges, and that was a fair illustration of their chances.

In the ring Grundy was a warm favourite, and he see-sawed between even money and 4/5 in price, being returned at the off a slight odds-on favourite at 9/10. There was solid support for King Pellinore and he wound up a firm 7/2 shot after opening at 4's. The

French challenger, Maitland, was well backed from 8/1 to 6/1, but no other horse attracted significant support in the market.

The omens looked good for the favourite as the race got under way. The day was fine and the going officially good to firm, the same as at Epsom. Given Grundy's known dislike of soft ground, it certainly appeared as if the gods were firmly back on his side. In fact the official description of the going probably erred on the conservative side. Con Houlihan, in his column in the *Evening Press*, described conditions memorably as follows: 'The grass was so thin that you could see the individual blades. And the narrow lawn by the rails was as unyielding as the adjoining asphalt . . .'

The thirteen runners set out on their long journey home and the two and a half minutes that were to follow would decide upon which contender the ultimate glory would be bestowed. Right from the outset the French challenger, Maitland, set off in the lead at a fair old clip. Maintaining a good gallop, Yves Saint-Martin's mount led at the mile marker and his nearest pursuers at this point were Hobnob, with Eric Eldin up, the outsider Giggery, ridden by Tommy Murphy, Anne's Pretender, partnered by Tony Murray, and Derby Court, the mount of George McGrath.

Grundy had been restrained in the early stages but was well in touch with the leaders as the race moved into its second half. On the downhill run towards the straight Walter Swinburn on the Relko colt, Irish Star, took closer order and pressed Maitland for the lead. Here the complexion of the race changed fairly dramatically. The Epsom

Derby third, Anne's Pretender, was pushed by Tony Murray past both Maitland and Irish Star and took up the running. Just behind the leader Lester Piggott on King Pellinore appeared to be going ominously easily. Grundy was only seventh entering the straight and perhaps for just a few strides his supporters must have wondered if his tough season was beginning to catch up on him.

Pat Eddery, however, soon set favourite backers' minds at rest. Switched into overdrive, Grundy made rapid headway and cut down those in front of him with a splendid burst of speed. The favourite powered into the lead with just under two furlongs to go and it was immediately obvious that the race was as good as over. Although King Pellinore gave chase, he had no hope of catching Grundy. As the first and second favourites raced throughout the final furlong, the inimitable Michael O'Hehir in his TV commentary colourfully and succinctly summed up the concluding stages in the following terms: 'The King is chasing Grundy, but the King is out in front!'

Pat Eddery was able to ease his mount down near the finish, so comfortably was Grundy travelling. Peter Walwyn's colt passed the post an easy two length winner from King Pellinore, who kept on well but was never going to finish better than second. It was a long six lengths back to the third home, Anne's Pretender, who stepped up a place on his Epsom run, but was in fact beaten just a little further than at Epsom by the impressive winner.

Joe Mercer's mount, Sea Anchor, finished fourth, half a length adrift of Anne's Pretender; the fifth horse home was Irish Star from the John Oxx stable, while Maitland had his limitations exposed in finishing in sixth place.

Grundy's victory enabled him to join a very exclusive club. He became only the second colt ever to win the Irish 2,000 Guineas, the Epsom Derby and the Irish Sweeps Derby. (The other was Santa Claus, the 1964 hero.) In addition, and perhaps a little more surprisingly, Grundy and Pat Eddery became the first horse/jockey combination to win both the Epsom and Curragh Derbies.

Grundy's successes marked the high water mark of the successful partnership between trainer Peter Walwyn and jockey Pat Eddery. Although their association was eventually to come to an end when Eddery joined the Sangster/O'Brien team, Eddery has maintained a close relationship with his former master and, indeed, he still rides quite regularly for the Walwyn stable.

After his tremendously popular Curragh victory, Grundy was hailed in many quarters as an outstanding champion. Although cheaply bought, his pedigree is worth examining. As previously stated, Grundy was sired by Great Nephew, who developed into a high-class racehorse after a relatively undistinguished juvenile career. He was a 66/1 outsider when he narrowly failed to land the 1966 Newmarket 2,000 Guineas behind Kashmir II. After finishing second in the Eclipse, Great Nephew was transferred subsequently to Etienne Pollet's stable at Chantilly, for whom he won four times, including the prestigious Prix du Moulin over one mile, and the ten furlong Prix Dollar, both at Longchamp.

Grundy's dam, Word from Lundy, although fairly moderate, won over two miles, even though her family was more noted for speed than stamina. It was from his dam that Grundy undoubtedly inherited his abundant stamina. Incidentally, reverting to Great Nephew, he was to go on to sire a second dual Derby winner. The horse in question was superior to Grundy and was without doubt one of the best thoroughbreds of the post-war era. This colt will feature in a later chapter.

As is traditional, champion three-year-olds, if they are to join the undisputed highest class of thoroughbreds, must test themselves against their elders. The stage chosen for Grundy's examination was Ascot, and the race, the King George VI and Queen Elizabeth Diamond Stakes. (Incidentally 1975 was the first year in which the De Beers connection was adverted to in the title of the race.) The 1975 race turned out to be a classic and in some quarters has been hailed as perhaps the greatest flat race ever run in England.

Too well known to bear extended re-telling, the duel between Grundy and the year older Bustino was one of the most thrilling battles between two high-class thoroughbreds in living memory. Both colts gave their all over the final gruelling stages of the race and at the line Grundy had half a length to spare over his most gallant rival. The time of the race — 2 minutes 26.98 seconds — was the fastest mile and a half race ever electrically recorded in Britain. Grundy's time smashed the previous course

record set by Dahlia by 2.36 seconds. In fact even the sixth horse to finish at Ascot, Ashmore, beat the old course record. It should be pointed out that both Grundy and Bustino appeared quite exhausted in the parade ring after the race, and there was some concern expressed as to whether perhaps too much had been asked of such game animals.

After Ascot, Grundy appeared to recover very quickly from his exertions and he was next prepared for the Benson and Hedges Gold Cup. Over the extended ten furlongs at York, Grundy finished a disappointing fourth to Dahlia (who had previously been a fairly remote third to Grundy at Ascot) and it was widely, and I think correctly, concluded that the Ascot race had got to the bottom of Peter Walwyn's gallant colt.

Grundy was straightaway retired and he stood at the British National Stud. His first crop of runners produced the Epsom Oaks winner, Bireme, and his career at stud seemed set fair. However, his next few crops contained no outstanding thoroughbreds and breeders lost confidence in him. He was exported to Japan in 1983.

A failure at stud he may have been, but Grundy was the epitome of the game, a courageous, genuine and high-class racehorse. A top of the ground specialist, his distinctive colouring, including a most eye-catching jagged blaze, ensured that this strong-galloping chestnut colt left a deep impression on the minds of all racegoers who warmed to his enthusiastic style of racing in the hot summer of 1975.

IRISH SWEEPS DERBY

1M 4F

SATURDAY 28 JUNE 1975

GOING: GOOD TO FIRM

WINNER: Dr C. Vittadini's Grundy by Great Nephew
out of Word from Lundy
P. Eddery

SECOND: King Pellinore by Round Table out of Thong
L. Piggott

THIRD: Anne's Pretender by Pretense out of Anne la
Douche
A. Murray

S.P. 9/10f 7/2 20/1
Winner trained by P. T. Walwyn

ALSO: Sea Anchor 4th, Irish Star 5th, Maitland 6th,
Hobnob 7th, Derby Court 8th, Dowdall 9th,
Masqued Dancer 10th, Phoenix Hall 11th,
Giggery 12th, Never So Gay 13th & last

Winner: favourite
Distances: 2 lengths, 6 lengths
Value to winner: £64,063
Time: 2 m 31.1 s
Timeform rating of winner: 137.

1976

IRISH SWEEPS DERBY

THE CURRAGH 26 JUNE 1976

Historically 1798 may have been the Year of the French, but in horse racing terms 1976 was its equine equivalent. Gallic raiders had already annexed the English 1,000 Guineas with Flying Water, the Epsom Oaks with Pawneese and the Epsom Derby with Empery. The last named headed a powerful five-strong French challenge for the 1976 Irish Sweeps Derby and with Lester Piggott seeking to make it a Derby double, Nelson Bunker Hunt's Vaguely Noble colt was a hot favourite to add the Curragh classic to his Epsom gains.

At Epsom, Empery had beaten Relkino by a comfortable three lengths, with the Irish raider Hawkberry just over one length back in fourth place and another French-trained challenger, No Turning, seventh of the twenty-three runners. Prior to his Epsom success, Maurice Zilber's colt had been third, beaten three-quarters of a length and one length in the Prix Lupin over an extended ten furlongs by his stable companion, Youth,

and Arctic Tern. At the half-way stage of the season, Youth, by the American sire Ack Ack, was being acclaimed as the probable champion of his generation. Unbeaten in four races, he followed up his Prix Lupin win with an impressive victory in the French Derby (the Prix du Jockey-Club), beating Twig Moss and Malacate by three lengths and three-quarters of a length.

As Malacate was also challenging for the Curragh classic, it was possible, through Youth, to link up the form lines of Empery and Malacate. Taking a strict reading of their respective performances against Youth, the inference was that Empery had a few pounds in hand on his compatriot. The reliability of the form line, however, was questionable. Empery's form with Youth was over an extended ten furlongs, while Malacate's Prix du Jockey-Club third placing was of course over twelve furlongs.

Prior to his defeat by Youth, Malacate had won all three of his three-year-old outings, each of them at Longchamp, with the most notable being his victory in the Prix la Force. It was known that the connections of Empery, while confident about their horse's chances, believed that Malacate, owned by Madame Maria Felix Berger and trained by François Boutin, was their most dangerous rival. Two years earlier the same combination of owner and trainer was responsible for Caracolero, the second favourite for the Sweeps Derby, but he had disappointed badly. On that occasion jockey Philippe Paquet had been replaced at the Curragh by Lester Piggott, but this time round the young French rider was allowed to keep the ride.

The French challenge was not confined to just two prime contenders. John Fellowes' Northern Dancer colt, Far North, was a far from forlorn hope; indeed there were some who fancied him to upset the big two. Looking at both his pedigree and his record it was easy to see why. A three parts brother to the brilliant Nijinsky, Far North had been a smart two-year-old and his two victories out of three outings included a two and a half length victory over Youth in the Prix Saint-Roman at Longchamp. On his seasonal reappearance he had won snugly over a mile at Saint-Cloud, but had subsequently run badly behind Youth in the Prix Daru, where he had become excitable before the race and never settled during it. His trainer believed he had got his beautifully bred colt back to his best, and if this was so he most certainly had to come into the reckoning.

No Turning, seventh at Epsom, was the fourth of the French raiders, but on the balance of his form he seemed unlikely to trouble the principals. The fifth French runner in the race was Oilfield, but he was expected to act as a pacemaker for Empery. In all seventeen runners went to post and the most remarkable feature was that there were no challengers from England. Clearly English trainers had come to the view that there was no point in taking on the French and thus it was left to Irish trainers to attempt to mount a defence of the Sweeps prize.

On paper, best of a fairly weak-looking home team was the Epsom fourth, Hawkberry. This lightly raced colt had run his best race to date at Epsom and Paddy Prendergast believed he was still improving. Hawkberry had finished well at Epsom, giving grounds for hope that the stiffer Curragh track would suit him better than Epsom.

The Northfields colt, Northern Treasure, had sprung a surprise by getting the better of the French-trained Comeram by the minimum distance in the Irish 2,000 Guineas. In inflicting one of the rare defeats on French challengers in 1976, Kevin Prendergast's colt proved that he was both game and had a touch of class. The big question about Northern Treasure was of course the obvious one. Would he stay?

Most of the rest of the Irish runners simply didn't seem good enough, although an interesting contender was the Seamus McGrath-trained Mart Lane, who was a half brother to the 1973 hero, Weaver's Hall. Lightly raced, Mart Lane was difficult to weigh up, but bearing in mind the phenomenal improvement registered by his half brother in producing a 33/1 shock three years earlier, his chances could not be entirely dismissed. Seamus McGrath saddled two other runners, King Mousse and Riot Helmet, and both were extreme outsiders. The latter, however, staked his claim for a place in racing history in that his jockey Joanna Morgan had the distinction of becoming the first woman to ride in a classic race in Europe.

The betting on the race followed a predictable pattern. Lester Piggott had ridden his eighth winner of the Epsom Derby when Empery was successful and clearly Irish punters expected him to follow up at the Curragh. After touching evens in the betting, Empery hardened to 5/4 on, poor enough value considering the strength of the opposition. In the face of the support for the favourite, both Malacate and Far North were easy enough in the betting. Malacate eased from 4/1 to 5's, while Far North drifted to 9/1 from 7's. Hawkberry was steady at 10/1, and it was 16/1 bar these four.

The attendance on what was a dry and warm day was disappointing and perhaps the relative weakness of the Irish, and the absence of an English, challenge accounted for this. The going was firm and the field of seventeen was led in the early stages by Empery's pacemaker, Oilfield. Empery raced in second place behind Oilfield throughout the first mile or so. The 200/1 chance King Mousse, ridden by Mick Kennedy, was third early on, with Malacate close behind. Entering the straight, Oilfield pulled out from the rails, leaving room for Empery to go on.

Empery and Piggott led into the straight, but Malacate and Philippe Paquet were sitting on his tail. In the words of Michael O'Farrell of *The Irish Times*, 'Once the field had turned for home, it was clear that

Malacate would win . . .' Called upon for his effort two furlongs out, Malacate eased past the hard-ridden Empery half a furlong later, and with Paquet scarcely straining a muscle, the second favourite won readily by two and a half lengths from the Epsom Derby winner.

Confounding those who asserted that he wouldn't get the trip, Northern Treasure stayed on strongly for Gabriel Curran to take third prize, just three-quarters of a length behind Empery. It was another three-quarters of a length back to the fourth-placed Hawkberry (it was not the first time that a horse had finished fourth at both Epsom and the Curragh — Tarqogan had done likewise in 1963), with Far North, who ran well but not well enough, in fifth place.

The benefit of hindsight frequently comes to the assistance of punters in the aftermath of defeat — all too late, alas. The most significant variable between the Derbies run at Epsom and the Curragh in 1976 was not the course, but rather the going. At Epsom where Empery won it was good; at the Curragh where he lost it was firm. As a son of Vaguely Noble, it might have been expected that Empery would have been suited by some cut in the ground. At the very least, firm ground would hardly have been expected to bring out the best in him. So it proved. Empery in fact never ran again after his outing at the Curragh. Perhaps he was jarred up on the fast ground? Who knows? Empery's defeat at any rate foiled his owner Nelson Bunker Hunt of a unique Derby treble, the oil magnate having already annexed the French and English equivalents.

As mentioned earlier, Malacate was owned by Madame Maria Felix Berger, who before her involvement with horses had been a film star of some renown. Born in Mexico, her best-known horse prior to Malacate was the 1974 English 2,000 Guineas winner, Nonoalco. Malacate's triumph certainly compensated Madame Felix Berger in style for her disappointment at the Curragh in 1974 with the strongly fancied Caracolero. American bred, Malacate was sired by the 1956 Kentucky Derby winner Lucky Debonair out of the My Babu mare Eyeshadow and was knocked down for $40,000 at the Keeneland sales.

After his Curragh triumph Malacate went on to contest the King George VI and Queen Elizabeth Diamond Stakes at Ascot. The expectation was that Malacate's stable companion, Youth, would confirm his standing as the pre-eminent colt among the classic generation. In the event Youth ran very poorly, finishing only ninth of the ten runners, while Malacate performed a good deal better than the 15/8 favourite. Although only fifth, Malacate was beaten just over two and a half lengths by yet another French raider, the Epsom Oaks winner, Pawneese, who maintained the Gallic stranglehold on the top European prizes.

Malacate and his connections evidently enjoyed their trip to Ireland for the colt was saddled up again later in the year to contest the inaugural running of the Joe McGrath Memorial Stakes at Leopardstown (later to become the Irish Champion Stakes). Ridden again by Philippe Paquet, Malacate stormed home in impressive style over the ten furlong trip, in the process confirming Curragh form with both Northern Treasure and Hawkberry. François Boutin's colt did not run in the Arc; instead he was held in reserve for the Champion Stakes at Newmarket. Here he was a slightly disappointing fourth to the 22/1 outsider, Vitiges, ridden by Pat Eddery, with Northern Treasure, whom he had beaten on their two previous encounters, finishing just ahead of Malacate in third place. Perhaps it was a case of one trip too many to the well for Malacate.

His stable companion Youth, meantime, contested the Arc and was a respectable third to the four-year-old filly Ivanjica, with the French-trained St Leger winner Crow dividing them. The result at Longchamp merely served to confirm the superiority of the French classic generation over their counterparts in both England and Ireland. It would be difficult to say which of the trio, Empery, Youth or Malacate deserved to be rated the best. Certainly Malacate, on his best form, was at least the equal of his two compatriots, and on his favoured fast going was arguably a little better even than that.

In 1970, Nijinsky became the last horse to win the English Triple Crown and added the Sweeps Derby to his list of triumphs with an easy win from Meadowville. (JC)

Michael O'Hehir interviewing Liam Ward, who piloted Nijinsky to success. (JC)

*French-trained Irish Ball was the winner of the 1971 race, beating two Paddy Prendergast-trained horses
into 2nd and 3rd places. (JC)*

Irish Ball, with Alfred Gilbert up, being led in after his easy victory in 1971. (JC)

Scobie Breasley, former champion jockey, was the trainer of the 1972 winner, Steel Pulse. (JC)

*Bill Williamson,
an Australian like
Scobie Breasley,
rode Steel Pulse
to victory. (JC)*

Steel Pulse wins the 1972 race from Scottish Rifle. (JC)

English Prince (left) *wins in 1974. (JC)*

English Prince being led in with his jockey, the great Frenchman Yves Saint-Martin, aboard. (JC)

Grundy won the 1975 race on a hot day in the middle of a particularly hot summer, ridden by a youthful Pat Eddery. (JC)

IRISH SWEEPS DERBY

1M 4F

SATURDAY 26 JUNE 1976

GOING: FIRM

WINNER: Mme M. Felix Berger's Malacate by Lucky
Debonair out of Eyeshadow
P. Paquet

SECOND: Empery by Vaguely Noble out of Pamplona
L. Piggott

THIRD: Northern Treasure by Northfields out of
Place d'Étoile
G. Curran

S.P.   5/1   4/5f   16/1
Winner trained by F. Boutin

ALSO: Hawkberry 4th, Far North 5th, Brandon Hill
6th, Niebo 7th, Navarre 8th, Finsbury 9th,
Oilfield 10th, No Turning 11th, Decent
Fellow 12th, Mart Lane 13th, Riot Helmet
14th, Talarias 15th, King Mousse 16th,
Imperial Fleet 17th & last

Winner: 2nd favourite
Distances: 2½ lengths, ¾ length
Value to winner: £66,016
Time: 2 m 31.2 s
Timeform rating of winner: 131.

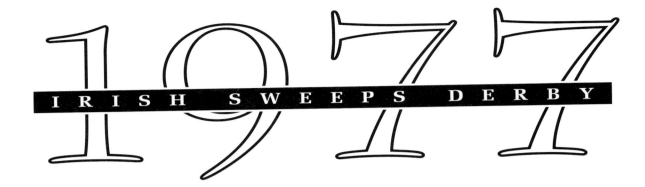

1977

IRISH SWEEPS DERBY

THE CURRAGH 25 JUNE 1977

In 1975 Robert Sangster and his partners Alan Clore, David Ackroyd and Simon Fraser, together with leading Irish trainer Vincent O'Brien, came together with one common purpose. That was to acquire the best-bred youngsters in the world, put them into training with arguably the greatest trainer of the century, win prestige races with the thoroughbreds in question, and then syndicate the horses at a suitably rewarding stallion fee.

Success is rarely instantaneous in such ventures, but this was an exception. The very first batch of yearlings acquired by the syndicate included the high-class colts, Be My Guest, Artaius and The Minstrel. It was at the 1975 Keeneland sales that Vincent O'Brien was taken by a flashy chestnut with four white stockings and a striking white blaze. The trainer was no less impressed by the colt's pedigree. By Northern Dancer, Nijinsky's sire, out of a mare called Fleur, who was herself a half sister to Nijinsky, the

colt who was to become known as The Minstrel was assuredly bred in the purple. Yet he was acquired at Keeneland for the comparatively modest sum of $200,000.

Possible competitors for the yearling dropped out of the reckoning because in the first instance they were put off by the colt's four white socks, usually not a good sign, and in addition The Minstrel was on the small side. But then so also was his sire, Northern Dancer. Vincent O'Brien was rarely wrong in assessing the potential of a thoroughbred, and with The Minstrel he was again to be triumphantly vindicated.

As a juvenile, The Minstrel made his début in the Moy Stakes over six furlongs at the Curragh. He started at 4/9 and won by five lengths, setting a new course record in the process. After another easy victory at Leopardstown, The Minstrel set the seal on his two-year-old career with a four length defeat of Saros in the Dewhurst Stakes at Newmarket.

The Minstrel seemed set for a splendid three-year-old career, but at the outset things did not go according to plan. A hard-earned victory in the Ascot 2,000 Guineas Trial in heavy ground was followed by two near misses in both the English and Irish 2,000 Guineas. He was third to Nebbiolo and Tachypous at Newmarket and second to Pampapaul, with Nebbiolo third at the Curragh.

Connections were both disappointed and perplexed. Both on breeding and on two-year-old performances, The Minstrel seemed a natural for the mile trip of the Guineas races. Vincent O'Brien was initially inclined to bypass the Epsom Derby with the Northern Dancer colt, but Lester Piggott, despite the Guineas setbacks, remained convinced that The Minstrel would stay the Derby distance. Ultimately, Vincent agreed with Lester's opinion and decided to run The Minstrel at Epsom rather than Alleged, whom he put by for an autumn campaign. It was to prove an inspired move, both for The Minstrel and for Alleged.

The Epsom Derby of 1977 will long be remembered by the many punters who put their faith in Lester Piggott's skill and judgment. Starting at 5/1, after opening at 7/1, The Minstrel got up in the last strides under a most vigorous and determined ride from Piggott to deprive Hot Grove of the spoils by a neck. For Piggott's legion of supporters it was 1972 and Roberto revisited.

After four very hard races there was some surprise engendered when Vincent O'Brien elected to send his Epsom winner on to the Curragh for the Sweeps Derby. Many felt that the gruelling race The Minstrel had had in winning at Epsom would take its toll, and as a result the colt's appearance at the Curragh was awaited with great interest.

There was no shortage of contenders prepared to take on the O'Brien colt at the Curragh. Apart from the suspicion that The Minstrel might be found out by his tough campaign, the record of Epsom Derby winners at the Curragh in the period since the inauguration of the Sweeps sponsorship was not especially encouraging. Larkspur, Relko, Charlottown, Sir Ivor, Blakeney, Roberto and Empery had all failed to complete the Derby double, with only Santa Claus, Nijinsky and Grundy going on from Epsom to success at the Curragh.

The opposition at the Curragh included three horses who had finished behind The Minstrel at Epsom. The French colt Monseigneur had finished fourth at Epsom, but had some eight lengths to make up on the winner. A well-bred horse by Ribot's son, Graustark, it was said that Monseigneur had not acted on the undulating Epsom track and in addition had encountered trouble in running.

Others which had run at Epsom were the Con Collins-trained Milverton and Harry Wragg's Lucky Sovereign, who had finished thirteenth and fifteenth respectively behind The Minstrel. Both had run below expectations at Epsom, but connections were hopeful of a more forward showing on this occasion, and the formbook suggested that there were grounds for some degree of optimism.

Milverton's main claim to fame was a victory in the Vauxhall Trial Stakes at the Phoenix Park over the subsequent

Newmarket 2,000 Guineas winner, Nebbiolo. Lucky Sovereign, for his part, had subsequently beaten Milverton into third place in the Mecca Dante Stakes at York, and as a result was quite well fancied at Epsom, only to disappoint.

Besides Monseigneur, the French fielded a further well-fancied contender in the unbeaten Sir Ivor colt, Ercolano, trained by Alec Head and to be ridden by his son Freddie. His French form was difficult to evaluate, and it was considered that he might not be at home on the fast going that was anticipated.

Among the other challengers to be feared were the Peter Walwyn-trained Classic Example, who had won the King Edward VII Stakes at Ascot from the Vincent O'Brien-trained Leonato. Connections of The Minstrel were entitled to feel that Classic Example should scarcely trouble their Derby winner who, it had to be assumed, was some way superior to Leonato.

On the day of the race there was a bit of a gamble on the Irish outsider, Orchestra. Backed from 20/1 to 12's, Orchestra had been beaten two and a half lengths by Alleged over course and distance on his most recent run and clearly was expected to go well. Not surprisingly, the punters at the Curragh made The Minstrel clear favourite. Varying between 5/4 and even money, he settled a very solid 11/10 favourite. Next in the betting was Monseigneur who eased to 5/1 from 4's, while compatriot Ercolano was a steady 10/1 shot. Of the others, Classic Example attracted some interest and finished at 14/1 from 16's.

In all, sixteen runners lined up to face the starter, and expectations of a first Irish win in the race since 1973 helped to create a great sense of anticipation among the crowds who had gathered to witness the 112th Irish Derby. The fact that Lester Piggott was bidding to win his first Irish Derby for Vincent O'Brien also added to the sense of occasion.

From the start the field broke fairly well, and as is so often the case, it was the rank outsider, King Ashoka, with Tommy Carmody up, who settled down to make the running. Lucky Sovereign was actually first to break the line, but Frankie Durr quickly reined him back into the middle of the pack. Ensuring a strong gallop for his fancied stable companion, Orchestra, who himself was close up, King Ashoka maintained his position at the head of affairs until beyond half-way. The Minstrel in the early stages was held up in the rear by Piggott.

After King Ashoka had cried enough, Orchestra and Raymond Carroll took over five furlongs out and set sail for home. Looking back through the field, The Minstrel could be noted making steady headway from the rear, while Lucky Sovereign was also closing on the leader. Turning into the straight, Orchesta still led, but both The Minstrel and Lucky Sovereign were poised to challenge.

Both horses made their move on the outside at almost the same time, with about two furlongs left to run. For a few seconds the outcome remained in doubt. The issue clearly rested between The Minstrel and Lucky Sovereign, although Classic Example was noted making a late bid in behind. Would the favourite oblige, or would Lucky Sovereign show that his Epsom running was all wrong?

At 22/1 only the bookmakers would be cheering if Harry Wragg's Nijinsky colt were to upset the Irish hot pot. However, the doubts raised were just as quickly quelled. The Minstrel produced the better turn of foot and soon put daylight between himself and his rival. The drama, however, was far from over. With the race seemingly won, The Minstrel suddenly swerved quite violently to his left and seemed to cross and perhaps impede Lucky Sovereign. Certainly, Frankie Durr switched his mount inside The Minstrel in the final furlong and from the stands it was impossible to say if there had been any interference.

The Minstrel asserted his authority in the final 100 yards and at the finish there was a length and a half between first and second, with Classic Example running on well to finish only a neck behind Lucky Sovereign in third place. Orchestra kept on to finish fourth, while the two French challengers Monseigneur (fifth) and Ercolano (sixth) were never sighted with a winning chance.

As soon as the horses passed the post a stewards enquiry was announced. At first the immediate reaction of the crowd, and indeed of the bookmakers, was that The Minstrel had not done enough to be disqualified. Shortly afterwards, however, it was announced that Frankie Durr, the rider of Lucky Sovereign, had objected to the winner for crossing his mount, and opinions, initially firmly against, began to shift in favour of the runner-up.

Betting on the outcome of stewards enquiries is notoriously fickle and confident assertions, without any basis in fact, can influence the market in the absence of any other tangible matter of substance. One invariable trend is that the longer the enquiry continues, the closer the odds become between the protagonists. This was certainly true of the 1977 Irish Derby enquiry. To the surprise of many, it dragged on and on, and the certainty which had marked early opinions on the outcome was soon dissipated.

In all of the enclosures spectators huddled together in heated debate. Closed circuit TV monitors were scanned, the fateful last furlong subjected to intense scrutiny, and still the enquiry went on.

For the connections of the two principals it must have been an agonising wait. Almost half an hour had elapsed before the announcement that all had been waiting for boomed out over the Tannoy system. 'Result of the stewards enquiry: there is no alteration in the judges' placings. Winner all right.' Loud and sustained cheering greeted the verdict. Of course, the majority of the attendance were Irish and national pride was suitably massaged. In addition, and not to be overlooked, many had doubtless backed the favourite.

Strangely, The Minstrel's success was to be Lester Piggott's first and only Irish Derby winner for Vincent O'Brien, despite the many Group 1 successes worldwide that the pair enjoyed in the course of their long association.

As a dual Derby winner, The Minstrel had little left to prove as regards his own age group. He was the undisputed three-year-old champion. Breeders, however, like to see their prospective stallions tried out against the older generation. The Northern Dancer colt was duly dispatched to Ascot for the King George VI and Queen Elizabeth

Diamond Stakes (incidentally The Minstrel's sixth race in sixteen weeks).

A truly international field was assembled for the all-aged classic. The second and third in the 1976 King George, Bruni and Orange Bay, were in the field, as well as Crow, the 1976 St Leger winner and Arc runner-up. Exceller, Coronation Cup hero, and Crystal Palace, the 1977 French Derby winner, were also in the line-up.

Starting 7/4 favourite, The Minstrel again proved what a durable, tough colt he was by battling to a very hard-fought short-head success over the five-year-old, Orange Bay. Lester Piggott once again demonstrated his immense strength in the saddle, and not even the best efforts of Pat Eddery on the runner-up could overturn the winning combination.

After his Ascot triumph, the O'Brien-Sangster syndicate sold a half-share in The Minstrel back to his breeder, E. P. Taylor, for a sum reputed to be in excess of $4 million. The original outlay of $200,000 on the colt had delivered a most handsome dividend. Of course, The Minstrel's success was another testament to the incomparable skill of Vincent O'Brien in spotting potential champion qualities in an unfurnished yearling.

Before an autumn campaign could be mapped out for The Minstrel an outbreak of contagious metritis forced the syndicate's hand. As there was a serious danger of a ban on the export of bloodstock resulting from the disease, The Minstrel was sent without further delay to the US to take up stallion duties at Windfields Farm in Maryland.

The Minstrel went on to become a highly successful sire, producing classic winners such as the 1989 1,000 Guineas heroine Musical Bliss and the 1988 Irish Oaks dead-heater Melodist. Sadly, however, he was put down in the summer of 1990, after contracting the chronic lameness disease, laminitis.

It is interesting to reflect on what a profoundly correct assessment both Lester Piggott and Vincent O'Brien made in weighing up the respective options for their two top-class three-year-olds in the early part of the 1977 flat season. The Minstrel's successes have been documented above. But Alleged, who bypassed both the English and Irish Derbies, went on to prove himself in the very highest class.

After winning the Great Voltigeur at York in a canter (in the process relegating Hot Grove to fourth), Alleged suffered the only defeat of his career in the Doncaster St Leger at the hands of the Queen's filly, Dunfermline. That, however, was to be the prelude to Alleged's greatest triumph. In October, the Hoist the Flag colt won the Prix de l'Arc de Triomphe in scintillating fashion. On contrasting ground in the following year, Alleged followed up with a second supremely impressive Arc victory. A very underestimated colt, Lester Piggott is on record as saying that Alleged was the easiest to ride of all the great horses he had partnered.

That could certainly not be said of The Minstrel. Often a slow starter, he did not possess the brilliance of a Nijinsky or the acceleration of a Sir Ivor. What the flashy chestnut with the distinctive markings did possess, however, were those qualities that students of the turf admire perhaps above all others in a racehorse — toughness, courage and an indomitable will to win.

IRISH SWEEPS DERBY

1M 4F

SATURDAY 25 JUNE 1977

GOING: GOOD TO FIRM

WINNER: Mr R. E. Sangster's The Minstrel by Northern
Dancer out of Fleur
L. Piggott

SECOND: Lucky Sovereign by Nijinsky out of
Sovereign
F. Durr

THIRD: Classic Example by Tudor Melody out of
Supreme Lady
P. Eddery

S.P. 11/10f 22/1 14/1
Winner trained by M. V. O'Brien

ALSO: Orchestra 4th, Monseigneur 5th, Ercolano
6th, Milverton 7th, Aristocracy 8th, Limone
9th, Remezzo 10th, Star Salute 11th, Ad
Libra 12th, Padroug 13th, Lath 14th, King
Ashoka 15th & last

Winner: favourite
Distances: 1½ lengths, nk
Value to winner: £72,795.50
Time: 2 m 31.9 s
Timeform rating of winner: 135.

IRISH SWEEPS DERBY

THE CURRAGH 1 JULY 1978

Mill Reef, in the view of one noted Irish trainer, perhaps the best horse he has ever seen, did not compete in the Irish Sweeps Derby of his year. His illustrious son, Shirley Heights, after emulating his sire by winning at Epsom, was by contrast dispatched to the Curragh in an attempt to land the prestigious Derby double. It is in the West Indian island of Antigua that Shirley Heights overlooks the landmark known as Mill Reef, hence the naming of the two thoroughbreds.

As a juvenile Shirley Heights had been a good consistent colt, but he was just short of top class. Unplaced first time out over an inadequate six furlong trip, he improved then to be second next time out in a six furlong maiden before winning over seven furlongs at Newmarket. Stepped up in grade, Shirley Heights was second to Sexton Blake in the seven furlong Seaton Delavel Stakes at Newcastle and followed that good performance with another

second, this time to Bolak on soft ground at Sandown. His best performance came in his final juvenile outing. In the Group 1 Royal Lodge Stakes at Ascot run on firm ground, Shirley Heights turned the tables on Bolak, beating his Sandown conqueror by three-quarters of a length. Interestingly, in third place on that occasion was a horse called Hawaiian Sound.

In the Free Handicap at the end of the season Shirley Heights was given a weight of 9 stone 1 lb, 6 lb behind the top-rated Try My Best. Vincent O'Brien's expensive US-bred did not quite make the grade as a three-year-old, although he was perhaps unfortunate in that his attempt to win the English 2,000 Guineas was undermined by untypically soft ground. Shirley Heights bypassed the Guineas and was instead prepared for a middle-distance campaign.

On soft ground and in need of the race, Shirley Heights finished a fairly distant second to Whitstead in the one and a quarter mile classic trial at Sandown on his seasonal début. He improved markedly for that outing, and in the ten furlong Heathorn Stakes at Newmarket gave Ile de Bourbon 10 lb and beat him a short head. Subsequent events would prove that this form was top class. In the Mecca Dante Stakes at York, one of the principal recognised Derby trials, Shirley Heights, with Greville Starkey easing him down close home, won impressively from Julio Mariner and Sexton Blake, again very good form.

Had punters at Epsom on the first Wednesday of June 1978 had the benefit of hindsight, sadly denied to them, it is inconceivable that Shirley Heights would have started an 8/1 shot for the Derby. The Epsom favourite was Vincent O'Brien's Inkerman, while also included among the opposition was Hawaiian Sound, whom Shirley Heights had of course beaten as a juvenile. Mill Reef's son duly won the Epsom Derby, but it was in fact a very close run thing.

The American legend, Willie Shoemaker, was aboard the Barry Hills-trained Hawaiian Sound at Epsom, and until the last fateful strides seemed certain to land the spoils. Quite inexplicably, given the camber of the ground at Epsom, Hawaiian Sound came off the rails and allowed Starkey on Shirley Heights to poke through on the inside and get up on the line to win by a head. The favourite, Inkerman, ran deplorably and finished twenty-first of the twenty-five runners. It was subsequently reported that Vincent O'Brien's Vaguely Noble colt had swallowed his tongue.

If Barry Hills and owner Robert Sangster were disappointed by Hawaiian Sound's defeat, they did not show it. They kept faith with the diminutive American jockey and Shoemaker was reunited with Hawaiian Sound in an attempt to gain revenge on Shirley Heights at the Curragh. The showdown between the Epsom winner and runner-up provoked a lively debate among racing *aficionados* as to the likely outcome, but of course it was anything but a two-horse race.

No less than four other horses who had competed at Epsom elected to take on the big two again. Chief among them was Remainder Man, third home at Epsom, but who had disappointed subsequently at Ascot. Also from England came Majestic Maharaj, fourteenth at Epsom and who, despite winning subsequently at Doncaster, was something of a long shot.

Two Irish-trained horses who had run poorly at Epsom were fancied to be better suited to the more galloping Curragh track. The disappointing Epsom favourite, Inkerman, to be partnered again by Lester Piggott, was expected to reproduce his earlier good Irish form. This included a six length victory over stablemate Encyclopaedia, who incidentally was also in the Derby field, over course and distance and in a very fast time. Paddy Prendergast's Exdirectory, thirteenth at Epsom, was the subject of very encouraging reports from the training grounds. It had been reported that Exdirectory had been unable to handle the Epsom track and, in addition, had met with trouble in running.

Of the remainder, the one with the best chance on form was John Oxx's Strong Gale. Beaten one and a half lengths by the aforementioned Exdirectory on his seasonal début, the Lord Gayle colt had looked all over a winner of the Irish 2,000 Guineas at the Curragh until picked off close home by Vincent O'Brien's Jaazeiro.

The lone French challenger was Maurice Zilber's El Badr, the mount of Yves Saint-Martin, successful in 1974 on English Prince. A son of the 1973 Sweeps Derby winner, Weaver's Hall, El Badr had won over the Derby trip at Chantilly but was not highly rated in France. He was no more than a lively outsider.

The competitive field brought a fine crowd to the Curragh on the first day of July 1978. The betting exchanges on the big race reflected a very strong market and five horses were supported to a greater or lesser degree. Weight of money forced Shirley Heights from an opening price of 7/4 down to a very miserly 5/4 chance. Despite the favourite's strength, the combination of Vincent O'Brien and Lester Piggott, going for their second successive Irish Derby, attracted considerable support and Inkerman settled at 3/1, having been backed initially from 7/2 to 5/2. Willie 'the Shoe' had his followers and Hawaiian Sound visited 7's before settling at 6/1.

A significant move came for Christy Roche's mount Exdirectory and he was backed from 12/1 down to 8/1. The Irish Guineas runner-up Strong Gale was also fancied, finishing up a 9/1 shot after opening at 10's. In the face of these market moves the Epsom Derby third, Remainder Man, weakened from 12/1 to 18/1, and it was any price the rest. The betting suggested that it was going to be a tremendous race and on this occasion at least money talked. The 1978

Sweeps Derby was destined to go down as the most thrilling battle for the Blue Riband of Irish racing for many years.

The going was officially good and in the early stages Hawaiian Sound and Willie Shoemaker, as anticipated, made the running. The American jockey, however, was not allowed to have things all his own way. Tommy Murphy on Vincent O'Brien's second string, Encyclopaedia, kept close tabs on the Epsom runner-up. Both Shirley Heights and Inkerman were towards the rear in the first half of the race, but in a compact field of only eleven runners were very much in touch. Continuing down the far side Hawaiian Sound still led from Encyclopaedia, with Valley Forge and Wally Swinburn, and Rathdowney, the mount of John Roe, close up.

At about the half-way point Hawaiian Sound was taken on by Encyclopaedia and for a couple of furlongs the two leaders raced side by side. There was some close riding in behind, but all the leading fancies were in close enough attendance at this point of the race. Some five furlongs out Encyclopaedia struck the front, with Hawaiian Sound, given a bit of a breather, staying a close second.

As the field turned into the straight, Encyclopaedia still led from Hawaiian Sound, but Shirley Heights, Inkerman, Exdirectory and Strong Gale were all poised to challenge. It was anybody's race at this point and in the packed grandstands few could have picked the winner with any confidence. Strong Gale was first to come under pressure and, probably failing to stay, faded out of contention. Encyclopaedia's dash for glory petered out approaching the two furlong marker and Hawaiian Sound and Shoemaker went on again. To a certain extent the race had been run to suit Barry Hills' American-bred colt, and having had the benefit of a breather, Hawaiian Sound got first run on the opposition.

However, no less than three horses sorted themselves out from the pack to lay down a serious challenge to the front runner. Shirley Heights, who had been fourth into the straight, made his move on the outside. Inkerman, who had been only ninth at half-way, made significant headway thereafter and made his bid on the far rails. Meantime Exdirectory, who like the favourite had also come very wide into the straight, simultaneously launched his determined challenge.

With four horses spread across the course, it was all but impossible to tell who was going the best. Having got first run, Hawaiian Sound still appeared to be in the lead with just over a furlong to run. The surprise packet of the race, Exdirectory, however, was responding very well to Christy Roche's urgings and to great cheering from his supporters struck the front inside the final furlong. It looked like a decisive move. At this stage Shirley Heights was under strong pressure from Starkey, but was still running on well. Over on the far rails Hawaiian Sound continued to make the best of his way home, with Inkerman still challenging.

From the packed enclosures supporters of all four horses were united in urging on their fancies to greater efforts. The gambled on Exdirectory, a son of Irish 2,000 Guineas winner Ballymore, seemed certain to win as the race entered its final 100 yards. But suddenly the picture changed. As Shirley Heights began to drift slightly to his left, Exdirectory, a relatively inexperienced colt, came off a true line and veered towards the Epsom Derby winner.

Meantime on the opposite side of the track Hawaiian Sound had got the better of Inkerman and was running on extremely well. With the three principals separated by virtually the entire width of the track, there was less than a neck between them as they entered the final fifty yards. It was here that the courage and experience of Shirley Heights proved decisive. Greville Starkey called for and got a renewed effort from the favourite, and in the dying strides Shirley Heights hit the front and just got to the winning post ahead of Exdirectory. Hawaiian Sound was a close-up third.

It had been a thrilling conclusion to a fine race. A photo finish was called for and the evidence of the camera confirmed the placings as set out above. The official distances were a head and a neck. It was close, but it was none the less a decisive outcome. Certainly supporters of both Exdirectory and Hawaiian Sound, whose hopes had been raised during the final dramatic surge for the line, were entitled to feel a little aggrieved, thinking perhaps that in different ways the race had got away from them. Shirley Heights, however, was a worthy winner and joined the select band of champions — Santa Claus, Nijinsky, Grundy and The Minstrel — who had added the Sweeps Derby to their Epsom spoils.

Vincent O'Brien's Inkerman ran a good race to be fourth, one length further back, but the rest of the field were well stretched out.

Strong Gale was a respectable fifth, the one-time prominent Encyclopaedia finished sixth and the disappointing Remainder Man a moderate seventh. In relation to Strong Gale, it is doubtful if his connections on Derby day 1978 could have quite foreseen the future that lay ahead for their classically placed Lord Gayle colt. Following Deep Run's demise, Strong Gale, standing at the Rathbarry Stud in County Cork, had established himself as Ireland's premier National Hunt sire before his untimely death in May 1994.

Shirley Heights' Derby triumphs represented trainer John Dunlop's biggest successes of his career to that point. His only previous classic victory was with Favoletta in the 1970 Irish 1,000 Guineas. He had of course come close to winning the Irish Derby before when his Scottish Rifle was runner-up to Steel Pulse in 1972.

It had been a gruelling race for those involved in the dramatic finish and it was immediately announced afterwards that Shirley Heights would not be trained for the King George VI and Queen Elizabeth Diamond Stakes. Instead he was to be aimed at the St Leger. These plans however never came to fruition. Lord Halifax's colt sustained a tendon injury and was in due course retired to stud.

In passing it is worth noting that Mill Reef, Shirley Heights' sire, was also responsible for Acamas, who won the 1978 French Derby, making it three Derbies for his sire in the one year, a feat to be repeated some years later by Nijinsky. Shirley Heights himself has developed into a

good-class sire and among his most successful progeny were Slip Anchor, winner of the 1985 Epsom Derby, and User Friendly, the 1992 Epsom Oaks and St Leger heroine. Shirley Heights also sired Deploy, who will figure prominently in one of the later chapters in this book.

In the absence of the dual Derby winner, the tough and consistent Hawaiian Sound reversed placings with Exdirectory in the King George at Ascot, but once again failed to gain first prize. Third to Ile de Bourbon, with Exdirectory sixth, Robert Sangster's colt gained a well-deserved Group 1 success when landing the one and a quarter mile Benson and Hedges Gold Cup at York. His season didn't end in a blaze of glory, however, although once again Hawaiian Sound ran respectably when finishing second to Paul Kelleway's filly, Swiss Maid, in the Champion Stakes.

Swiss Maid's success brought down the curtain on a quite tremendous year for his jockey Greville Starkey. Including his two Derby victories on Shirley Heights, Starkey won no less than nine Group 1 races for his patrons in 1978, his other principal victories being in the Epsom and Irish Oaks and the Ascot Gold Cup.

Because he failed to compete against his elders, Shirley Heights could not be ranked in the very top flight of Irish Derby winners. Like the 1977 winner The Minstrel, however, he was unquestionably a very game and genuine colt who had the priceless knack of knowing exactly where the winning post was.

1M 4F

SATURDAY 1 JULY 1978

GOING: GOOD

WINNER: Lord Halifax's Shirley Heights by Mill Reef out of Hardiemma
G. Starkey

SECOND: Exdirectory by Ballymore out of Regal Bell
C. Roche

THIRD: Hawaiian Sound by Hawaii out of Sound of Success
W. Shoemaker

S.P. 5/4f   8/1   6/1
Winner trained by J. L. Dunlop

ALSO: Inkerman 4th, Strong Gale 5th, Encyclopaedia 6th, Remainder Man 7th, Rathdowney 8th, Valley Forge 9th, El Badr 10th, Majestic Maharaj 11th & last

Winner: favourite
Distances: hd, nk
Value to winner: £73,087.50
Time: 2 m 32.3 s
Timeform rating of winner: 130.

1979

THE CURRAGH 30 JUNE 1979

After the excitement of the 1978 renewal, it seemed improbable that the 1979 Irish Derby could produce another equally enthralling race. This supposition was based rather more on the evidence of public form than on the presumed laws of probability. Only nine runners went to post for the Curragh classic on the final day of June 1979 and the principal reason for the compact field was the presence in the line-up of the impressive Epsom Derby winner, Troy.

The Dick Hern-trained colt had been a revelation at Epsom. His previous form had stamped him a good-class colt, but the manner in which Troy had spreadeagled his field in the Epsom classic was quite breathtaking and suggested that he was a thoroughbred of the highest class.

Owned by Sir Michael Sobell and bred at the Ballymacoll Stud in County Meath, Troy had run four times as a juvenile. First time out, he was second in a six furlong maiden at Salisbury. Subsequently, he won a seven

furlong maiden at Newmarket. Stepped up in class, he proved equal to the task, winning the seven furlong Lanson Champagne Stakes at Goodwood from Ela-Mana-Mou. The latter horse gained revenge on Troy by beating him by three-quarters of a length in the Group 1 Royal Lodge Stakes at Ascot.

Clearly there wasn't much between the two protagonists and in the Free Handicap the Ascot form was accepted at face value, for Troy was given a weight of nine stone, with Ela-Mana-Mou rated two pounds higher. Troy was obviously a nice prospect for the future, but as a son of Petingo, some entertained doubts as to what his best trip as a three-year-old might turn out to be.

Petingo was a top-class two-year-old, winning both the Gimcrack and Middle Park Stakes. He was unfortunate enough to come up against Sir Ivor in his year and was a good second to Vincent O'Brien's superb colt in the English 2,000 Guineas. Petingo did not stay a yard beyond a mile, but proved his class (and at the same time paid a handsome tribute to his Newmarket conqueror) by winning two of the top mile races in the calendar, the St James's Palace Stakes at Ascot and the Sussex Stakes at Goodwood.

A glance at the distaff side of Troy's pedigree, however, must have given every encouragement to Dick Hern and his team as they mapped out a middle-distance campaign for their charge. Troy's dam was La Milo, who was herself by that game stayer, Hornbeam. In turn, Hornbeam was a son of the great Hyperion, the winner of the Epsom Derby and St Leger in 1933 and widely regarded as the greatest 'little horse' of the century. (He stood only 15.1½ hands high.) The blend of speed and stamina in Troy's pedigree was close to perfection, and Troy's three-year-old career must have been anticipated with keen excitement by his connections.

Troy's first outing as a three-year-old was in the Classic Trial Stakes at Sandown over a mile and a quarter. A hard-earned and not very convincing neck win over Ace of Diamonds didn't set the ante-post market on the Epsom Derby alight. It was in his next run, however, that Troy suggested that stamina was his strong suit. In the Predominate Stakes at Goodwood over the full classic distance of a mile and a half, Troy hacked up by seven lengths from Serge Lifar and two other moderate opponents.

It was difficult to evaluate Troy's Goodwood victory and punters were uncertain as to the merit of the form. At Epsom, Troy's old adversary, Ela-Mana-Mou, was preferred in the market and he started the 9/2 favourite in an open betting race.

Troy was second favourite at 6/1. Badly placed and being scrubbed along in the early stages, Troy suddenly sprouted wings once in the straight and stormed home to a stunning seven length victory from Dickens Hill. Ela-Mana-Mou was only fourth.

Besides being a popular winner for both his owner Sir Michael Sobell and trainer Dick Hern, Troy was live-wire lightweight jockey Willie Carson's first Epsom Derby success. There had of course been several near misses in the past for Carson, in particular his heartbreaking defeat on Hot Grove in 1977 at the hands of Lester Piggott and The Minstrel. Troy more than made up for all the disappointments.

And so on to the Curragh and Troy was, as might have been expected, a hot favourite to make it a hat trick of dual Derby successes following upon the achievements of both The Minstrel and Shirley Heights. Willie Carson was certainly entitled to feel confident that Troy would bring him his first Irish Derby success on this, only his second ever ride in the premier Irish classic.

In the face of what appeared to be the inevitable, how was one to gauge the strength of the opposition to Troy? Mick O'Toole, more renowned for his exploits at Cheltenham than on the flat, must have thought long and hard before committing his Epsom Derby runner-up, Dickens Hill, to take on Troy again. Appreciably more optimistic were the connections of the English-trained Laska Floko, who had finished last of the twenty-two runners at Epsom. Surely not even the presence of Lester Piggott on board Clive Brittain's charge could serve to work the oracle?

Realistically, besides Dickens Hill, only the French could have hoped to make a race of it with Troy. The Northern Dancer colt, Fabulous Dancer, had an impressive winning streak behind him, including in particular a victory over Northern Baby by a head at Longchamp over a mile and a quarter. Given, however, that Northern Baby had finished all of ten lengths behind Troy at Epsom when crossing the line in third place, on the evidence of the formbook Fabulous Dancer had a lot of ground to make up on the hot favourite. The other French challenger, Scorpio, appeared held by Fabulous Dancer on French form.

One interesting riding arrangement which attracted media attention was Adrian Maxwell's decision to bring Willie Shoemaker all the way from the States to partner his outsider, Bohemian Grove. Doubtless Willie 'the Shoe' was hoping to improve on his close-up third on Hawaiian Sound in the previous year, but given that his mount had finished no less than twenty-two lengths behind Ardross on his outing prior to the Derby, his prospects of stepping up did not look too bright.

The betting on the Derby, the third on a seven-race card, was predictable. Varying between 1/2 and 2/5, Troy settled at 4/9, scarcely a price to entice the average punter. Perhaps because of this, there was a good measure of support for Dickens Hill and he visited 4's from 6's, before closing at 9/2. Fabulous Dancer eased slightly from 6's to 7's, while Scorpio, after opening at 10's and touching 14's, finished a 12/1 shot. You could all but name your price about the rest, Bohemian Grove, for instance, being returned a 66/1 shot.

In fine, dry conditions the premier Irish classic got under way. The first half of the race went very much as might have been anticipated. Troy's stable companion, the rank outsider, Rivadon, set a strong pace and led until just beyond half-way. Ted Curtin's The Bart, with Christy Roche up, tracked Rivadon and took over when the pacemaker began to wilt. At this stage both Troy and Dickens Hill had a fair bit to do, but few anticipated that they would encounter any difficulty in doing it.

Under a vigorous ride from Roche, The Bart soon opened up a useful lead as the field approached the half-mile marker. There was a momentary flutter of concern among Troy's supporters as for a few strides Carson appeared to get a bit serious with the supposed 'good thing'. The response was not instantaneous and those who had laid the odds on the favourite were perhaps beginning to ponder the wisdom of the move.

The Bart continued to lead into the straight and for a few strides those who had supported the outsider must have had their hopes raised. Troy, meantime, was beginning to close on the leader and was looking full of runnning. With about two furlongs to go Roche began to send out distress signals on the American-bred colt, and all the while the ominous presence of Troy was looming up behind. From somewhat further back Dickens Hill too had been driven closer and the race was taking shape very much as the formbook had predicted.

With about a furlong and a half to go, Willie Carson on Troy ranged alongside The

Piggott to administer a corrective slap. Monteverdi immediately resented the chastisement and cocked his head to one side. In that instant the colt's chequered future loomed up for all to see. So much for Monteverdi! With the Epsom Derby winner Henbit having gone lame in the latter stages of his surge for victory, he too was destined to miss the Curragh equivalent.

After three winning favourites in succession Irish racegoers were probably beginning to feel that the task of picking the winner of the 1980 Irish Derby was an eminently straightforward affair. Even in the enforced absence of Henbit, at first glance the 1980 renewal offered every hope to punters that the sequence of successful favourites would be maintained. The Epsom Derby runner-up, Master Willie, was the obvious form choice and seemed to have everything going in his favour.

Apart from the evidence of the formbook, many believed that the Henry Candy-trained colt had been unlucky at Epsom. Besides encountering trouble in running — what horse at Epsom does not encounter trouble in running, you may ask — Master Willie had suffered a setback when contracting an infected throat at a crucial stage of his preparation for the premier English classic.

An open and shut case, on the face of it. Racing, of course, is never quite so simple. Among those who chose to take on the Epsom runner-up again was the trio which had finished directly behind Master Willie in third, fourth and fifth places. One and a half lengths behind Master Willie, Rankin had finished a half-length in front of Pelerin, with Garrido just a short head back in fifth.

In all just over two lengths covered the four horses at Epsom, so it is relatively easy to understand why connections of the vanquished chose to do battle again.

Master Willie's pre-Epsom run was in the Mecca Dante Stakes at York, where he had been beaten by a neck by Hello Gorgeous, with Tyrnavos almost two lengths back in fourth place. Over the extra distance of the Epsom Derby, however, Master Willie comfortably reversed the form with Hello Gorgeous and indeed increased further his advantage over Tyrnavos, who finished in the ruck. The mount of Philip Waldron, Master Willie had a favourite's chance at the Curragh.

Dangers clearly abounded, however, and the three above mentioned — Rankin, Pelerin and Garrido — were top of that particular list. It had taken Pelerin, Lester Piggott's mount at the Curragh, a long time to lose his maiden certificate and it was not until the Glasgow Stakes at York in May that the Harry Wragg-trained colt was first past the judge. On that occasion he was a 16/1 chance when he beat Winslow Boy by one and a half lengths in a field of eight. The form was not considered exceptional and Pelerin was an 18/1 outsider at Epsom.

Rankin, from the Guy Harwood stable, was only marginally more fancied than Pelerin at Epsom. A 14/1 chance, he had been a three-quarter length second to Prince Bee — a Sweeps Derby rival — in the Predominate Stakes over ten furlongs, which in 1980 was run at Kempton Park due to rebuilding work at Goodwood. Like Pelerin, Rankin had to be given a serious chance at the Curragh, but both seemed to have it to do to reverse Epsom placings with Master Willie.

Similar observations applied to the French-trained Garrido, who prior to Epsom had won the Italian Derby. Garrido only came into the Epsom picture after the defection of his unlucky stable companion Nureyev — controversially disqualified in the English 2,000 Guineas — but trainer François Boutin and jockey Philippe Paquet had tasted Irish Derby success before with Malacate in 1976 and certainly knew what was required to win.

A number of the Epsom also-rans took up the challenge afresh. The aforementioned pair, Nikoli (eighth) and Tyrnavos (twelfth), together with Noble Shamus (nineteenth), had less obvious chances than those who had finished in front of them, but doubtless their presence was an illustration of the undeniable proposition that if you're not in you can't win.

Henbit had won the Epsom Derby at 7/1 second favourite. The favourite, perhaps surprisingly, was the Irish-trained Nikoli. Even though Nikoli had shown great courage in holding off the English-trained trio — Last Fandango, Final Straw and Posse — in the Irish 2,000 Guineas, it was probably sentiment that propelled the Great Nephew colt into Epsom favouritism.

The great Paddy Prendergast, who had won every race of consequence with the exception of the Epsom Derby in a fabulous career, was gravely ill, and the racing world collectively hoped that Nikoli would crown his illustrious career with classic success at Epsom Downs. It was not to be, and sadly Paddy Prendergast died just a few weeks afterwards at his home at Meadow Court, Maddenstown, in County Kildare. His son

Kevin took charge of the stable and hopes were high that Nikoli might yet posthumously honour the memory of his greatly admired and respected father.

Nikoli was a heavy-topped colt and it was considered that he had been unsuited to Epsom's undulations. He was expected to run a big race at the Curragh. Apart from Nikoli, the only other Irish contender who was given a chance was Dermot Weld's Ramian, who had won Leopardstown's Nijinsky Stakes, although the form had not worked out too well.

The only other horse worth mentioning was Dick Hern's Prince Bee. Though basically only a substitute for his unfortunate stable companion, Henbit, the Sun Prince colt had that Kempton verdict mentioned earlier over Epsom third, Rankin, to his credit. However, Prince Bee was 5 lb worse off with Rankin as compared to Kempton, and in addition Rankin's Epsom run appeared to represent improved form.

Thirteen runners in all went to post and much discussion centred on what effect the heavy overnight rain might have on the outcome of the race. The going was officially yielding, although there was debate as to how accurate that description was. The betting exchanges were lively, to say the least, and it appeared as though most punters were taking the view that the rain-softened going would not hinder the chances of the principal contenders.

There was a wholesale on-course gamble on the English-trained favourite. Master Willie was backed from opening offers of 3/1 down to a very short 7/4 favourite. The support for Henry Candy's runner did not

1981

IRISH SWEEPS DERBY

THE CURRAGH 27 JUNE 1981

Probably no racehorse has captured the headlines to the same extent as has the Aga Khan's Shergar since the days of the peerless Arkle's domination of his jumping counterparts in the 1960s. For many observers, Shergar was the best horse to have appeared on a racecourse since the Second World War. Others are more circumspect in their opinions, but whatever the truth of it, Shergar dominated the classic generation of 1981 in a manner unequalled since. Sadly, however, it is not for his prowess on the racecourse that Shergar is now remembered in the public consciousness.

Trained by Michael Stoute, Shergar made two appearances as a juvenile. After winning his maiden impressively over a mile at Newbury, he was upped in class to contest the traditional end of season juvenile trial, the William Hill Futurity at Doncaster. Under a sympathetic ride from Lester Piggott, Shergar finished a respectable two and a half length second to the more experienced Beldale Flutter. Although he had given no proof of greatness, several shrewd judges believed that the best was yet to come from the promising son of Great Nephew.

Engaged as a stable jockey by Michael Stoute at the start of the 1981 season, the 19-year-old Walter Swinburn took over from Lester Piggott on Shergar for his three-year-old campaign. The race chosen for Shergar's seasonal début was the Guardian Newspaper Classic Trial over ten furlongs at Sandown. A few eyebrows were raised when Michael Stoute's colt absolutely demolished the opposition, winning in a canter by ten lengths from Geoff Wragg's Kirtling.

When a horse wins as easily as Shergar did in a recognised classic trial, there is always a tendency to question the strength of the opposition. Some chose this route. Veteran racing journalist Richard Baerlein, however, nailed his colours to the mast after Shergar's spectacular Sandown triumph.

He urged his Guardian readers in his famous rallying cry to 'bet like men' on Shergar for the Epsom Derby, for which incidentally he was still available at 8/1 after his scintillating Sandown success. Some, wisely, followed his advice.

After Sandown, Shergar was routed towards Chester and the long-established Derby trial, the Chester Vase. At Sandown Shergar had put ten lengths between himself and the opposition. At Chester, over the full Derby distance, Shergar's winning margin over his nearest pursuer, Sunley Builds, was a staggering twelve lengths! Following upon his Chester triumph it seemed that only an act of God could have prevented Shergar from romping home at Epsom and no such divine intervention was to come to the aid of the bookmaking fraternity.

With Walter Swinburn again in the plate Shergar hacked up at Epsom, clearly demonstrating his vast superiority over his contemporaries, with the second horse, Glint of Gold, all of ten lengths adrift. The ground at Epsom was on the softish side and the time the slowest since Airborne's win in 1946, yet few if any were prepared to question the majestic ease of Shergar's victory. Seeing is believing. Swinburn was quoted after the race in the following terms: 'It was just like putting Steve Ovett in with a bunch of schoolchildren.'

Next stop after Epsom for Shergar was the Curragh and, not surprisingly, none of those who had finished behind him in the Derby elected to take on the winner again. It is frequently said that the presence of a top-class horse often serves to frighten the opposition away. In Shergar's case perhaps the truth was that there was no opposition, or at any rate no effective opposition.

Hoping for the proverbial miracle, however, at the Curragh were the connections of eleven thoroughbreds whose owners at least deserved credit for taking on the wonder horse. The principal opposition to Shergar came from overseas. There were three challengers from Britain and a lone French raider. Geoff Wragg again threw down the gauntlet with Kirtling who had of course been well beaten by Shergar at Sandown. That Sandown run was Kirtling's second run of the season and Wragg had made it absolutely clear that there were no excuses for his Grundy colt.

Since being outclassed by Shergar in the Guardian Classic Trial, Kirtling had gone on to win the Dee Stakes at Chester with impressive ease, before taking the Gran Premio d'Italia over one and a half miles in Milan. Kirtling's form was progressive, but doubtless Shergar had not exactly stood still either.

An interesting English challenger was Dick Hern's Cut Above, a half brother to the Irish 2,000 Guineas winner Sharp Edge. Twice placed to Kalaglow on his only juvenile runs, Cut Above reappeared in the White Rose Stakes at Ascot in April. Though not fully wound up, Cut Above had beaten Ridgefield by three lengths over the ten furlong trip. He had suffered a slight setback subsequently and hadn't run after that. A fresh horse and relatively unexposed, he looked a useful long-term prospect whatever his fate at the Curragh.

The other English runner, Baz Bombati, just didn't seem good enough and the lone

French raider, Gap of Dunloe, was a more likely sort. Third, beaten four lengths and two and a half lengths by Bikala and Akarad in the French Derby, Patrick Louis Biancone's Sassafras colt looked to be improving, but he had a fair bit of improving to do if he was to trouble Shergar.

Of the Irish contenders the most interesting was Dermot Weld's Dance Bid, a quite lightly raced Northern Dancer colt. He had finished a promising fifth to the initially disqualified and subsequently reinstated winner, Kings Lake, in the Irish 2,000 Guineas on his most recent run, and if he stayed the trip, had place prospects. Kevin Prendergast's Ore had won the Queen's Vase over two miles at Royal Ascot, but on earlier form was held by Dance Bid. It seemed improbable that any of the other Irish runners could possibly take a hand in the finish.

As well as being a top-class jockey, Lester Piggott was also a lucky one. Not for the first time in his illustrious career, fate was about to deal Piggott a winning hand. At Royal Ascot Walter Swinburn had fallen foul of the stewards over his riding of Centurius in the King Edward VII Stakes and the resulting period of suspension unfortunately ruled him out of the Irish Derby. By an ironic coincidence, at the start of the season Swinburn believed that Centurius, and not Shergar, would turn out to be his most likely classic prospect! With Swinburn sidelined, Lester Piggott who had ridden Shergar in his two juvenile outings was snapped up for the Curragh ride.

The betting on the Irish Derby reflected the seemingly one-sided nature of the contest. After opening at 2/7, Shergar eased slightly to 1/3, still prohibitive odds for the average punter. Opposition to the favourite in the ring was slight. Kirtling eased out to 12/1 from opening offers of 8's. Cut Above, after some early support from 12's to 10's, drifted out to 16/1 before settling at 14/1. It was 20/1 bar these three.

The details of the race are easily enough described. Willie Carson on Cut Above cut out most of the running. Shergar, with Lester aboard, was always close up and throughout the race it was clear that he was galloping over the opposition. Briefly Pat Eddery and Kirtling moved up to dispute the lead with Cut Above approaching the straight, but it was only on sufferance. Lester Piggott was sitting motionless on Shergar, and entering the straight he switched to the outside, let out an inch of rein and the race was as good as over. Shergar quickened smoothly to go clear of the toiling opposition, and throughout the final furlong Piggott had greater difficulty easing his mount down than beating off his challengers.

It was as easy a victory as could be imagined and after the race Piggott confided that he could have won by any distance that he had wanted. For Lester it was his fourth classic success of the year, following upon the Newmarket 1,000 Guineas (Fairy Footsteps), the English Oaks (Blue Wind) and the French Oaks (Madam Gay). For the record, Cut Above ran on gamely to be second to Shergar, with Dermot Weld's Dance Bid taking the third prize. Kirtling was fourth, Ore fifth and Gap of Dunloe sixth. The official distances were four lengths, one and a half lengths, five lengths, three-quarters of a length and a short head. The bare statistics don't tell the full story. Shergar had simply outclassed the opposition.

Shergar, like the 1975 dual Derby winner, Grundy, was sired by Great Nephew, about whom I have already written in an earlier chapter. Great Nephew's dam, Sybil's Niece, was good enough to win the Queen Mary Stakes at Royal Ascot and his second dam was by the great Hyperion. Shergar's dam was Sharmeen, who had won over ten and a half furlongs and had been placed at up to a mile and a half. Sharmeen herself was by the French Derby winner, Val de Loir, who also produced the Epsom Oaks winner La Lagune. Shergar's grand dam was by another French Derby winner, Charlottesville, who had sired the Epsom Derby winner and Sweeps Derby runner-up Charlottown. If ever a horse possessed a classic pedigree, then Shergar was that horse.

Interestingly Shergar, like another of the great thoroughbreds of the modern era, Northern Dancer, was not an especially big horse. (As mentioned elsewhere, Hyperion, who also figures in Shergar's pedigree, was also a small horse.) In fact Shergar stood only 15.2 hands high, even smaller than Northern Dancer at 15.3 hands, but what an engine he had! The doyen of racing journalists, Richard Baerlein, writing in the *Manchester Guardian* on the Monday after the Sweeps Derby, made the following observations about Shergar's Curragh success: 'In my opinion Nijinsky was the best winner of the Irish Sweeps Derby I have seen prior to Saturday's performance by Shergar. Now, I must give the latest winner preference.'

As pointed out earlier, Baerlein was a Shergar fan from early in the season, but as a respected commentator on racing over a long number of years his views are worthy of the closest attention. Following upon his Curragh triumph, Shergar was prepared for the King George VI and Queen Elizabeth Diamond Stakes. To prove himself an outstanding champion, Shergar would have to deal summarily with whatever opposition was mustered against him in the first major clash of the three-year-olds and the older generation. One horse who would not be in opposition at Ascot was the Curragh runner-up, Cut Above. His trainer Dick Hern was emphatic that his colt would not take on Shergar in the King George and would instead wait for the St Leger.

The field for Ascot's July show-piece was perhaps not the strongest ever assembled, but if no one was prepared to take Shergar on, well that was hardly his fault. Best of the opposition on paper was the four-year-old Master Willie who, it will be remembered, had finished a disappointing fifth on ground softer than he liked in the 1980 Sweeps Derby to Tyrnavos. Master Willie's overall record was however top class, and details of his principal successes have been set out in the previous chapter. In the event Master Willie never really settled in the Ascot race and he finished a disappointing fourth.

Shergar, as expected, won the King George with comparative ease, beating the Epsom Oaks runner-up and Prix de Diane winner, Madam Gay, by four lengths. Shergar encountered some slight trouble in running, but once clear early in the straight he again demonstrated his vast superiority over his contemporaries. After Ascot it only remained for Shergar to put the crowning achievement of an Arc triumph at the top of his honours list for him to be ranked among the great racehorses of all time.

After a short rest Shergar was brought back into training and to many racing fans' surprise the Doncaster St Leger was chosen as his preparatory race for the Arc. The St Leger had been unpopular with owners since 1970 when Nijinsky's participation in it was widely held to have cost him his chance in the Arc. This, I believe, as I have pointed out in the chapter on Nijinsky, is a simplistic and inaccurate view; however, the plain fact is that the St Leger had become unfashionable and Shergar's participation in it therefore was quite a surprise.

Not, indeed, that stamina ought to have been a problem for Shergar: as indicated earlier, his pedigree was laden with stamina. There were rumours running up to the day of the St Leger that he had not been working well, and at one point the ante-post bookmakers had started to field against him. On the day, however, Shergar was the only horse the punters wanted to know about and he started at 9/4 on.

In the event Shergar ran a listless race and finished a moderate fourth, beaten all of eleven and a half lengths by Cut Above, whom Shergar had so easily diposed of in the Irish Sweeps Derby. The turn-around in form was in fact fifteen and a half lengths. It will be remembered that the connections of Cut Above had made it their business to avoid Shergar after the Curragh! Horses are not machines, of course, but another illustration of the

perplexing nature of the Doncaster result can be mentioned briefly.

The second horse home at Doncaster was Glint of Gold, who finished nine lengths in front of Shergar. At Epsom in the Derby Shergar had beaten Glint of Gold by no less than ten lengths! It could not be argued that lack of stamina had beaten Shergar, for he was not going to win from fully three furlongs out. For whatever reason Shergar simply ran at least a stone and a half below his best.

Various excuses were put forward for Shergar's below-par performance at Doncaster, including the trip and the going, but none of them was convincing. Afterwards Michael Stoute's team could find no physical reason for Shergar's Doncaster flop and so the matter became one of racing's many imponderables. There still remained a possibility after Doncaster that Shergar might be aimed at the Prix de l'Arc de Triomphe, but the Aga Khan, being of the view that there was not enough time to find out if there was anything wrong with Shergar, ruled out the Paris option. There was criticism of the decision from some quarters of the racing press, but I think it is fair to say that it was not an unreasonable one in all the circumstances.

And so Shergar was retired to stud, and if things had gone according to plan the rest of this piece might have focused on his success or otherwise as a stallion. That particular script, however, was shredded to pieces by the appalling event which occurred on the night of Tuesday 8 February 1983. At about 8.40 p.m. on that night Shergar, one of the best, some might say the best, of the post-war classic winners, was kidnapped from the Aga Khan's Ballymany Stud on the edge of the Curragh in County Kildare.

The story aroused massive public interest and generated a flurry of publicity in the mass media which even to this day has not abated. It is outside the scope of this book to detail the events which followed the kidnapping of Shergar by a group of armed men: the story is already widely known.

A number of different theories as to what happened to Shergar have been floated in the years since his kidnapping and disappearance, but the almost certain truth is that the stallion was put to death at the hands of his kidnappers. The probability is that the kidnappers, who almost certainly had paramilitary connections, were ill prepared for the task of looking after a highly strung and temper-amental stallion and, tragically for all concerned, resorted to the only strategy which they felt was open to them to bring the ill-conceived affair to a conclusion.

And so Shergar, whose bloodlines trace back to the famous flying filly, Mumtaz Mahal, one of the first ever winners for the third Aga Khan (grandfather of the present Aga Khan) back in the 1920s, was lost forever to the breeding industry. In his only season at stud Shergar had covered forty-four mares, resulting in seventeen live colts and nineteen live fillies. Among this crop were included Maysoon, placed in both the 1986 1,000 Guineas and Epsom Oaks, and Authaal who won the Irish St Leger for David O'Brien. There seems little doubt that had he been allowed to establish himself at stud, Shergar would have stamped future generations with the marks of his pre-eminent brilliance.

It was not fated to be. Those privileged to have been in attendance at the Curragh on 27 June 1981 will always be able to recall with pleasure and some nostalgia their memories of a fabulous racehorse at the peak of his powers. Michael Stoute is on record as saying that in his view Shergar was more impressive in his winning performance at the Curragh than anywhere else. The bay colt with the distinctive white face had given pleasure to millions; it was an unmitigated tragedy that the rest of Shergar's story was to take such an unpredictable and bitter turn.

1M 4F
SATURDAY 27 JUNE 1981
GOING: GOOD TO FIRM

WINNER: H. H. Aga Khan's Shergar by Great Nephew out of Sharmeen.
L. Piggott

SECOND: Cut Above by High Top out of Cutle
W. Carson

THIRD: Dance Bid by Northern Dancer out of Highest Trump
W. Swinburn

S.P. 1/3f   14/1   33/1
Winner trained by M. R. Stoute

ALSO: Kirtling 4th, Ore 5th, Gap of Dunloe 6th, Young Kildare 7th, Baz Bombati 8th, Jolly Heir 9th, Crowned Hare 10th, Wolver Heights 11th, Bustineto 12th & last

Winner: favourite
Distances: 4 lengths, 1½ lengths
Value to winner: £117,075
Time: 2 m 33.2 s
Timeform rating of winner: 140.

1982

IRISH SWEEPS DERBY

The field for the 1982 running of the Sweeps Derby was frankly disappointing. Ten runners went to post and few of them could be given any realistic chance of winning. The obvious form choice was David O'Brien's French Derby winner Assert, whose chances had been immeasurably increased by the defection of the Epsom Derby winner Golden Fleece from the line-up.

At Epsom, with Pat Eddery on board, Golden Fleece had produced a devastating display to spreadeagle the opposition in a manner which had to be seen to be believed. Badly placed coming off Tattenham Corner into the straight, and with at least ten horses ahead of him, the Nijinsky colt had been produced by Eddery on the outside of the field, and in a matter of a couple of hundred yards had cut down the opposition as if they were selling platers.

It was a breathtaking performance and the evidence of the clock supported the view that Golden Fleece was a horse of exceptional ability. His time was the fastest electrically recorded for the Derby since electronic timing was introduced in 1964. In interviews since, both Vincent O'Brien and Lester Piggott have included Golden Fleece in the same exalted company as their two superstars of earlier generations, Sir Ivor and Nijinsky.

Following upon the victories of Golden Fleece at Epsom and Assert at Chantilly, the dream prospect of a clash between the two Derby winners at the Curragh was mooted as a distinct possibility. Sadly, however, the fates conspired to prevent such a mouth-watering contest taking place. Within a fortnight of his Epsom triumph Golden Fleece became ill. Later a swelling appeared on his hind leg and he was retired from racing. Tragically, Golden Fleece died of cancer eighteen months later.

Golden Fleece's death completed a miserable triumvirate of incalculable losses to the breeding industry. Within the space of a few short months, three of the most impressive Epsom Derby winners of the past several decades — Troy, Shergar and Golden Fleece — had died prematurely (I am assuming that Shergar was killed) and consequently their prospects of significantly influencing future bloodstock generations were all but eroded.

With Golden Fleece sidelined, Assert's task in the Irish Sweeps Derby appeared to be a relatively straightforward one. Assert had enjoyed a reasonably successful juvenile campaign. He made his racecourse début at Leopardstown where he was second, beaten two and a half lengths by no less than Golden Fleece! Assert stepped up on that performance in his next outing, beating Longleat by four lengths over a mile at the Curragh. He was sent then to Doncaster to contest the William Hill Futurity. Assert was a disappointing eighth to Count Pahlen, but he did encounter some trouble in running.

Put by for the winter, Assert made his seasonal reappearance in the Nijinsky Stakes at Leopardstown. Among the opposition was Golden Fleece. Both horses were in the ownership of Robert Sangster and there was some surprise expressed that two such exciting prospects were meeting in the same classic trial.

In the event Golden Fleece won the race named after his sire, once again finishing two and a half lengths ahead of Assert, just as he had done on their previous encounter. Just how accurate the result was as a gauge of the merits of the two thoroughbreds is open to question. Roger Mortimer,

commenting on the race in his book on the Epsom Derby, was not guilty of overstating the issue when he said that 'it would be an exaggeration to suggest [that Assert] had been subjected to a hard race'.

On his next outing Assert left no one in any doubt as to his true ability when he thrashed the opposition in the Gallinule Stakes over ten furlongs at the Curragh, winning by no less than ten lengths from Rivellino. His third outing of the season was at Chantilly where he became the first ever foreign-trained winner of the French Derby, beating Real Shadai and Bois de Grace by three lengths and two lengths. In doing so he recorded a famous victory for his young trainer. David O'Brien, the son of Vincent, only trained for a number of years during the 1980s, but in that time he showed that he had inherited many, if not all, of the training skills of his legendary father. Without doubt his most notable achievement during his short but extremely successful career as a trainer was in 1984, when at 28 years of age he became the youngest ever trainer to saddle an Epsom Derby winner. His decision to quit training horses at the end of the 1988 season was a sad blow to the Irish horse racing industry.

The principal danger to David O'Brien's Assert at the Curragh was the Michael Albina-trained Silver Hawk, the mount of Tony Murray, who had been successful in the 1980 Sweeps Derby on Tyrnavos. Silver Hawk had followed up a creditable five and a half length fifth to Zino in the English 2,000 Guineas with an even better run in the Epsom Derby. Despite being hampered in running, Silver Hawk had finished third to the flying Golden Fleece, beaten only four lengths. The son of Roberto obviously had a very fair chance and at the very least he would provide a useful line of form as between Golden Fleece and Assert. Trainer Michael Albina had gone to the trouble of bringing Silver Hawk to the Curragh on the Tuesday before the race and had personally supervised his colt's final preparations at the headquarters of Irish racing.

It is interesting to contrast Albina's optimism in taking on Assert at the Curragh with the views expressed by François Boutin whose charge Persepolis had finished fourth at Epsom, only a head behind Silver Hawk. Declining the Curragh engagement, Boutin told Tony Power of the *Irish Press* that there was 'no point in opposing Assert. It would be an expensive waste of time.'

There were eight other contenders for the first prize of almost £130,000. Each-way chances were perhaps held by the likes of Royal Rendezvous who had a juvenile victory over Pas de Seul to his credit, and Patcher who had finished fourth in the Queen's Vase over two miles at Ascot. Besides Silver Hawk, Favoloso was the only other English challenger, but three successive unplaced efforts hardly inspired maximum confidence.

26 June 1982 was a very warm day but, reflecting perhaps the public perception that the big race was somewhat uncompetitive, the attendance at the Curragh was a bit on the thin side. The betting on the race, which had threatened to be desultory, was however given renewed vigour by the rain which fell on the track in the days leading up to the Derby. There was some suggestion that Assert's connections were a little concerned about the forecast give in the ground.

In the circumstances Assert, which some betting forecasts had suggested might be a 3/1 on shot, eased from an opening 4/9 down to 4/6 on some boards, before strengthening to finish 4/7 at the off. There was good support for Silver Hawk and he closed firm at 3/1 from opening offers of 7/2. Jim Bolger's Condell, which had run up a string of three straight victories in races somewhat below top class, was third favourite at 11/1 after opening at 10's. It was 28/1 from 20's Patcher, and any price the rest.

The race took shape very much as might have been predicted. From the outset Assert's stable companion Raconteur, ridden by Wally Swinburn, father of Walter, made the running. He was closely attended by Christy Roche on Assert, with second favourite Silver Hawk next. From an early stage none of the others really counted. Raconteur continued to dictate the pace until over a mile had been covered. With some three and a half furlongs to go, Roche made his move and pushed Assert into the lead. Silver Hawk was unable to respond immediately and indeed Raconteur kept on going in second place until well into the straight.

Meantime, Assert had quickened clear early in the straight and it was already patently obvious that the race was as good as over. Silver Hawk finally got past Raconteur about a furlong and a half out, but by then the bird had flown. Assert came home on his own, winning very easily by no less than eight lengths from the one-paced Silver Hawk. It was two and a half lengths back to Patcher, who ran on best of the rest to land some nice each-way bets at the returned odds. A further eight lengths elapsed to the fourth-placed Favoloso, with Condell fifth and Raconteur eventually sixth after his gallant front-running efforts. The simple truth of it was that Assert had won in a canter.

While it cannot be said to prove anything, it is none the less worth noting that in winning, Assert had finished eight lengths in front of Silver Hawk, precisely twice as far as the latter had been beaten by Golden Fleece at Epsom. Of course, it must be borne in mind that on their only two racecourse clashes Golden Fleece had twice finished ahead of Assert. If the two horses had ever met again, there is little doubt that Golden Fleece would have started favourite. But would he have won? Who can say? As a postscript to the above, I recall that in the Nijinsky Stakes at Leopardstown (referred to earlier) some bookmakers had bet without the favourite (Golden Fleece). Odds of 7/4 against were freely offered about Assert to win or come second to Golden Fleece. Was it the bet of the century?

Certainly François Boutin's opinion that it would have been folly to take on Assert at the Curragh was comprehensively vindicated. In fact, it is difficult in retrospect to understand quite why connections of Assert were believed to be concerned about the state of the ground at the Curragh. Officially good to yielding, the going had been good to soft at Chantilly, where Assert had won the French Derby so convincingly. In addition, Assert was by Be My Guest, and the progeny of that sire usually act with a bit of give in the ground.

Although he had scaled the heights, Assert was a cheaply bought yearling. Bred by the Moyglare Stud, he was purchased for approximately £16,000 at the Goffs Paris sales in October 1980. By Vincent O'Brien's former high-class miler Be My Guest, who was himself a son of Northern Dancer, Assert's dam was Irish Bird, who was a Sea Bird II mare. Well related, Assert's half brother Bikala won the 1981 French Derby, while the dam Irish Bird was a half sister to the 1971 Irish Derby winner Irish Ball. Certainly Robert Sangster got a bargain and a half when he acquired Assert.

For the owner, Assert's victory at the Curragh crowned a remarkable achievement for the former football pools magnate. With Golden Fleece and Assert having already taken the English and French Derbies, Assert's Curragh success meant that Sangster became the first ever owner to complete the hat trick of the most prestigious European Derbies.

In many respects 1982 marked the high point of Robert Sangster's outstandingly successful involvement in horse racing. He would continue to enjoy many successes including classic triumphs on the racecourse with his horses, but his unchallenged hegemony of the upper echelons of the bloodstock industry was about to be tested and seriously eroded by a concentrated Arab-led onslaught over the following number of years.

With Golden Fleece sidelined, the way seemed clear for Assert to dominate proceedings for the rest of the season. The David O'Brien-trained colt's next assignment after his Curragh victory was the King

George VI and Queen Elizabeth Diamond Stakes. He was installed a slight odds-on favourite for the annual mid-summer show-piece and for much of the race looked certain to justify his backers' confidence. But in the end Assert was just edged out of first place by the year-older Kalaglow, who beat him by a neck. It was three lengths back to the useful Glint of Gold, who had finished second to Shergar in the 1981 Epsom Derby, and among those in arrears was coincidentally Assert's half brother, Bikala, who as mentioned above had won the 1981 French Derby.

Some regarded Assert's defeat as a disappointing effort, but this was to underrate Kalaglow. Unbeaten in five outings as a two-year-old, Kalaglow's three-year-old season was cut short when he was struck into and injured in Shergar's Epsom Derby of 1981. He reappeared as a four-year-old and after taking the Brigadier Gerard Stakes at Sandown, he impressed greatly when winning the Coral Eclipse Stakes also at Sandown by four lengths from Lobkowiez.

Assert's performance in running the older horse to a neck in the King George was a performance which in no way diminished his ranking. Assert ran in the Arc, but the conditions had gone against David O'Brien's colt. Heavy rain had turned the going soft and Assert finished a disappointing eleventh of seventeen behind the François Mathet-trained Aga Khan-owned Akiyda. His season was over. Assert was a good, though not outstanding, Irish Derby winner and his Curragh success is now best remembered as the race which announced the arrival of trainer David O'Brien as a name to be reckoned with at the highest levels of the sport of horse racing.

Less happily, from the point of view of the centre-piece of Irish racing, Assert's stroll to victory was the third time in the space of four years that Ireland's premier race had turned out to be little more than a lap of honour for the one outstanding horse in the field. Significantly, too, the declining attendance figures for the years in question — 1979, 1981 and 1982 — showed that the Irish racing public were less than enthused about the developing state of affairs. Better quality all round fields were required to win back the support of the public for the Irish Derby. Fortunately for all concerned, the 1983 renewal was to produce a significantly more competitive contest for the Blue Riband of Irish racing.

IRISH SWEEPS DERBY

1M 4F

SATURDAY 26 JUNE 1982

GOING: GOOD TO YIELDING

WINNER: Mr R. E. Sangster's Assert by Be My Guest
out of Irish Bird
C. Roche

SECOND: Silver Hawk by Roberto out of Gris Vitesse
A. Murray

THIRD: Patcher by Patch out of Alace
G. Curran

S.P. 4/7f   3/1   28/1
Winner trained by D. V. O'Brien

ALSO: Favoloso 4th, Condell 5th, Raconteur 6th,
Bruckner 7th, Remanded 8th, Royal
Rendezvous 9th, Grateful Heir 10th & last

Winner: favourite
Distances: 8 lengths, 2½ lengths
Value to winner: £129,600
Time: 2 m 33.2 s
Timeform rating of winner: 134.

1983

THE CURRAGH 25 JUNE 1983

After the successes of three odds-on favourites in the space of four years, a good class competitive field lined up for the 1983 renewal of the Irish Sweeps Derby, a welcome boast for all involved in staging the race. Twelve runners went to post and as these included the first and second in the Epsom Derby, the winner of the French Derby and the winner of the Irish 2,000 Guineas, the Curragh classic was arguably the true championship test for the classic generation. Interestingly, too, the 1983 contest marked the first ever clash on Irish soil between the winners of the English and French Derbies (a portent of similar duels in the years to follow).

The Epsom Derby winner Teenoso was the mount of Lester Piggott and Geoff Wragg's colt was bidding to provide the 'long fellow' with his sixth Irish Sweeps Derby, following upon Meadow Court in 1965, Ribocco in 1967, Ribero in 1968, The Minstrel in 1977 and Shergar in 1981.

Teenoso had had an inauspicious juvenile campaign during which he failed to win, his best effort being to finish fourth of seventeen in a maiden race at Newmarket. The spring of 1983 was the wettest for many years in England and the rain-softened ground brought about a vast improvement in Teenoso's form. After losing his maiden tag in a modest affair at Newmarket, Geoff Wragg's colt was upped in class and contested the recognised Derby trial at Lingfield. The ground was extremely testing but Teenoso revelled in it, beating Shearwalk by three lengths.

Ground conditions were again favourable at Epsom and Teenoso and Piggott strode to a comfortable success, beating the Irish-trained outsider Carlingford Castle and his old rival Shearwalk by three lengths and the same. Teenoso had proved himself a top-class performer on soft going, but how would he handle contrasting conditions? That was a question that would most certainly be answered at the Curragh where the going was officially good to firm.

Liam Browne's Carlingford Castle had been a surprise runner-up to Teenoso at Epsom and he was another for whom the changed going might pose problems. His best performance prior to Epsom, however, was a very useful one and a half length victory over the subsequent Lancashire and Irish Guinness Oaks winner, Give Thanks, and on that form he was a very worthy contender. A son of Le Bavard (more noted as a national hunt sire), Carlingford Castle was a bargain-basement purchase for his popular owner Frank Roe, a long-time respected member of the Irish judiciary and a former amateur jockey. Success for the popular Judge Roe would have been greeted enthusiastically by the Irish racing fraternity.

If the Epsom winner and runner-up were to be overturned, the animal most fancied to upset them was Vincent O'Brien's Caerleon. Bred by the great Nijinsky, Caerleon was bidding to set a unique record for his sire, for no horse who had won the Sweeps Derby had gone on to sire the winner of Ireland's premier classic. In his only two outings as a two-year-old Caerleon had registered victories in two of the principal Irish juvenile races. He went into winter quarters after his successes in the Tyros & Anglesey Stakes as one of Ballydoyle's principal classic hopes for the following season.

Caerleon's three-year-old career had been a bit disappointing to begin with. Only eighth on his seasonal reappearance to the outsider Evening M'Lord in the Ballymoss Stakes at the Curragh, he next finished a close second to his stable companion Solford at the Phoenix Park, giving that horse 8 lb. It did not prove possible to get Caerleon ready in time for the Epsom Derby, and instead the $800,000 colt was sent to Chantilly to contest the French Derby (the Prix du Jockey-Club).

At Chantilly Caerleon had dispelled any stamina doubts that may have been entertained about him by easily brushing aside the French colt L'Emigrant by three lengths in a time which in 1983 was the fastest French Derby time for thirty years and the second fastest ever. In crediting Vincent O'Brien with the only major European prize which had eluded him, Caerleon had impressed many race readers with the style of his Chantilly success.

Even though it is unwise to compare times on different courses and on different going, Caerleon's Chantilly time of 2 minutes 27.3 seconds was no less than 22.4 seconds faster than the time posted by Teenoso when winning the slowest ever Epsom Derby. Caerleon's supporters were extremely confident and Pat Eddery's reported comments that the French Derby winner rated among the best he had ridden fuelled that confidence.

The Irish 2,000 Guineas winner Wassl was on something of a recovery mission. A big disappointment in the English 2,000 Guineas when quite well fancied, Wassl, by Mill Reef, turned the form right around at the Curragh when he beat Vincent O'Brien's Newmarket winner, Lomond, into second place. Wassl was then a poor fourteenth to Teenoso at Epsom, but evidently trainer John Dunlop, who had won the 1978 Irish Sweeps Derby with Shirley Heights, took the view that it was the going rather than the distance which had led to his colt's undoing at Epsom.

Of the others, the two who seemed most capable of springing a surprise were Dermot Weld's Parliament and the Michael Stoute-trained Shareef Dancer. Parliament, a colt by Lord Gayle, had run only three times in his career. On his most recent outing he had been third to Wassl and Lomond in the Irish 2,000 Guineas, beaten one and three quarter lengths in all. He obviously had a touch of class, but as a son of Lord Gayle there had to be some doubt about his ability to handle the fast ground.

Costing his owner £3.3 million as a yearling, Shareef Dancer was the most expensive colt ever to race in Britain at that juncture. Lightly raced, he had begun his three-year-old career in a Sandown handicap where he had finished second. The significant thing about that Sandown race was that it was run on heavy ground. On his only other three-year-old outing at Royal Ascot, Shareef Dancer on contrasting going had shown much improved form to beat Russian Roubles by a length in the King George VI Stakes over one and a half miles.

It was perhaps significant that trainer Michael Stoute, successful with Shergar in the 1981 Irish Derby, had chosen Shareef Dancer in preference to his Epsom Derby third, Shearwalk, to represent him at the Curragh. Having missed the winning ride on Shergar in 1981, for jockey Walter Swinburn Shareef Dancer was his first ride in the premier Irish classic.

The attendance at the Curragh for the 1983 Derby was some 9 per cent up on the 1982 figures. A more competitive race was undoubtedly largely responsible for the increase in attendance. If there had been uncertainty in the pre-race betting forecasts as to who might start favourite, punters were quick to make their preference known in the ring. Put in at a scarcely generous 6/4, Caerleon was pursued down to evens before easing slightly to 5/4 at the off. Opening up a tight 7/4 shot, Teenoso eased out to 5/2 before sustained support caused Lester Piggott's mount to wind up 2/1 second favourite.

The two Derby winners cornered the market, but there was some interest in Shareef Dancer who opened at 9/1 and was backed down to 7/1 before settling a point longer. Carlingford Castle, the mount of Michael Kinane, was weak from 6/1 out to 17/2, while Wassl varied between 14/1 and 16/1, closing at the longer price. Dermot Weld's Parliament eased right out from 12/1 to 20/1, and little was seen for the rest.

There were no problems at the start, and in the early stages of the race the outsider Sir Simon, ridden by Jackie Coogan, made the running. The Epsom Derby second, Carlingford Castle, tracked him early on, with Caerleon quite prominent. Shareef Dancer pulled hard for his head in the first couple of furlongs and Walter Swinburn had quite a job to restrain the Northern Dancer colt. In contrast to the way he had been ridden at Epsom, Teenoso was held up towards the rear by Lester Piggott.

Sir Simon continued to lead until approaching the half-way stage, where Mick Kinane took up the running on Carlingford Castle. Caerleon remained in third place, while the rest of the field were quite tightly bunched. Sir Simon, who was a natural front runner, moved back up to dispute the lead with Carlingford Castle as the field began to make the downhill run towards the straight. The leading twosome had quite a joust up front as meantime the big guns were lining up to position themselves for a challenge. Caerleon, Teenoso and Shareef Dancer were all well placed as the field swung into the straight, and it was anybody's race at this stage.

There was an amount of scrimmaging as the two front runners, Sir Simon and Carlingford Castle, dropped away early in the straight. Caerleon appeared to be hampered; certainly Pat Eddery's mount didn't get the clearest of runs at a vital stage of the race. Meantime Shareef Dancer, who had been switched by Walter Swinburn from the inside entering the straight, moved between horses to take the lead two furlongs out. Teenoso attempted to go with him but was soon struggling. Trapped on the rails, Eddery had to pull Caerleon out to make a challenge and in so doing lost ground. Finally seeing daylight, Caerleon set off in pursuit of Shareef Dancer, but by now he had far too much to do.

Walter Swinburn on Maktoum Al Maktoum's Northern Dancer colt was not going to be denied, and at the finishing line he had a clear three lengths to spare over a somewhat unlucky Caerleon. Two lengths further back came Teenoso, and the conventional wisdom was that the Epsom winner had been unsuited to the fast ground. Mick O'Toole's outsider Quilted, whose main claim to fame was that he had finished second earlier in the season to the talking horse, Danzatore, was a surprisingly good fourth, beaten six and a half lengths by the winner. Of the remainder, Wassl, who plainly didn't get the trip, was fifth, Carlingford Castle, unsuited by the going, seventh, while Parliament, likewise ill at ease on the firm ground, never got into the hunt and finished tenth of the twelve runners.

Shareef Dancer's Irish Sweeps Derby success is significant for one reason above all. His victory represented the most prestigious prize yet annexed by Europe's fastest growing racing empire, the Maktoum brothers from Dubai. There are four brothers in all — Maktoum, Hamdan, Mohammed and Ahmed, in order of age — and they are the sons of the ruler of Dubai. The brothers, besides their bloodstock interests, are also full-time politicians. Sheikh Maktoum, for instance, is Deputy Prime Minister, while Sheikh Mohammed is Minister for Defence. Known as the Venice of the Gulf, Dubai is one of seven sheikhdoms which comprise the United Arab Emirates and it is the second richest in terms of oil reserves.

Sheikh Mohammed and Hamdan Al Maktoum are the two brothers who have become most closely identified with the racing of thoroughbreds and both have enjoyed outstanding success since their first entry on to the European racing stage in the late 1970s. In the spiralling market for yearlings in the United States in the first half of the 1980s, the brothers were right in the thick of some ferocious bidding and spent an astonishing $240 million at the principal US yearling sales over a period of some six years.

Among the most expensive yearlings purchased in that spectacular splurge was Shareef Dancer and the successful bidder was in fact Sheikh Mohammed. However, he passed on the colt to his elder brother Sheikh Maktoum and it was in his royal blue colours with a white chevron and light blue cap that the Northern Dancer colt won at the Curragh.

In more recent years, while the Maktoums continue to be among the biggest buyers at the principal yearling sales worldwide, they have increasingly bred their own thoroughbreds in a select number of stud farms which they have bought in Europe. Stud farms in Ireland which have been acquired for this purpose include the Woodpark, Derrinstown and Kildangan Studs.

The emergence of wealthy Arab owners spearheaded by the Maktoum brothers but involving a number of other oil-rich princes, ushered in an era of almost total Arab domination of the upper echelons of the bloodstock industry in Europe, which is even more pronounced today than it was back in 1983. Whether this increasing concentration of ownership in the hands of just a few wealthy patrons is for the long-term good of horse racing is a subject upon which there are widely divergent views.

Perhaps, though, there is at least a sense of poetic irony in the manner in which once prominent European owners have been elbowed aside by the wealth and power of the newcomers from the Middle East. After all, the thoroughbred in Europe traces back to three Arabian stallions — perhaps the Maktoum brothers and their Arab allies are only reclaiming what is properly theirs!

It is easy to see why Shareef Dancer's pedigree attracted the attention of his wealthy owner. By Northern Dancer out of a mare called Sweet Alliance, Shareef Dancer was the first foal of her dam. Sweet Alliance was a high-class racehorse who won the Kentucky Oaks. In addition, she was a daughter of Sir Ivor who seemed to specialise in producing quality fillies. Shareef Dancer's sire, Northern Dancer, has already been considered in the chapter on the 1970 winner, Nijinsky, and nothing further need be added.

For successful jockey Walter Swinburn, Shareef Dancer's success meant that he had emulated his unique Epsom achievement. His first Epsom Derby ride produced a winner, Shergar, and with Shareef Dancer he repeated the feat at the Curragh.

How good was Shareef Dancer? Unfortunately the colt never ran again after his Curragh victory and thus it is impossible to be dogmatic about the merits of the 1983 Irish Derby winner. The time of the 1983 race was very good — the only faster time recorded prior to that was by Tambourine II in 1962 — but that of itself cannot be taken as conclusive. On his preferred fast ground, my guess is that Shareef Dancer was potentially up to the highest standard and it is very much to be regretted that commercial breeding considerations intervened to prevent the racing public from having any further opportunities to gauge his true worth. (It should be pointed out that following upon his Curragh success Shareef Dancer was due to run in the Benson and Hedges Gold Cup at York, but he was taken out on the day of the race after heavy rain changed the forecast good to firm ground to good to soft — shades of Zafonic at Royal Ascot in 1993.)

The only way to assess Shareef Dancer is to attempt to measure the strength of the opposition he faced at the Curragh. Based on 1983's form alone, one could not be too enthusiastic about the Irish Derby winner. Two of his victims ran in the King George VI and Queen Elizabeth Diamond Stakes at Ascot, but neither ran well. Carlingford Castle, once again unsuited by the going, finished sixth of the nine runners to Time Charter, while Caerleon was last. In mitigation, however, it should be pointed out that Caerleon, who was joint favourite at Ascot, lost both of his front plates in the course of the race. Caerleon did, however, go on to win the Benson and Hedges Gold Cup at York, beating Hot Touch by a neck, to shed some lustre on the Curragh form.

Teenoso's 1983 campaign ended prematurely when in the Great Voltigeur Stakes, also at York, he injured an off foreleg when only third to Seymour Hicks. Bravely, it was decided to keep Teenoso in training as a four-year-old and on this occasion fortune favoured the brave. After an encouraging third first time out in the John Porter Stakes at Newbury, Teenoso won the Ormonde Stakes at Chester before contesting the Grand Prix de Saint-Cloud. Overcoming fast ground, Teenoso was a game short-head winner from the French-trained Fly Me.

Next on the agenda for the son of Youth was the King George. A very strong field was assembled for the mid-summer highlight including the 1983 winner Time Charter, the Coral Eclipse winner Sadler's Wells, the Prix du Jockey-Club winner Darshaan and the 1983 Oaks and St Leger heroine Sun Princess. On good to firm going it was widely assumed that Teenoso would not be able to show his best form and he was allowed to start at 13/2 third favourite. The doubters however were to be confounded. With Piggott riding a masterly race, Teenoso made much of the running to win impressively by two and a half lengths from Sadler's Wells in a time which was the second fastest in the history of the race and bettered only by that recorded in the epic duel between Grundy and Bustino in 1975.

Due to a recurrence of his old foreleg injury, Teenoso could not be trained for the Arc for which he had been installed ante-post favourite, and he was retired to stud. As well as having consolidated his own reputation, Teenoso's tremendous King George victory paid a handsome compliment to his 1983 Curragh conqueror, Shareef Dancer.

In summary, therefore, Shareef Dancer probably beat a very good-class field at the Curragh in 1983. His victory, though, is now best remembered as the race in which the oil-rich sheikhs gained their most notable success to that date and inaugurated an era of Arab domination of the European bloodstock industry.

IRISH SWEEPS DERBY

1M 4F

SATURDAY 25 JUNE 1983

GOING: GOOD TO FIRM

WINNER: Maktoum Al Maktoum's Shareef Dancer by Northern Dancer out of Sweet Alliance
W. R. Swinburn

SECOND: Caerleon by Nijinsky out of Forseer
P. Eddery

THIRD: Teenoso by Youth out of Furioso
L. Piggott

S.P. 8/1   5/4f   2/1
Winner trained by M. R. Stoute

ALSO: Quilted 4th, Wassl 5th, Kalaminsky 6th, Carlingford Castle 7th, Sir Simon 8th, Avalanche Way 9th, Parliament 10th, Heron Bay 11th, Slaney Prince 12th & last

Winner: 3rd favourite
Distances: 3 lengths, 2 lengths
Value to winner: £134,425
Time: 2 m 29.4 s
Timeform rating of winner: 135.

1984 IRISH SWEEPS DERBY

W ednesday 6 June 1984. The most hotly debated race of the past dozen years took place at Epsom Downs on that not easily forgotten day. In a moment indelibly imprinted on the minds of countless thousands of horse racing fans, David O'Brien's 14/1 chance, Secreto, beat his father Vincent's El Gran Senor, the odds-on favourite, by a short head in a pulsating finish to the Epsom Derby.

In Pat Eddery's autobiography, the Irish-born champion admits candidly that his defeat on El Gran Senor represented 'the greatest disappointment of my life in racing'. An 8/11 favourite, El Gran Senor was considered unbeatable by many professional judges and started the hottest Epsom Derby favourite since Tudor Minstrel in 1947.

The final stages of the Epsom race will bear one more re-telling. Always well placed, El Gran Senor, who appeared to be travelling supremely easily, struck the front well over a furlong out. The only possible danger was

Secreto, but Christy Roche was already hard at work on the Northern Dancer colt, and nothing else had a chance.

Roger Mortimer in his book on the Epsom Derby describes what happened next:

'Perhaps at that point, with Secreto under extreme pressure . . . it would have been better if Eddery had headed for home as hard as he could go . . . As it was Eddery had a look behind him and then, *possibly because he lacked confidence in El Gran Senor's stamina* (author's italics), he seemed reluctant to really get to work on the favourite.'

Certainly there are instances in the history of the Epsom Derby where enterprising tactics have helped to offset any lingering doubts about stamina. The most notable example perhaps was Charlie Smirke's early dash for glory on doubtful stayer Hard Ridden in 1958 — a move which seemed to take his rivals by surprise.

The final 100 yards of the 1984 Epsom Derby were agony for the many, many backers of the favourite. Secreto, responding to Roche's vigorous riding, belatedly began to draw closer to El Gran Senor. Suddenly Eddery had to get serious with the favourite. Asked for an effort, El Gran Senor could not respond immediately and indeed hung slightly to the right in the closing stages. In the very last strides Secreto got his nose in front and amid tremendous heart-stopping excitement passed the post a few inches ahead of El Gran Senor.

The outcome of the race led to a torrent of criticism of Eddery's riding of the beaten favourite. The substance of the case against Eddery is succinctly summed up in the extract quoted above from Roger Mortimer's book. The jockey remains convinced, however, that the tactics adopted by him on El Gran Senor were absolutely correct, and the only ones open to him.

The questions raised by the Epsom Derby result looked likely to be resolved just a few weeks later at the Curragh. The connections of both first and second indicated that they planned to take each other on again on the last day of June in the Irish Sweeps Derby. The projected clash captured the imagination of the Irish racing public as never before. Advertisements were placed by the Curragh management in the national newspapers promising racegoers a dramatic return bout between the Epsom Derby protagonists.

At the four-day declaration stage, besides Secreto and El Gran Senor, others declared included Darshaan, the French Derby winner, and Sadler's Wells, the Irish 2,000 Guineas winner. On paper it looked like being perhaps the greatest flat race ever staged in Ireland. It is virtually certain that all

attendance records would have been smashed had the principals gone to post. Sadly, however, the dream race never materialised.

Secreto was pulled out on the Wednesday before the race. A half-share in the Epsom Derby winner had been purchased by an American stud for a figure reputed to be in excess of $20 million, which made Secreto the most valuable horse in training ever sold. Because of the sale he was taken out of the Irish Derby and it was stated that Secreto was to be prepared for a campaign which included the King George VI and Queen Elizabeth Diamond Stakes, the Prix de l'Arc de Triomphe and the Breeder's Cup — an ambitious programme indeed, but one that Secreto was destined not to fulfil. Various reasons combined to prevent the Northern Dancer colt from ever running again and so the unanswered questions that lingered after Epsom remained just that — unanswered.

Worse was to follow, for the firm ground at the Curragh was deemed unsuitable for Darshaan and he too was withdrawn. With Sadler's Wells also defecting (he had only been in the race as a precaution in case El Gran Senor picked up an injury), considerable disappointment was expressed in the Irish media at the combination of circumstances, both commercial and natural, which had deprived Irish racegoers of the opportunity to see a re-match between the two sons of Northern Dancer and indeed between Vincent and his son David.

Only seven horses were left to take on the Epsom Derby runner-up and the sense of anticlimax in the newspaper previews of the Sweeps Derby was absolutely pervasive. Some commentators suggested, indeed, that

Irish racegoers might choose to voice their disgust at the commercialism which had undermined the ostensible purpose of horse racing by staying away in droves on Derby day. No such thing happened. In fact a fine crowd turned up on the day, the attendance being over 5 per cent up on the 1983 figures.

The scribes had underestimated the drawing power of a great horse, for El Gran Senor, despite his Epsom reverse, was surely a top-class thoroughbred. His record spoke for itself. A bay colt by Northern Dancer out of Sex Appeal, a Buckpasser mare, El Gran Senor was unbeaten in four races as a juvenile. Not seriously extended in his opening three races in Ireland, which included victories in the Railway and National Stakes, El Gran Senor was sent off 7/4 favourite for the end of season juvenile championship, the Dewhurst Stakes at Newmarket. Vincent O'Brien's colt did not disappoint his admirers. He beat Rainbow Quest impressively in the Dewhurst, recording the fastest time in the race for many years.

As a three-year-old El Gran Senor won on his reappearance over seven furlongs at the Curragh, handing out a comfortable two length beating to another Northern Dancer colt, and indeed another Vincent O'Brien-trained colt, the aforementioned Sadler's Wells. The value of that form was underlined when Sadler's Wells went on to win the Irish 2,000 Guineas and the Coral Eclipse Stakes, as well as finishing second to Darshaan in the French Derby, and also second to Teenoso in the King George VI and Queen Elizabeth Diamond Stakes.

After his Curragh win El Gran Senor went to Newmarket and demolished a strong field in the most convincing fashion in the English 2,000 Guineas. The quality of the opposition is amply illustrated when it is considered that Chief Singer was two and a half lengths back in second place, with the strongly fancied Lear Fan a further four lengths adrift third. Rainbow Quest was back in fourth place. The three horses named above, all of whom had been put so firmly in their places by El Gran Senor, went on to win Group 1 races subsequently.

The unbeaten, and some felt, unbeatable Northern Dancer colt was next seen in action at Epsom, with the unfortunate consequences as outlined above. For El Gran Senor, therefore, the Curragh represented an opportunity to put the record straight, to prove to all concerned that the colt truly stayed a mile and a half. Sceptics however contended that the weakness of the opposition meant that the question would not be decisively resolved in the Irish Sweeps Derby.

The majority of the seven horses who opposed Vincent O'Brien's long odds-on favourite could be eliminated as serious contenders straightaway. The English-trained pair, Telios which had finished sixth and Long Pond seventh at Epsom, renewed rivalry, but even their fondest supporters would have been pleasantly surprised if either of these colts were to prove capable of turning the tables on El Gran Senor. Besides the favourite, the pick of the other Irish runners was Dermot Weld's Inflation Beater, whose best performance was to get within a neck of Sadler's Wells over ten furlongs at the Phoenix Park, admittedly when receiving 6 lb from the O'Brien colt. Both Liam

Browne's March Song and Mick O'Toole's Nino Volador were extreme outsiders, with little chance on the book.

The two principal dangers to the hot favourite came from overseas. Rainbow Quest had twice finished behind El Gran Senor, but given the paucity of the opposition, if there was to be an upset then the Jeremy Tree-trained colt was the one most likely to cause it. Following upon his fourth placing behind El Gran Senor in the English 2,000 Guineas, Rainbow Quest had finished third to Darshaan and Sadler's Wells in the Prix du Jockey-Club, beaten one and a half lengths and half a length. In tenth place in that race came Dahar, trained by Maurice Zilber, for whom excuses were made. Beautifully bred, by Lyphard out of the dual King George heroine Dahlia, Dahar had previously won the Prix Lupin impressively over ten furlongs at Longchamp and connections obviously felt that he was best judged on his winning form, and so the French-trained colt was duly dispatched to the Curragh to take on the short-priced favourite.

Betting on the race was predictably light, reflecting the widespread opinion that whatever doubts there were about El Gran Senor's stamina, the opposition at the Curragh was simply not good enough to put it to a severe test. Despite the poor value, however, the favourite hardened from opening offers of 1/3 to 2/7, making El Gran Senor the hottest favourite in the history of the Sweeps Derby. Rainbow Quest eased from 9/2 to 5/1, and Dahar drifted to 10/1 from 8's. There was no money for anything else.

It was a warm day and the ground was riding fast. The early pace in the Derby was quite leisurely which must have delighted both Vincent O'Brien and jockey Pat Eddery. If stamina doubts were entertained about El Gran Senor, the slow early pace ensured that stern questions were not going to be asked in this area. The suspicion remains that perhaps the connections of the other runners had elected to fight it out for the placings.

Early on, Geoff Baxter on Telios cut out the running, followed by Long Pond, Rainbow Quest and Dahar. Eddery on the favourite was tucked in behind the leading quartet at this stage. The pace improved as the race wore on, but the order remained the same until well after half-way. Telios continued to lead and didn't give way until, with less than three furlongs to run, Steve Cauthen pushed Rainbow Quest into the lead.

El Gran Senor, who was fifth into the straight, progressed smoothly to move into a challenging position just behind Rainbow Quest with over a furlong to go. Rainbow Quest battled on well for Cauthen and for a few moments there was just a doubt as to whether El Gran Senor had enough in reserve to tackle the leader. Eddery was sitting comfortably, though, and he delayed his challenge until inside the last furlong before asking his mount to go on. For just a moment El Gran Senor hung fire, but it was just for a moment. The Northern Dancer colt quickened nicely and won snugly by a length.

It was five lengths back to Dahar, with Liam Browne's March Song taking almost £8,000 prize money for fourth place. This was substantially in excess of any earnings that might have accrued to his connections had March Song taken up his alternative engagement in an apprentice race at

Roscommon on the following Monday. The decision to go for glory was handsomely rewarded.

In passing it should be mentioned that El Gran Senor hasn't been quite the success that had been anticipated at stud. Infertility problems have been a factor, although included among his good winners are Belmez, who will feature prominently later on in the book, and Rodrigo de Triano, who numbered both the Newmarket and Irish 2,000 Guineas among his four Group 1 triumphs in 1992.

And so El Gran Senor had won over the classic distance of a mile and a half. Did it prove that he truly stayed the trip? What do the bare facts about his performance tell us? The time of the race, on firm going, was 2 minutes 31.5 seconds. There were only five faster Irish Derbies in the period since the inauguration of sponsorship, a point in favour of those who argued that El Gran Senor had no stamina problems. Maybe it's worth bearing in mind though that in a handicap over the Derby distance on the same day, the far from top-class four-year-old Sheer Gold won in a time almost a second faster than that recorded by El Gran Senor.

Time comparisons are notoriously unreliable, however, as race-times are influenced far more by the pace at which a race is run than by the quality of the field. It is interesting to note a point made by Vincent O'Brien in his assessment of the two racetracks, Epsom and the Curragh. It is traditionally held that the Curragh is a stiffer track than Epsom, yet the standard time for Epsom is 2 minutes 36 seconds, while that for the Curragh is 2 minutes 32 seconds.

The difference in standard time is accounted for by the differing contours of the two tracks. While Epsom is undulating, with sharper turns, the Curragh is by contrast relatively flat with easier bends. Accordingly, at Epsom a jockey will often have to take a few pulls at his mount to get him balanced properly, whereas the Curragh is a more galloping track and thus horses usually handle it better and can maintain a more even gallop. It is because horses can be given a breather at strategic times at Epsom that the standard time there is four seconds outside the Curragh's equivalent. The argument as to which is the stiffer track is a more difficult one, but certainly the final uphill two furlongs at the Curragh puts a considerable premium on stamina.

None of this, sadly, answers the questions posed above. In Pat Eddery's autobiography the jockey freely admits that in his heart he did not truly believe that El Gran Senor stayed a mile and a half. This belief, in my view, undermined Eddery's appreciation of the tactical requirements of the particular situation in which he found himself at Epsom. At another point in his most revealing account of the Epsom race, Eddery goes on to talk of those whom he perceived as dangers to his mount. He baldly states, 'one [danger] that I discounted was Secreto . . .'

Given this admission it is certainly arguable that when Pat Eddery, at the two furlong marker at Epsom, realised that the horse nearest to him, and the only possible danger, was Secreto, was he not perhaps guilty of a fatal error — the error of underestimating the opposition? Put another way, was Pat Eddery guilty of over-confidence?

If perhaps the horse that was closest to him at the two furlong marker at Epsom was, say, second favourite Alphabatim with Lester Piggott on board, would Eddery have waited so long before asking his mount for the supreme effort?

It is in the end a matter of opinion. Pat Eddery, in commenting on the Irish Derby, states that the race was not truly run at all and no test of stamina. Furthermore, he adds that Steve Cauthen on Rainbow Quest set the race up for him by giving him a lead. On the other hand it should be noted that Rainbow Quest proved as a four-year-old that he was a horse of the highest class and a true stayer, finishing a close-up third in the King George VI and Queen Elizabeth Diamond Stakes, and following that up with a win (on the disqualification of Sagace) in the Prix de l'Arc de Triomphe. No one would question Rainbow Quest's right to be regarded as a top-class mile and a half horse, and yet El Gran Senor beat him easily at the Curragh over that trip.

In an interview with Noel Reid of RTE, broadcast immediately after El Gran Senor's Curragh victory, Vincent O'Brien was emphatic in stating that Eddery had ridden his colt at the Curragh in the way that he needed to be ridden. Whilst he didn't add to that, the inference was that he had not been quite as happy with the way his horse had been ridden at Epsom.

The issue of whether El Gran Senor truly stayed a mile and a half will be debated for decades to come. The fact that neither El Gran Senor nor Secreto ever ran again after their Derby successes means that there is no fresh evidence to bring to bear on the question. What is not in dispute is that El Gran Senor was a class act at the Curragh on the last day of June 1984. At 2/7, clearly Irish bookmakers believed that he would have no trouble staying the Derby distance! Certainly those intrepid punters who helped make the Northern Dancer colt the shortest-priced Epsom Derby favourite for almost forty years will take a lot of convincing that it was stamina limitations alone that accounted for his failure in the first of the two Derbies he contested.

1M 4F
SATURDAY 30 JUNE 1984
GOING: FIRM

WINNER: Mr R. E. Sangster's El Gran Senor by
Northern Dancer out of Sex Appeal
P. Eddery

SECOND: Rainbow Quest by Blushing Groom out of
I Will Follow
S. Cauthen

THIRD: Dahar by Lyphard out of Dahlia
A. Laqueux

S.P. 2/7f   5/1   10/1
Winner trained by M. V. O'Brien

ALSO: March Song 4th, Inflation Beater 5th, Telios
6th, Long Pond 7th, Nino Volador 8th & last

Winner: favourite
Distances: 1 length, 5 lengths
Value to winner: £134,241
Time: 2 m 31.5 s
Timeform rating of winner: 136.

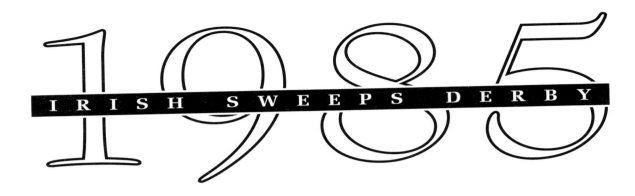

1985 IRISH SWEEPS DERBY

The 1985 Irish Derby was to mark the final year of sponsorship by the Irish Hospitals Sweepstakes organisation. Despite the absence through injury from the line-up of the spectacular Epsom Derby winner, Slip Anchor, the field was one which held high promise of a splendid renewal of Ireland's premier classic. The fourteen runners due to face the starter included four horses who had competed at Epsom — Law Society who had finished second, Damister third, Theatrical seventh, and Snow Plant tenth. All but the last of these were well fancied to land the prestigious prize.

In a difficult year for the stable, Law Society had helped to keep Vincent O'Brien's name to the fore. A good-class two-year-old — he had finished second in the Dewhurst Stakes to Kala Dancer — Law Society's breeding suggested that he would improve as a three-year-old. Early season form was encouraging. A comfortable two and a half length win from Petoski in the

Dalham Chester Vase over a mile and a half preceded his Epsom placing, and connections were hopeful that Law Society would step up a place at the Curragh. The doubt surrounding Law Society, however, was the poor form of the stable. With only five winners to show at the half-way stage of the season, there was concern that the virus which had affected so many of the Ballydoyle horses might perhaps have passed on to Law Society.

Such concerns undoubtedly fuelled the hopes of the connections of both Damister and Theatrical. The form of the Jeremy Tree-trained Damister prior to Epsom was quite impressive. He had beaten Petoski by a length at Sandown over ten furlongs and had subsequently won the Dante Stakes at York in good style by four lengths from Vin de France. He had made up a lot of ground at Epsom in the straight to finish third, and there was a body of opinion which favoured him to turn the tables on Law Society.

Dermot Weld's Theatrical was also well fancied despite his disappointing showing at Epsom. He had been impressive beforehand in his two preparatory races at the Curragh and Leopardstown and Lester Piggott, who had ridden him at Epsom, reported that he had not acted on the track.

Besides those who had run at Epsom there were others who had to be given serious consideration. The remarkable Triptych, who had become the first filly ever to win the Irish 2,000 Guineas earlier in the season, was strongly fancied in certain quarters to upset the colts and become the first of her sex to win an Irish Derby since the turn of the century. On her most recent run Triptych had been no match for the high-class Oh So Sharp in the Epsom Oaks, but her second placing there proved conclusively that she stayed the one and a half mile trip.

The French mounted their usual strong challenge for the Curragh classic. Their principal hope was the Nishapour colt, Mouktar, unbeaten in all of his five starts. Impressive in winning the Prix Greffulhe and the Prix Hocquart, Mouktar had displayed a fine blend of stamina and speed in winning the Prix du Jockey-Club (the French Derby) at Chantilly. Betting forecasts predicted that Mouktar would start favourite for the Derby and many expected him to credit the French with their first win in the race since Malacate in 1976.

Baillamont, a Blushing Groom colt, was another French challenger. Trained by François Boutin and to be ridden by Cash Asmussen, he had never won over a mile and a half and there were obvious stamina doubts. In addition, his best form had been on soft ground.

29 June 1985 was a fine warm day and with the prospects of a competitive race, and perhaps an Irish win, a good crowd descended on the Curragh for the annual mid-summer highlight. The going was officially good although the drying conditions perhaps tended to make the ground ride on the fast side. These conditions were thought likely to suit the Irish-trained colts, Law Society and Theatrical, better than their overseas rivals.

The underfoot conditions certainly influenced the betting exchanges. Put in at joint favourite with Mouktar, punters backed the expertise of Vincent O'Brien and his charge, Law Society, ended up 15/8 clear favourite. Mouktar edged out from 2/1 to 5/2, but was returned at 9/4. Damister eased slightly from 9/2 to 5/1. There was substantial support for Theatrical from 12/1 all the way down to 6/1. Indeed one leading layer reported a bet of £60,000–£5,000 on Dermot Weld's Nureyev colt. David O'Brien's Triptych had her supporters at 12/1 and she closed at 10/1. There was also some interest in the other French challenger, Baillamont, and he wound up a 16/1 shot from 20's.

For some perverse reason delays at the start of Irish Derbies have occurred all too frequently. Regrettably, 1985 marked another such occasion. The English outsider, Mango Express, broke through the stalls and after unshipping Paul Cook proceeded to gallop off riderless in the general direction of Kildare town.

Even though it was patently obvious to onlookers that Mango Express would not take part in the race, it took the best part of fifteen minutes before the official announcement of withdrawal was made. For Paul Cook, who had to miss race riding for a couple of days after his fall, the unfortunate incident was to prove a sad augury of the career-ending injury he sustained at Doncaster some four years later.

With the field reduced to thirteen, the starter finally got the horses dispatched. Right from the outset the outsiders Snow Plant, Bel Havrais and Outrider were to the fore. More to the point, the strongly fancied Mouktar was always close up and led at various stages throughout the first mile. The favourite Law Society was in touch throughout, but to the dismay of his supporters inexplicably lost ground some five furlongs out. It later transpired that he had been hampered by another runner. The well-fancied pair, Theatrical and Damister, were held up towards the rear in the early stages, but began to make progress from about the six furlong mark.

Turning into the straight the field of thirteen were quite closely bunched and few, if any, could have confidently named the winner at this point. Mouktar had regained the lead at this stage and appeared to be going particularly well. However, the complexion of the race underwent a rapid change as a series of challengers emerged to take on the French leader.

After encountering problems in running, Law Society and Pat Eddery had picked their way through the field to get back in touch with the leaders early in the straight. However, the Vincent O'Brien-trained colt still had a lot to do at this point. Damister,

too, had been noted making good headway, but it was Theatrical who looked the most likely winner some two furlongs out. From cruising, entering the straight, Mouktar had collapsed like a pricked balloon in a matter of strides. As Mouktar dropped tamely away, Dermot Weld's colt struck the front and the hopes of those who had helped to halve Theatrical's odds to 6/1 must have soared as Mick Kinane's mount made his dash for the line.

Hope, however, was rapidly transformed into doubt as a challenger emerged from the pack. The well-known colours of Stavros Niarchos — dark blue with light blue crossbelts and striped sleeves — sported by Pat Eddery on Law Society suddenly appeared on the wide outside with a spirited challenge. With none of the other leading contenders making any significant headway, it was clear that it was going to be an Irish one-two, but in which order?

Both horses were put under maximum pressure from their respective pilots and both responded well to the urgings. With a furlong to go, Theatrical, in Bert Firestone's green with white diamond colours, still held a decisive advantage, but Law Society was making relentless progress. The huge crowd broke into two camps, one supporting the favourite and an equally vociferous segment rooting for Dermot Weld's colt. It was an absorbing struggle and until well inside the final furlong it seemed certain that the lead poached by Theatrical early in the straight would prove decisive.

With about a hundred yards to go, however, Vincent O'Brien's colt drew level with his rival. Could Theatrical respond?

The game Nureyev colt gave his all, and for a few strides it seemed possible that he could regain his advantage. It was not to be. The more stoutly bred Law Society stuck his head in front and, although Theatrical never gave up, Law Society edged on and at the line had half a length to spare over the courageous runner-up.

It had been a thrilling battle between the two Irish-trained colts and in fact, as the time demonstrated, quite a fast-run race. In third place, two and a half lengths back, was Damister, who had had every chance but just wasn't good enough. Doubtless, connections were quite pleased with his second successive Derby third placing.

Damister had only a head to spare over the surprise packet of the race, Barry Hills' Infantry, who in turn finished one and a half lengths in front of the filly, Triptych, in fifth place. David O'Brien's very genuine filly had run well, though finding the ground a little on the firm side. The strongly fancied Mouktar was a huge disappointment, partic-ularly to those who had backed him, and he finished in the rear. The suspicion beforehand that the ground might be too lively for the Aga Khan's colt turned out to be well founded.

Although it wasn't known at the time, the 1985 renewal marked a fitting epitaph for the Irish Hospitals Sweepstakes' involvement in the premier Irish classic. Law Society's victory was a tremendous training feat; producing a Derby winner fit and well in the midst of a stable decimated by the virus was a phenomenal achievement by the O'Brien team. There is little doubt, too, that the master of Ballydoyle must have derived

particular pleasure from the success of his £2.7 million Keeneland purchase.

Alleged, the dual Arc winner, had been responsible for a number of good-class winners without however up to that time producing one of the highest class. Law Society changed all that and there were to be further top-class winners in the following years. The dam of Law Society was Bold Bikini, who was herself a half sister to the US champion two-year-old of 1968, Top Knight. The third dam was a full sister to Gallant Man, who had won the Belmont Stakes, the third leg of the US triple crown and the only one run over the traditional European classic distance of a mile and a half.

There were other influences for stamina in Law Society's pedigree and in former years there is little doubt that the Alleged colt would have been aimed at the St Leger. However, as mentioned earlier, the Leger is no longer favoured by breeders and so Law Society was sent to Ascot for the King George VI and Queen Elizabeth Diamond Stakes.

In one of the most exciting races of the season, Law Society ran a gallant race to finish a good fourth on ground that was very firm and probably too firm for his liking. The race was won by Petoski who, earlier in the season it will be remembered, had finished second to Law Society at Chester. The runner-up at Ascot was the dual classic winner, Oh So Sharp, who went on to beat the colts in the St Leger. As if to underline the quality of the race, third place went to Rainbow Quest, who had been second to El Gran Senor in the 1984 Sweeps Derby and who was to enjoy his greatest moment later in 1985 when being awarded the Prix de l'Arc de Triomphe on the disqualification of Sagace.

It is fitting, when reviewing the 1985 Sweeps Derby, to reflect on the achievements which had been brought about as a result of the involvement of the sponsors. Over the twenty-three years of the Irish Hospitals Sweepstakes' association with the premier Irish classic, the prestige of the event had been qualitatively improved and the race elevated on to an altogether higher plane in the international racing calendar. By 1985, however, there were disturbing signs that the dynamism which had marked the early years of the Sweeps involvement had been dissipated over time.

The Irish Hospitals Sweepstakes organisation was the product of an era which had all but passed away. There were other competitors both extant and on the horizon for the disposable income that the Sweeps draws used to mop up. The organisation was in terminal decline and symptomatic of that was the fact that there had been no increase in the contribution made by the Irish Hospitals Sweepstakes to the prize fund for the Derby over the twenty-three years of its sponsorship. The contribution was £30,000 in 1962 and it remained the same, effectively much reduced in real terms, in 1985.

In the 1960s the newly sponsored race was responsible for an unparalleled display of enthusiasm among all those connected with staging the event. By the 1980s the attention to detail, which had marked those early days, had disappeared. In a critical article in the *Irish Independent* on the Tuesday after the 1985 race, racing correspondent Tom McGinty articulated the concerns of racegoers.

The fundamental point made by Mr McGinty was that there had been a deterioration in the arrangements made for catering for the vast crowds which assembled at the Curragh on Derby day. Among the observations made by him was that the capacity of the racecourse was so severely stretched that many patrons endured considerable discomfort as a consequence of attending the showcase event of the flat racing season in Ireland. Stewarding, he pointed out, left something to be desired. The facilities for the overseas press, he considered, were totally inadequate.

Tom McGinty's call for a new broom was one that would have been echoed by most racegoers. What he asked for was a serious effort to be made by the authorities to restore Irish Derby day to the standards that had been set by the late Joe McGrath and Captain Spencer Freeman. The long-serving racing correspondent could scarcely have known it, but the new broom that he yearned for was in the course of being fashioned across the wide Atlantic in far-away St Louis, Missouri.

1M 4F

SATURDAY 29 JUNE 1985

GOING: GOOD

WINNER: Mr S. S. Niarchos's Law Society by Alleged out of Bold Bikini
P. Eddery

SECOND: Theatrical by Nureyev out of Tree of Knowledge
M. J. Kinane

THIRD: Damister by Mr Prospector out of Batucada
L. Piggott

S.P. 15/8f   6/1   5/1
Winner trained by M. V. O'Brien

ALSO: Infantry 4th, Triptych 5th, Baillamont 6th, Mouktar 7th, Sun Valley 8th, Rising 9th, Dundalk Bay 10th, Outrider 11th, Snow Plant 12th, Bel Havrais 13th & last

NR Mango Express
Winner: favourite
Distances: $\frac{1}{2}$ length, $2\frac{1}{2}$ lengths
Value to winner: £168,919
Time: 2 m 29.9 s
Timeform rating of winner: 130.

1986

BUDWEISER IRISH DERBY

B y a happy coincidence, as the Irish Hospitals Sweepstakes organisation was contemplating its future as sponsor of the Irish Derby, in the United States of America a major new sponsor was casting around for a prestigious sporting involvement. Anheuser-Busch Incorporated, brewer of Budweiser, keen to market its famous beer in Europe, saw in the Irish Derby an opportunity to link its name to an event which enjoyed a high standing worldwide.

It was more than coincidental that the Executive Vice-President and Director of Marketing for Anheuser-Busch, Michael J. Roarty, was a first-generation Irish American whose father, John, came originally from Meenamara, Co. Donegal. A keen racing enthusiast, John Roarty returned on a number of occasions to Ireland from the US and often visited the Curragh for the running of the Irish Derby. Clearly the association forged by John Roarty with the

Curragh classic transmitted itself to his son Michael with the most beneficial consequences for Irish racing.

The sponsorship deal which was negotiated between Anheuser-Busch and the Irish racing authorities could hardly have been better timed from the standpoint of the future of Ireland's premier classic race. The imagination and enthusiasm which had marked the early years of the Irish Sweeps sponsorship and which had transformed the Irish Derby into a race of worldwide importance, had been eroded with time, and the centre-piece of the Irish flat racing season was in urgent need of a dramatic improvement in both organisation and image. It got precisely that.

A comparison of the prize money alone, as between the last running of the Irish Derby under the Sweeps banner and the new beginning with Anheuser-Busch, dramat-ically underlines the transformation that took place. In 1985 Law Society won a first prize of just under £169,000 for his connections. The 1986 winner, by contrast, would collect for his lucky owner a sum just £1,350 short of £300,000. Reflecting the desire to attract the very best thoroughbreds to the Curragh, place money for the second, third and fourth was also raised by an even greater percentage. Echoing their predecessors in 1962, the new sponsors of 1986 were able to proclaim proudly that once again the Irish Derby, now known as the Budweiser Irish Derby, was the richest race ever run in Europe.

For many Irish racing fans the first Budweiser-sponsored Irish Derby had a sad prelude. On the previous day, at Auteuil, that great mare Dawn Run, the only horse ever to win both the Champion Hurdle and the Cheltenham Gold Cup, had to be put down after a tragic fall at the fifth hurdle from home in the French Champion Hurdle. Probably the most popular racehorse in Ireland since Arkle, the shattering news from France was a desperate blow for national hunt racing, and an incalculable loss to the sport in general.

Eleven runners were declared for the 1986 Budweiser Irish Derby, headed by the Epsom Derby winner, Shahrastani. Widely regarded as a very fortunate winner of the Blue Riband of English racing, all the post-race publicity after Epsom centred on the runner-up, Dancing Brave. Jockey Greville Starkey was mercilessly panned by journalists and punters alike for his riding of Dancing Brave at Epsom.

Coming around Tattenham Corner, Starkey had only two of his sixteen rivals behind him. Switched to the outside in the straight, as Shahrastani set sail for home, Channel 4's commentator Graham Goode, noting that Dancing Brave was making ground from the rear, summarised in an agonised cry the feelings of the favourite's countless supporters, 'But oh! So much to do!' Guy Harwood's colt made a valiant bid to retrieve what looked like a hopeless cause. Relentlessly cutting down his rivals, Dancing Brave's dramatic bid for success failed by a rapidly diminishing half-length. It is interesting to note that Dancing Brave's sire, Lyphard, himself a son of Northern Dancer, had finished fifth in the Irish Derby of 1972 behind Steel Pulse.

With so much attention focused on the runner-up, it is probably true to say that the Michael Stoute-trained Shahrastani was not given due credit for his Epsom triumph. Prior to Epsom the Nijinsky colt had done everything asked of him in winning two recognised Derby trials, the Guardian Classic Trial and the Mecca Dante Stakes at York. Shahrastani's style of winning was workmanlike rather than spectacular, but the end result was what mattered, and unbeaten in his three-year-old campaign, he lined up at the Curragh as the horse they all had to beat.

Dancing Brave was being aimed at the King George VI and Queen Elizabeth Diamond Stakes and so did not renew rivalry with Shahrastani on this occasion. The third home at Epsom, Mashkour, however, was in the field and had three lengths to find on Shahrastani on Epsom running. It was argued by some that he was unlucky at Epsom and if that was indeed so, certainly he had to have a chance of reversing placings. Mashkour had previously won the

Lingfield Derby Trial by half a length from Bakharoff, and was Steve Cauthen's choice of Henry Cecil's two runners.

England also supplied two other challengers who were well fancied to test the Epsom Derby winner. Although only Henry Cecil's second string, the Pat Eddery-ridden Bonhomie was no forlorn hope. Sheikh Mohammed's colt had been beaten four lengths by Shahrastani on his seasonal début in the Guardian Classic Trial, but was found afterwards to have had a low blood count. Bonhomie's only other run was at Royal Ascot, where he had been an impressive winner of the King Edward VII Stakes, often a very useful guide to the Irish Derby. Trainer Cecil had stressed that Bonhomie was in the race on his own merits, and not simply to act as a pacemaker for Mashkour.

Representing Guy Harwood, so unlucky with Dancing Brave at Epsom, was the aforementioned Bakharoff. A son of the 1977 Curragh hero, The Minstrel, Bakharoff, after his close Lingfield second placing to Mashkour, next ran in France in the Prix du Jockey-Club. He was third there, beaten four and a half lengths by the most impressive winner, Bering, whom the French strongly fancied to go on and win the Arc. Bering had broken the course record at Chantilly and Bakharoff had probably run a fine race in the circumstances. After his controversial defeat on Dancing Brave at Epsom, it was certain that Bakharoff's partner, Greville Starkey, would be straining every muscle to wipe out the memory of that unhappy experience.

Two Irish-trained contenders who had competed at Epsom were also in the field for the first running of the Budweiser

Derby. Flash of Steel and Mr John, who had fought out the finish of the Irish 2,000 Guineas, with victory going to the former, had both disappointed at Epsom finishing sixth and ninth respectively. Doubtless connections hoped that a return to the scene of their Guineas duel might bring about a change in fortune.

None of the other runners had a realistic chance on form. Michael Halford's Fighting Hard was unbeaten, but as his sole outing was in a modest race at Roscommon, his participation was fuelled more by hope than by expectation. The closest that Barry Kelly's Pacific Drift was likely to get to a Derby winner was through his sire, Henbit, who had won the Epsom Derby back in 1980. King Retain was a stable companion of Mr John and, like World Court, was something of a forlorn hope. The only other runner, Ostensible, was in the race to act as pacemaker for his stablemate, Bakharoff.

Considering that Shahrastani was unbeaten and a Derby winner, he was quite fairly priced at even money after touching fractions either side of his starting price. There was very good support for Steve Cauthen's mount, Mashkour, and he closed at 3/1 from 4's. By contrast, Bakharoff eased out to 9/2 from a point shorter. Reflecting divided stable opinion, Bonhomie also came in for support and wound up a 7/1 shot from 8/1. Best of the Irish were the 2,000 Guineas principals, Flash of Steel and Mr John who were both returned at 20/1, although Flash of Steel eased from 16's and Mr John came in from 25's.

Rain on the day before the race had taken the sting out of the ground and the going, though officially good, was perhaps just a little on the easy side. It was a very hot day, but despite this the weather forecast was uncertain, with the distinct possibility of thunderstorms. Fortunately for everyone, and in particular the new sponsors, the rain held off and the race was run in fine, dry conditions.

The third race on the card, the Budweiser Irish Derby got under way without undue delay and as predicted Guy Harwood's Ostensible made the early running. Right from the start the pacemaker was tracked by Pat Eddery on Bonhomie, with Walter Swinburn on Shahrastani a close-up third. In the first half of the race both Mashkour and Bakharoff were held up, off the pace.

Ostensible's pacemaking exertions took their toll just after half-way, and straightaway Bonhomie and Pat Eddery moved into the lead. Shahrastani and Swinburn quickly covered Eddery's move, and even at this early stage it was looking like a two-horse race. Bonhomie led Shahrastani into the straight and from the stands it appeared simply a matter as to when Swinburn would press the button on the favourite. Sensing how easily his rival was going, Eddery got to work on Bonhomie. For a short while Bonhomie appeared to be responding to the pressure, but with just two furlongs to go, Swinburn asked Shahrastani to go on and the favourite did just that.

Sweeping past his hard-ridden rival, the combination lengthened most impressively and soon opened up a winning lead. Despite veering slightly to the left inside the final furlong, Shahrastani kept up the gallop and at the line had no less than eight lengths to

spare over the game but outclassed Bonhomie. A length and a half further back came Bakharoff who, although under pressure before entering the straight, ran on late to claim third prize. The disappointing Mashkour was a neck behind Bakharoff in fourth place, never having held out any hope for his supporters at any stage. Best of the Irish was Mr John who finished a respectable fifth, two places in front of his Irish Guineas conqueror, Flash of Steel, for whom the ground was not soft enough.

Shahrastani's spectacular victory, which showed him in an even better light than at Epsom, was notable on several counts. For trainer Michael Stoute it represented his third success in the Irish Derby in the space of five years, following upon Shergar in 1981 and Shareef Dancer in 1983. And for Shahrastani's sire, Nijinsky, it completed a fabulous Derby treble in 1986, for his son Ferdinand had in May won the Kentucky Derby at Churchill Downs. Nijinsky claimed another slice of the glory as well. Shahrastani's win meant that Nijinsky became the first horse in the sponsorship era to win the Irish Derby and go on subsequently to sire the winner of the race.

As things transpired, it was as well that the Derby was concluded when it was. At the end of the day's racing a violent thunderstorm broke over the Curragh, lighting up the sky in spectacular fashion and turning the nearby Naas dual carriageway into a waterway. The storm was but a prelude to a night of continuous thunder and lightning storms over the eastern half of Ireland which ensured that few, if any, slept easily in their beds that night. For the connections of Shahrastani, however, it probably added an extra dash of piquancy to the doubtless lively celebrations.

Shahrastani's splendid Curragh triumph forced many to revise their opinions of the merits of his Epsom victory. Whereas it had been widely assumed that Shahrastani had been a winner more or less by default, it was now increasingly argued that with all the attention on the luckless runner-up, perhaps Shahrastani might have won anyway, whatever way the Epsom race was run.

Clearly a re-match between Shahrastani and Dancing Brave would go a long way towards settling the argument. It says much for the sporting instincts of the connections of both horses that neither camp side-stepped the obvious mid-summer target, and so both lined up at Ascot a month after Shahrastani's Curragh victory.

The betting on the King George VI and Queen Elizabeth Diamond Stakes was most interesting. Contrary to expectations, Shahrastani was returned the 11/10 favourite, with Dancing Brave a 6/4 shot. In the parade ring, however, the dual Derby winner's physical appearance did not please experienced observers. Worse was to follow. Down at the start, the Aga Khan's colt began to exhibit unexpected signs of temperament. He was sweating profusely and in addition took quite an amount of coaxing before consenting to go into the stalls.

The forebodings aroused by Shahrastani's pre-race behaviour were to prove all too prophetic. Never going partic-ularly well, once the race started in earnest Shahrastani dropped out of contention and finished almost ten lengths back in fourth place behind Dancing Brave. Guy Harwood's colt had in fact to be quite vigorously ridden to get the better of Shahrastani's lesser fancied stable companion, Shardari, making the favourite's performance all the more puzzling.

Plainly, Shahrastani ran below his best and it has to be assumed that the exertions of his classic successes left a greater mark than was apparent to the naked eye. It is greatly to the credit of his connections that, rather than packing him off to stud forthwith, Shahrastani was kept in training and prepared for his farewell outing in the Prix de l'Arc de Triomphe. Here he was to have his final joust with his great rival, Dancing Brave.

Now universally accorded a position of pre-eminence as the top three-year-old of his generation, the Pat Eddery-ridden Dancing Brave won the Paris showdown with a quite devastating turn of foot inside the final furlong. The high-class French challenger, Bering, was in second place, one and a half lengths behind Dancing Brave, and in third place half a length back came that durable mare, Triptych, who had of course run in the 1985 Irish Derby. Shahrastani was only a short head behind in fourth place, beaten a little over two lengths by his Epsom victim, Dancing Brave. Considering that the ground at Longchamp was very firm, which would have suited Dancing Brave better than most of his rivals including Shahrastani, the first Budweiser Irish Derby winner ran a fine genuine race in the Arc, more than making up for his moderate display at Ascot.

Summing up the 1986 generation, Dancing Brave had to be rated some few pounds superior to Shahrastani, but given the exalted rating accorded to Guy Harwood's champion, Shahrastani must go down as a very good-class Irish Derby winner. From the point of view of the American sponsors, the 1986 renewal of the premier Irish classic represented a successful inauguration of their newly formed partnership with Irish racing. The storm clouds, however, that hovered after the conclusion of the day's racing on Derby day were a gloomy augury of a rather less happy experience in 1987.

BUDWEISER IRISH DERBY

1M 4F

SATURDAY 28 JUNE 1986

GOING: GOOD

WINNER: H. H. Aga Khan's Shahrastani by Nijinsky out of Shademah
W. R. Swinburn

SECOND: Bonhomie by What a Pleasure out of Chatter Box
P. Eddery

THIRD: Bakharoff by The Minstrel out of Qui Royalty
G. Starkey

S.P. 1/1f   7/1   9/2
Winner trained by M. R. Stoute

ALSO: Mashkour 4th, Mr John 5th, World Court 6th, Flash of Steel 7th, King Retain 8th, Ostensible 9th, Pacific Drift 10th, Fighting Words 11th & last

Winner: favourite
Distances: 8 lengths, 1½ lengths
Value to winner: £298,650
Time: 2 m 32.1 s
Timeform rating of winner: 135.

1987

BUDWEISER IRISH DERBY

THE CURRAGH 27 JUNE 1987

Unfortunately the 1987 renewal of the Irish Derby, in its second year under the Budweiser banner, will long be remembered for all the wrong reasons. Overnight rain had ensured that the going at the Curragh would be particularly testing, but regrettably many racegoers were to experience the underfoot conditions at first hand in circumstances that they could not possibly have envisaged.

A splendid crowd turned up on what was a fine day and the foresight of race organisers and sponsors in developing a new spectator area in the Curragh infield was warmly welcomed as a means of catering with greater comfort for the crowds. The actions, however, of one misguided prankster contrived to spoil the day for most if not all of the attendance, as well as presenting a dreadful image worldwide of one of the country's premier sporting attractions.

The hoax bomb scare call was of course timed to cause maximum disruption, and

this is precisely what it did. It took an unconscionable length of time to clear the reserved stand — almost forty minutes — for the simple reason that most of the patrons steadfastly refused to obey repeated and ever more urgent appeals on the public address system to vacate the area.

Irish racegoers' disregard of the broadcast requests to vacate the alleged location of the bomb was a source of baffled amazement to the many American visitors who had flown in for the occasion. A Mr Bill Lang of Washington DC, quoted in *The Irish Times*, described his reaction in the following terms: 'I was absolutely terrified. I expected the worst. If you had announced a bomb scare in a major stadium in the US there would have been a stampede, people would have hurt each other.'

Eventually the reserved stand was cleared although one consequence of this was that, due to the subsequent overcrowding, many of the spectators had to be allowed on to the racecourse. High heels and summer attire were ill fitted to the soft ground, with the result that a sizeable number of fashionably dressed racegoers ended up wiping the Curragh mud off their expensive footwear and summer finery.

It was a frustrating and unhappy occasion for spectators and the projection of these scenes to a worldwide audience via satellite television was not calculated to present the best possible image of a high summer sporting occasion in Ireland. *The Irish Times* report, referred to earlier, outlined how the American network ABC broadcast from the Curragh, lasting some eighteen minutes, had used the news of the bomb scare as a suspenseful lead into a commercial break. After the break, viewers in the United States were told that all had ended well and that the bomb scare had been a hoax.

Of course it was not only the patrons who were inconvenienced by the frustrating and tedious delay. The Derby field, eight in all, were obliged to walk around at the start for the best part of an hour, while the jockeys glumly sat around on the wet grass. None of the losing jockeys afterwards blamed his mount's failure on the delay, but it was scarcely an ideal preparation for such a prestigious contest.

By common consent the field for the 1987 Budweiser Irish Derby was not the best ever assembled for Ireland's premier classic. The Epsom winner Reference Point was being held in reserve for the King George, while the third horse at Epsom, Bellotto, was taken out of the Curragh race because of the soft ground. However the second, fourth, fifth and eighth horses

home behind Reference Point renewed rivalry, and as it turned out these four colts occupied the first four places in the betting market, although not in the order that might have been anticipated.

At Epsom Most Welcome had been beaten one and a half lengths by Reference Point, with Sir Harry Lewis fourth, beaten three and a half lengths, Entitled a further half a length back fifth, and Sadjiyd close up in eighth place, beaten about six lengths in all. On the book Most Welcome was the clear form choice, for in addition to his second placing at Epsom he had crossed the line in third place in the 2,000 Guineas at Newmarket behind Don't Forget Me, only to be disqualified subsequently. Geoff Wragg's Be My Guest colt was to be partnered by Paul Eddery and was bidding to give his sire his second success in the Irish Derby in the space of five years.

Sir Harry Lewis was trained by Barry Hills and this son of Alleged was bound to be suited to the galloping Curragh track. Prior to his prominent showing at Epsom he had been quite impressive in winning the Dee Stakes at Chester, upsetting the odds laid on Shady Heights in the process. Best of the Irish was expected to be Vincent O'Brien's Entitled, a beautifully bred but relatively inexperienced Mill Reef colt. His Epsom run was only his third ever race and there was every reason to expect that he would improve on that encouraging performance. Unraced as a two-year-old, Entitled, after winning a minor race at the Curragh, had surprised connections by forcing the English 2,000 Guineas winner, Don't Forget Me, to pull out all the stops before going under by half a length to the Richard Hannon-trained colt in the Irish equivalent.

Quite the most intriguing horse in the race, however, was Sadjiyd, representing the Aga Khan, bidding to make it three Irish Derbies for his sporting owner in a matter of six years. The subject of a massive gamble for the Epsom Derby, Sadjiyd had disgraced himself on that occasion, paying more attention to some nearby gypsy ponies than to the matter in hand. He had practically refused to race in the early stages at Epsom, but late on he began to run on to such effect from a seemingly hopeless position, that many were of the view that had he consented to race properly from the start Sadjiyd would have asked the front-running Reference Point a very stiff question indeed in the concluding stages.

Prior to Epsom Sadjiyd had excellent form in France, having run up a four-race unbeaten sequence. His performance in the Prix Hocquart over a mile and a half at Longchamp was particularly impressive. Boxed in for much of the way up the straight, Sadjiyd flew the final furlong and won going away in near record time without having to be subjected to any discernible pressure. He had winning form on very soft ground and it was that consideration which had prompted the Aga Khan to saddle Sadjiyd in preference to his Prix du Jockey-Club winner Natroun in the Irish Derby.

Of the other runners, Vanvitelli was a maiden from the Liam Browne stable with no apparent prospects, while Golden Isle, by the ill-fated Golden Fleece, was in the race to act as a pacemaker for his stable companion,

Entitled. Dollar Seeker was an English-trained outsider from the Michael Ryan stable, who would have to step up on all previous form to have a realistic chance.

A far more potent threat from across the Irish Sea was David Elsworth's runner, Naheez, from the first crop of Critique, who was trained by Vincent O'Brien to finish runner-up in the Grand Criterium. Naheez had won twice from three starts as a two-year-old and had run reasonably well when seventh to Don't Forget Me in the 2,000 Guineas at Newmarket. However, when stepped up in distance to a mile and a half in the Prix du Jockey-Club (the French Derby), Naheez really came into his own and finished a good third to the aforementioned Natroun and Trempolino, beaten just over two lengths. The merit of the form was to be clearly underlined later in the season when Trempolino went on to win the Prix de l'Arc de Triomphe.

The betting of the race was, despite the protracted delay before the off, very lively. As at Epsom there was a torrent of money for the French challenger Sadjiyd. Put in at 2/1, the Aga Khan's colt was backed down to 6/4, although he eased slightly to be returned at 13/8 at the off. Most Welcome was a solidly supported second favourite, opening at 3's, touching half a point longer but settling at his opening price. Entitled too attracted plenty of support and after visiting 4/1 ended at 7/2. Sir Harry Lewis wasn't totally ignored at 6/1 although he had opened a point less. Naheez was weak, drifting out to 10/1 from 7's, and there were only small amounts for the rest.

The advertised starting time of the Derby was 3.40 p.m., but due to the unanticipated delay the field of eight runners was not dispatched until 4.29 p.m., to the great relief of all concerned. On settling down, Golden Isle, as had been expected, made the running but at a fairly sedate pace. Entitled and Sir Harry Lewis were closest to the front runner in the early stages, while the heavily backed favourite Sadjiyd was in rear but in touch. The maiden Vanvitelli moved into second place seven furlongs out and with Golden Isle having fulfilled his pacemaking duties and dropped away, Michael Kinane pushed the Ela-Mana-Mou colt into the lead.

At this point backers of the first and second favourites were looking to their fancies to take closer order, but Sadjiyd and Most Welcome were not giving their supporters any grounds for optimism. Vanvitelli continued to lead into the straight, being most closely attended by Sir Harry Lewis, with Entitled next and Naheez beginning to make significant headway.

The outsider Vanvitelli began to feel the strain not long afterwards as Sir Harry Lewis, with John Reid up, struck the front over two furlongs out. Entitled and Cash Asmussen tried to go with him, but the partnership was soon struggling in the soft ground. Backers of Sadjiyd and Most Welcome were by now ruefully shaking their heads, for neither colt was in any position to play a part in the business end of the race. It was in fact Naheez who emerged as the most serious challenger to the leader Sir Harry Lewis.

Under strong pressure from Ray Cochrane, Naheez closed the gap somewhat on Sir Harry Lewis and with 150 yards to go there was just a chance that he might get up. John Reid's mount, however, was galloping on resolutely, clearly appreciating the give in the ground, and although Naheez gave his all Sir Harry Lewis had his measure all the way to the line, eventually winning by three-quarters of a length from the gallant runner-up. Vincent O'Brien's Entitled plugged on to be third, four lengths further back, and the 50/1 outsider Vanvitelli delighted connections by finishing fourth, another four lengths back.

Most Welcome was a disappointing fifth and it was reported that the Epsom runner-up simply could not handle the ground. The favourite Sadjiyd never gave his supporters a moment's hope and was a very moderate sixth. Clearly he had developed a mind of his own about the game. The time of the race was slow, 2 minutes 40.2 seconds, the fourth slowest since Tambourine II won the first Sweeps Derby in 1962. Only the races won by Ragusa, Meadow Court and Tyrnavos were run in a slower time.

None of this mattered to the colt's owner, New York businessman Mr Howard Kaskel, who owns the Doral Hotel and Country Club in Miami. The horse was named, Mr Kaskel explained, after his late father-in-law, the title being added without reference to Queen Elizabeth. Bred by Joseph Allen and Regent Farm in Kentucky, Sir Harry Lewis was by Alleged out of a mare called Sue Babe. She herself was by the top American sire, Mr Prospector, and won three of the four races that she contested, including two Stakes races at Belmont, as well as finishing second in the Grade 1 Sorority Stakes. Sue Babe was in fact named after Mr Kaskel's wife and it is to be presumed that she was happy about that.

Besides Mr Kaskel, one man who must have been quite pleased at the outcome of the race was Vincent O'Brien. Besides saddling the third horse home, Entitled, he must have derived considerable satisfaction from the fact that both first and second were sired by horses formerly trained by him. In addition, for Alleged, who had made a slow start to his career at stud, Sir Harry Lewis's victory represented his second Irish Derby winner in the space of three years following upon Law Society, trained of course by O'Brien, in 1985.

For Cash Asmussen, Entitled's third placing was one of the few bright spots in a difficult year as first jockey to the powerful Vincent O'Brien stable. In fact in the Irish 2,000 Guineas Asmussen had chosen to ride the stable's first choice, Baba Karam, who disappointed, leaving Declan Gillespie to pick up the ride on Entitled, who of course surprised everyone by finishing a close second. This example more or less typified Asmussen's year in Ireland and by mutual agreement his contract with Ballydoyle was terminated at the end of the season.

As it transpired John Reid, who had ridden such a competent and confident race on Sir Harry Lewis, became stable jockey at Ballydoyle in 1988, and one wonders if perhaps his performance on the Barry Hills-trained colt helped to clinch for the Northern Irish-born jockey his prestigious appointment.

Sir Harry Lewis was not in the front rank of Irish Derby winners and his subsequent performance, when a moderate seventh of nine to Reference Point in the King George VI and Queen Elizabeth Diamond Stakes on ground which should have suited him, was frankly very disappointing. He was kept in training as a four-year-old, but he failed to reproduce his best three-year-old form.

However, as stated at the outset, the 1987 Budweiser Irish Derby will not be remembered for the rather substandard nature of the race itself, but for the regrettable prelude to the entire affair, hopefully never to be repeated.

For the sponsors the 1987 débâcle was a very trying test of their commitment to Irish horse racing. Happily, Anheuser-Busch was prepared to be patient with its fledgling venture and in the years that followed that patience was to be handsomely rewarded.

Shahrastani, the 1986 winner, is surrounded by photographers after his victory. (CN)

Old Vic, with Steve Cauthen up, strolls to victory in 1989. (CN)

(CN)

Under a vigorous ride from Ray Cochrane, Khayasi gets home from a whipless Richard Quinn on Insan in 1988. Afterwards, Khayasi relaxes in the winner's enclosure.

(INPHO)

*The 1985 and 1987
winners, Law Society and
Sir Harry Lewis, were both
sired by the great dual Arc
winner, Alleged. Law
Society's owner, Stavros
Niarchos, is shown with
the trophy (above), while,
two years later, Sir Harry
Lewis storms home. (CN)*

Hamdan Al Maktoum leads in his 1990 winner Salsibil, the first filly to win the Irish Derby for 90 years. (CN)

Famous faces at the Curragh: Michael Smurfit, Robert Sangster, His Highness the Aga Khan and Paul Newman.

Christy Roche's two wins were separated by a ten year gap, Assert (1982) and St Jovite (1992).

(INPHO)

succeeded subsequently in reversing placings with the winner at the Curragh. Hours After's French Derby win was difficult to evaluate and apart from that Gerald Mosse's mount would be facing contrasting going at the Curragh.

The most intriguing runner in the race was Paul Cole's Insan. With only one run as a three-year-old behind him prior to the Curragh, Insan was likely to strip fresh and well and the form of that solitary outing bore the closest inspection. In the Lingfield Derby Trial, Insan had been beaten two lengths by no less than Khayasi and significantly Paul Cole's charge had been conceding 5 lb to the subsequent Epsom winner. As a juvenile Insan's main claim to fame was a victory in the Beresford Stakes at the Curragh in soft ground from Gold Discovery and Safety Catch, form which seemed at the time to be some way below the required standard.

Khayasi, for his part, had run only once as a two-year-old, winning a modest event at Newmarket in October, and as such his name was not to the fore in the annual winter speculation on the upcoming year's classics. His Lingfield Trial win was adjudged to be no more than average form and he started a comparatively unfancied 11/1 shot at Epsom. Clearly, however, nobody had told Khayasi that he should not win and he took the Blue Riband of English racing in authoritative fashion. He came from some way back at Epsom and was certainly not stopping at the finish. In that well-honed racing phrase, whatever beat him would almost certainly win.

Among the optimists hoping to bring off this seemingly unlikely feat were no less than six Irish-trained runners, whose chances on form fell within the range of outside possibility to absolutely no hope. In the first category was John Oxx's Curio, which had won a listed race by five lengths at the Phoenix Park and was touted in some quarters as a good each-way prospect. Second in a Group 2 event at the Curragh behind Project Manager, David O'Brien's Baltic Fox had to be considered, if only because of the tremendous record of his young trainer.

The long shots included the President of Ireland's Cúileann, a narrow winner of a mile and three quarters race at Leopardstown, and another with similar credentials was Kevin Prendergast's Magistro. Little Bighorn, trained by Liam Browne, had won a modest race over ten furlongs at the Phoenix Park and while his chances appeared slim, stable companion Wagon Load's most recent piece of form, last of twelve in a listed race at the Curragh, suggested that sentiment alone was responsible for his place in the line-up.

The sun shone pleasingly to welcome the tremendous crowds who descended upon the Curragh on 26 June for the first Sunday running of Ireland's premier flat race. A liberal sprinkling of both national and international celebrities added to the glamour of the occasion. Among the famous names who graced the unique occasion were glamorous model Jerry Hall, wife of Rolling Stone Mick Jagger. Photographed in one of the Irish national newspapers entertaining John Forsyth with a tune on a guitar, it was not recorded whether Jerry's musical performance was up to gaining her a place in her husband's band. Robert Sangster, whose Glacial Storm was a strong fancy for the Derby, was in attendance with his third wife, Susan. It is not known if Jerry and Robert, who were at one stage romantically linked, crossed each other's path in the course of the afternoon.

Dr Michael Smurfit was in attendance and there was some disappointment for the gossip columnists in that his new Swedish bride, Birgetta, was not with him. The American Ambassador Margaret Heckler was present, helping to foster the US connection with Ireland's most prestigious racing occasion. The sponsors of course flew in a large party for the day and Michael J. Roarty — the man credited with initiating Anheuser-Busch's involvement with Irish racing — was right at the centre of things. On that lovely summer's day in June 1988 Mr Roarty must have sensed that the gods had conspired to ensure that Budweiser's association with the Irish Derby was to develop into something more than just a passing fancy.

The betting on the race took a fairly predictable course. The favourite was Khayasi who see-sawed between 4/5 and 4/6, settling at the former price. Glacial Storm who opened at 3's initially eased out to 4/1, but good money forced him back to 3/1 at the off. Insan, for whom there had been significant support in the betting offices in the days before the race, was steady at 10/1. The each-way fancy, Curio, attracted patriotic cash and finished at 12/1, having opened two points longer. By contrast, the French Derby winner, Hours After, was very weak in the market and drifted from 9/1 out

to 14/1. The other French challenger, Port Lyautey, was a 20/1 shot, and it was 66/1 and better the others.

On going that was officially described as good to firm, the field of eleven was dispatched on the one and a half mile trek around the Curragh. The 300/1 rank outsider Wagon Load, with John Reid up, made the early running at a pace which was no more than sensible. In the early stages the fancied Insan ran second behind the leader, with another English challenger, Glacial Storm, third. The favourite Khayasi, ridden by Irish-born jockey Ray Cochrane, was held up towards the rear early on. There was little change in the order throughout the first mile of the race. The Liam Browne-trained long shot, Wagon Load, continued to blaze a front-running trail and he was followed by Insan and Glacial Storm.

Ray Cochrane was in no hurry on Khayasi and with five furlongs to go he had only two horses behind him. Wagon Load's gallop came to an end about half a mile out and he weakened rapidly out of contention. Richard Quinn then took over on Insan, who was followed into the straight by Glacial Storm. Supporters of the favourite, though not unduly worried, were a bit concerned that Khayasi had still a fair bit to do entering the straight, being only sixth at this stage.

The race, however, changed complexion quickly once the horses straightened up for home. Insan still led and he was followed by Steve Cauthen on Glacial Storm. Khayasi, meantime, had made smooth headway and was a closing third with less than three furlongs to run. A gap was beginning to open up between the leading trio and the rest of the field. Those who had invested their cash on either the French Derby winner, Hours After, or the leading Irish fancy, Curio, were already starting to count the cost of their folly, for their chances of collecting had effectively disappeared.

Khayasi went past Glacial Storm into second place with just under two furlongs to run and set off in pursuit of Insan, who was now beginning to come under pressure. However, the game Insan responded well to the pressure and suddenly it was clear that Khayasi had a battle royal on his hands.

Both horses were under the whip as they entered the final furlong, but all the while Insan held a narrow lead. Supporters of the two colts roared encouragement for their respective fancies as both Richard Quinn and Ray Cochrane sought to wrest the prestigious prize away from the other. Glacial Storm meantime was running on at one pace behind the two principals. There was less than 100 yards to go, with Insan still about a neck to the good, when arguably the decisive moment in determining the destination of the race occurred.

Jockey Richard Quinn on Insan dropped his whip and so was unable to call upon the 'persuader' in the final dramatic stages of the race. By contrast, Ray Cochrane was able to extract every response from his willing partner, and as the two jockeys and their gallant mounts strained every muscle in the exhilarating dash for the line, it appeared as if Khayasi was closing the gap on Insan slowly but inexorably.

As the two horses flashed past the post it was impossible to tell with the naked eye whether Insan had held on or if Khayasi had

got up to claim victory in the dying strides. A tense wait ensued for the connections of the two principals. It must have been a particularly trying time for Richard Quinn and trainer Paul Cole, in that both men realised the importance that would be attached to the jockey's loss of the whip, should the verdict go against them. Their worst fears were to be confirmed.

The judge announced the result and number seven, Khayasi, was named the winner. The distance was the minimum one, a short head, and it was two and a half lengths back to the one-paced Glacial Storm in third place. It was ten lengths further back to the fourth home, the 100/1 outsider Little Bighorn, who finished best of the Irish, half a length ahead of Curio in fifth place. The big disappointment of the race was the French challenger, Hours After, who was a poor ninth of eleven, clearly not appreciating the fast ground. It emerged afterwards that Hours After had been involved in a bit of a barging match with Wagon Load, and although the stewards enquired into the incident they were unable to apportion blame.

Khayasi's success was a popular one, and not alone with the big punters who had waded in on the favourite. A massive £300,000 was in fact wagered with the course bookmakers on the big race. For the third time in eight years the Aga Khan had seen his famous green colours with red epaulettes carried to success in Ireland's principal flat race. Not only that, but the three winners concerned — Shergar, Shahrastani and Khayasi — had all completed the prestigious Epsom-Irish Derby double. If the tragic loss of Shergar was a terrible blow to the bloodstock world, it was only fitting that the Aga Khan, who had kept faith with the Irish industry despite his misfortune, should have enjoyed such heartening success in the years immediately afterwards.

It is worth noting that Khayasi came back to the unsaddling area after his narrow win with a nasty gash over the knee on his near foreleg. Naturally both trainer and owner were very concerned as to the extent of the injury, but neither attempted to claim that Khayasi's mishap had in any way affected the result. In fact, it should be pointed out that Khayasi and Insan had reproduced their Lingfield Derby Trial running to the pound.

Paul Cole, for his part, did not attempt to suggest that Quinn's loss of his whip had contributed to Insan's defeat. The trainer remained commendably loyal to his stable jockey. How much, however, the incident contributed to owner Prince Fahd Salman's decision a few years later in 1991 to engage Alan Munro to ride all his horses in Cole's stable is impossible to say. As it happened, the wealthy potentate had another change of heart later on, and Richard Quinn is now again riding in the Prince's famous dark green colours.

If Insan's jockey was understandably unhappy with the outcome, for Ray Cochrane Khayasi's victory was splendid compensation for his second placing on Naheez in the previous year's race. Khayasi provided trainer Luca Cumani with his first Irish classic success. His previous visit to Ireland, however, had brought glory when Lester Piggott guided the St Leger winner

Commanche Run to victory in the Phoenix Champion Stakes of 1985.

The two Curragh principals were to clash again later in the season. After an eleven week lay-off, Khayasi returned to action at Longchamp in the Prix Niel over twelve furlongs and among the opposition was Insan. Chosen as a preparatory race for the Arc, under the conditions of the race Khayasi had to give 6 lb to Insan. The Paul Cole-trained colt had run once since the Curragh and had been a somewhat disappointing three-quarter length second to the Royal Ascot winner, Sheriff's Star, in the Great Voltigeur Stakes at York.

In the event neither horse won, but in a close finish Khayasi came out the better, finishing a neck second to the French horse, Fijar Tango, with Insan just over half a length back in fourth place. The run satisfied trainer Luca Cumani and Khayasi was allowed to take his chance in the Prix de l'Arc de Triomphe.

In a thrilling race at Longchamp, the Italian-owned and trained Tony Bin, ridden by John Reid, beat the unlucky Mtoto by a neck. Khayasi finished a respectable sixth, a place in front of Fijar Tango, with Curragh third Glacial Storm fifteenth of the twenty-four runners. It was to be Khayasi's last race and he was retired to stud forthwith.

Bred at the Ballymany Stud, just down the road from the Curragh, Khayasi is by the 1978 King George VI and Queen Elizabeth Diamond Stakes winner, Ile de Bourbon, himself a son of Nijinsky. Bred in the purple, Khayasi has every chance of making a name for himself as a stallion.

Khayasi was no more than an average winner of the Irish Derby, but the manner of his victory and the general circumstances surrounding the staging of the race did much to restore the prestige of the Curragh classic after several years in the doldrums. The move to Sunday was an outstanding success, the weather was at its kindest and organisationally the whole meeting was a triumph. A few years on, it can be appreciated now that the 1988 renewal represented a decisive turning point in the process of restoring Ireland's premier flat race to its rightful place as one of the top European attractions for the classic generation.

BUDWEISER IRISH DERBY

1M 4F

SUNDAY 26 JUNE 1988

GOING: GOOD TO FIRM

WINNER: H. H. Aga Khan's Khayasi by Ile de Bourbon out of Kadissya
R. Cochrane

SECOND: Insan by Our Native out of Artania
T. Quinn

THIRD: Glacial Storm by Arctic Tern out of Hortensia
S. Cauthen

S.P. 4/5f 10/1 3/1
Winner trained by L. M. Cumani

ALSO: Little Bighorn 4th, Curio 5th, Baltic Fox 6th, Port Lyautey 7th, Magistro 8th, Hours After 9th, Wagon Load 10th, Cúileann 11th & last

Winner: favourite
Distances: sh. hd, 2½ lengths
Value to winner: £329,250
Time: 2 m 32.5 s
Timeform rating of winner: 130.

1989

BUDWEISER IRISH DERBY

Henry Cecil, master of the powerful Warren Place stables, though a dominant figure on the English racing scene over many years, has until comparatively recently campaigned but rarely in Ireland. Interestingly enough, though, Cecil won his first ever classic, the Irish 1,000 Guineas, with Clodagh in 1973. His next major Irish success took all of fifteen years and this time it was another filly, Diminuendo, who dead-heated with Melodist in the 1988 Kildangan Stud Irish Oaks.

Together with jockey Steve Cauthen and owner Sheikh Mohammed, Henry Cecil set out in 1989 to repair a gap in all their auspicious records with a formidable challenge for the 1989 Budweiser Irish Derby. Old Vic, a son of Sadler's Wells, carried their hopes and aspirations and his chances on paper were second to none.

As a juvenile Old Vic was lightly campaigned, winning the second of his two races, an uncompetitive affair at Haydock Park, by six lengths from Rendezvous Bay. He was on nobody's list of future classic winners when the 1988 crop of two-year-olds retired to their winter quarters. In the early part of 1989 one horse in fact dominated the classic scene in England. Nashwan, owned by Sheikh Mohammed's brother, Hamdan Al Maktoum, supplemented a game victory in the Newmarket 2,000 Guineas with an impressive success in the Epsom Derby over the outsider, Terimon, and the well-fancied Cacoethes.

Old Vic meantime had started off in humbler surrounds and his first outing of the season was rewarded with a victory in the Burghclere Stakes at Newbury. Stepping up in class, Old Vic then gave first notice of above average ability when winning the Dalham Chester Vase in good style. It is worth recording that he handed out a two and a half length beating there to a horse then trained by Clive Brittain called Golden Pheasant.

There was talk of running Old Vic in the Epsom Derby, but believing that neither the course nor the probable going would suit him, Cecil held the Sadler's Wells colt in reserve for the French Derby (the Prix du Jockey-Club). It was at Chantilly that Old Vic demonstrated that he was a racehorse of exceptional ability. He thrashed the opposition at Chantilly, beating Dance Hall by no less than seven lengths, with eight lengths back to the third horse home. It was a performance which drew superlatives from some expert race readers, although others questioned the value of the form. Doubts on that score were significantly removed, however, when Dance Hall reappeared subsequently and won the Grand Prix de Paris.

Even at this early stage of the season, there was considerable debate as to the merits of the two Arab-owned Derby winners. Each camp had its partisans, but several private handicappers adjudged Old Vic to be superior to Nashwan following upon their respective classic triumphs. It was a debate that would intensify as the season progressed.

Only seven opponents lined up to take on Old Vic at the Curragh. Three of them were from Britain and four from the home country. The home challenge looked distinctly substandard. The best of them was probably Dermot Weld's Vision colt, Phantom Breeze. Although he had won the Derrinstown Stud Derby Trial Stakes over ten furlongs at Leopardstown well enough, he had been readily beaten in the Gallinule Stakes over the same distance at the Curragh by Old Vic's stable companion, Porter Rhodes, who was not regarded as being in the top class.

The other three Irish runners were outclassed to varying degrees. Glowing Star from the Joe Canty stable had won a modest event at the Phoenix Park, but at best was a contender for a slice of the place money, while both Galliero and Stone Drum almost certainly were competing for the honour of finishing second last.

The three English challengers represented more of a threat to Old Vic. The Ile de Bourbon colt, Ile de Nisky, was on form the biggest danger to the favourite. Fourth to Nashwan at Epsom, beaten seven and a half lengths, Geoff Huffer's colt had previously won a minor event at Doncaster on his seasonal début, but was obviously improving.

Over twenty years had elapsed since Fulke Johnson Houghton had won successive Irish Derbies with Ribocco and Ribero, and his challenger this time was the Aga Khan's Darshaan colt, Zayyani. To be ridden by Pat Eddery, Zayyani had run three times as a three-year-old and was something of a 'dark horse'. After an impressive performance when winning the Greenham Stakes at Newbury, Zayyani was a leading fancy for the English 2,000 Guineas, but was a moderate eighth to Nashwan. He improved, however, when stepped up in distance and finished a good second, beaten three-quarters of a length by Cacoethes in the King Edward VII Stakes over the full Derby distance at Royal Ascot. On a line through Epsom Derby third Cacoethes, Zayyani had at least as good a chance as Ile de Nisky.

The other English runner was the Barry Hills-trained Observation Post. After a successful juvenile campaign, this Shirley Heights colt had been a leading fancy for the Epsom Derby, but his two length second to Tourjon in the William Hill Dante Stakes at York had been rather disappointing, and as a consequence Robert Sangster's colt had bypassed Epsom. The same combination of owner and trainer had been third in the previous year's race with Glacial Storm and doubtless they were hoping that Observation Post would improve on that performance.

There was an overnight scare for the supporters of the odds-on favourite when Old Vic developed a warble on his back, directly where the saddle would be placed. Trainer Henry Cecil seriously considered withdrawing Old Vic, but after a discussion with owner Sheikh Mohammed and following upon suitable veterinary treatment, it was decided to run the horse provided there was no sign that he was suffering in any way.

Because of the warble, Cecil requested permission from the stewards to have the colt brought down to the start without a rider and saddle. The intention was to saddle Old Vic down beside the starting stalls. The stewards, however, were unable to comply with the trainer's request, as under rule 205 of the Rules of Racing a horse competing in a race must be ridden past the judge before going down to the start. While in the circumstances the stewards' decision might have appeared harsh, none the less a moment's reflection will allow one to appreciate that any relaxation in the relevant rule would not help to promote the integrity of the sport of horse racing.

What happened in fact was that Steve Cauthen complied with the necessary requirement, but once past the judge he dismounted from Old Vic and, accompanied by Ile de Nisky, walked his mount all the way across the Curragh to the starting point. Despite this late blip in Old Vic's preparation, neither the bookmakers nor the punters were disposed to believe that the favourite's chances would be impaired significantly by his mishap.

After opening at 2/5, Steve Cauthen's mount hardened to 1/3 before settling at 4/11 at the off. Ile de Nisky was a clear second favourite and after some initial support from 9/2 to 4/1, he eased back out to 5/1. Zayyani, bidding to win the Irish Derby for the fourth time in the 1980s for the Aga Khan, was steady on 10's, while Willie Carson's mount, Observation Post, eased from an opening 10/1 to 12's. It was 20/1 Phantom Breeze and 33/1 and upwards the rest.

The going was officially good although there had been extensive watering of the course in the days preceding the race. The watering had in fact provoked some muted criticism from those who felt that the Curragh executive was bending over backwards to accommodate the going preference of the favourite, in that it was known that Old Vic was not at his best on firm ground. This tendency to like a cut in the ground is one that has been noted in most of the stock of Sadler's Wells.

As the horses were being loaded, supporters of Zayyani must have feared the worst as Walter Swinburn's mount was quite fractious in the stalls. Indeed as the stalls opened the Darshaan colt banged himself against the stalls, which can hardly have improved his chances. Straight from the outset it was Ile de Nisky and Pat Eddery who were first to show. After less than a furlong, however, Steve Cauthen pushed the favourite Old Vic into the lead. Dictating a relentless gallop Old Vic led the way, with Ile de Nisky and Observation Post tracking the favourite, and the rest of the field just about managing to keep tabs.

From a long way out supporters of the favourite were on good terms with themselves. Old Vic was clearly enjoying himself out in front and neither Pat Eddery on Ile de Nisky nor Willie Carson on Observation Post seemed to have enough horse under him to pose a serious challenge to the long-striding Sadler's Wells colt. The rest were already struggling. The order remained unchanged as the field galloped on past half-way, and at this point the four English-trained challengers led the four home-trained contenders.

Old Vic continued to lead into the straight going like a winner. Both Eddery and Carson on their respective mounts tried to raise a challenge to the front-running favourite, but neither made any significant impression on Old Vic. Although Cauthen had to shake up his mount to put paid to his nearest rivals, Old Vic pulled well clear in the run for home, and in the final stages the only question was who would be second.

It was Observation Post in fact who ran on best of the rest to finish a four length runner-up to the very easy winner. Ile de Nisky was two and a half lengths back in third place, and best of the Irish was Phantom Breeze who earned £24,000 for his connections by finishing fourth, a further five lengths away. Glowing Star was fifth, Zayyani a disappointing sixth (his antics at the start perhaps a factor), and Stone Drum won his private duel with Galliero in the battle to finish second last.

It had not been an exciting race; indeed it proved positively uneventful. However, the attraction of seeing an outstanding thoroughbred in action is one that purists will always relish, and Old Vic satisfied even the sternest critics with the ease of his victory. On the well-watered Curragh ground, the time was a particularly impressive 2 minutes 29.9 seconds. Doubtless if Old Vic had been asked a serious question, an even better time might have been recorded. In completing his Curragh victory Old Vic became only the second horse (the other was Assert) to win both the French and Irish Derbies.

The result was particularly noteworthy for jockey Steve Cauthen. As well as winning his first Irish Derby, Old Vic's success meant that the popular American became the first jockey ever to win the four principal Derbies — successes in the Kentucky, Epsom and French equivalents having preceded his Irish triumph.

Old Vic's success marked the arrival of Sadler's Wells as a stallion of the highest quality, and at this stage he would appear to be the natural successor to his sire, Northern Dancer. Though somewhat overshadowed in his three-year-old year by the exploits of both his stable companion, El Gran Senor, and by the Epsom Derby winner, Secreto, Sadler's Wells had campaigned very successfully for Vincent O'Brien, numbering the Irish 2,000 Guineas and the Eclipse Stakes among his triumphs. A resolute, game and genuine colt, Sadler's Wells, like his brilliant sire, has imbued all his stock with the attributes of toughness and courage. In the years following Old Vic's successes, Sadler's Wells went on to embellish his record as an outstanding sire, and this will be dealt with more thoroughly in a later chapter.

The dam of Old Vic was a mare called Cockade. It was clearly from Cockade that Old Vic derived his abundant stamina. When trained by Dick Hern, Cockade won only one small race, but that was over two miles. Cockade, though not very good herself, was very well related and was an own sister to the good-class milers, High Top and Camden Town. Her half sister Green Lucia was trained by the late John Oxx to finish second in both the Irish Oaks and the Yorkshire Oaks.

After the successes of Nashwan at Epsom and Old Vic at Chantilly and the Curragh, the racing world wondered if perhaps the two champions would ever meet. The possibility of a clash at Ascot in the King George VI and Queen Elizabeth Diamond Stakes was mooted, but as often happens, fate intervened to rule out any such projected encounter. Not long after his Curragh triumph Old Vic was cast in his box, pulled a muscle and was sidelined for the rest of the season.

This left the way open for Blushing Groom's son, Nashwan, to lord it over his rivals in the major all-aged races in the second half of the season, or at least it should have done. However, things did not work out quite as planned. Nashwan duly

won the King George at Ascot, but his performance in getting the better of Cacoethes by a neck on ground that should have suited him was frankly disappointing. Cacoethes was fully seven lengths behind Nashwan at Epsom, so either Cacoethes had improved or Nashwan had gone backwards. As Cacoethes subsequently proved disappointing, it would have been difficult to argue that Guy Harwood's colt had shown improved form at Ascot.

Nashwan was given a short rest and then prepared for the Arc. To test his well-being, Nashwan was sent over to Longchamp to contest the Group 2 Prix Niel over one and a half miles. Nashwan proved a sad disappointment, admittedly on softish ground which he didn't like, and was beaten two lengths into third place behind the formerly English-trained Golden Pheasant. It will be recalled that Old Vic had handed out a two and a half length beating to the self-same Golden Pheasant at Chester.

On the bare form lines it is certainly arguable that Old Vic was a better colt than Nashwan. The latter's record in winning the English 2,000 Guineas, Epsom Derby, Eclipse and King George is impressive, indeed unique, but there is a serious question mark over the quality of the opposition he met in those races. The case of Cacoethes has already been dealt with. To take another example, Terimon, who had finished a five length second at 500/1 to Nashwan at Epsom, did little afterwards to advertise the form. He finished down the field in a poor-class St Leger behind Michelozzo which was run at Ayr after the Doncaster course suffered subsidence problems. In any event, in the 1989 international classifications Old Vic was rated 3 lb better than Nashwan and, on the balance of their form, this seems fair.

After a long lay-off Old Vic returned to action as a four-year-old. His initial run was satisfactory, but no more than that. He finished a ten and three quarter length third of seven to Assatis in the Hardwicke Stakes at Royal Ascot. Ile de Nisky, who had been six and a half lengths behind Old Vic at the Curragh, was no less than ten lengths ahead of Old Vic in this, his comeback race. Sufficiently encouraged, connections then prepared Old Vic for a tilt at the King George VI and Queen Elizabeth Diamond Stakes. On ground that was probably a shade too fast for him, Old

Vic narrowly lost the Ascot show-piece, although he did reverse earlier form with Assatis, who was third.

The King George of 1990 will be dealt with in greater detail in the next chapter. Suffice to say that Old Vic lost nothing in defeat, although regrettably he did not run again after Ascot and was subsequently retired to stud. As a top-class son of a top-class stallion, it will be interesting to see how Old Vic's progeny perform in the years to come. Certainly for the crowds who had the pleasure of watching Old Vic perform at his very best at the Curragh on Budweiser Derby day 1989, he will be remembered fondly as among the best Irish Derby winners of recent years.

1M 4F

SUNDAY 2 JULY 1989

GOING: GOOD

WINNER: Sheikh Mohammed's Old Vic by Sadler's
Wells out of Cockade
S. Cauthen

SECOND: Observation Post by Shirley Heights out of
Godzilla
W. Carson

THIRD: Ile de Nisky by Ile de Bourbon out of Good
Lass
P. Eddery

S.P. 4/11f 12/1 5/1
Winner trained by H. R. A. Cecil

ALSO: Phantom Breeze 4th, Glowing Star 5th,
Zayyani 6th, Stone Drum 7th, Galliero 8th &
last

Winner: favourite
Distances: 4 lengths, 2½ lengths
Value to winner: £366, 500
Time: 2 m 29.9 s
Timeform rating of winner: 136.

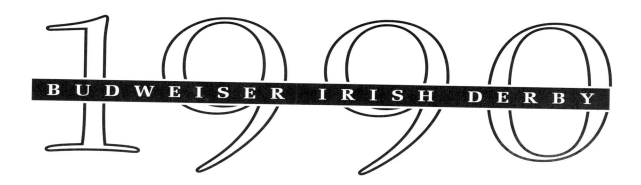

1990 BUDWEISER IRISH DERBY

THE CURRAGH 1 JULY 1990

In the racing calendar, 1 July 1990 was the date assigned for the fifth running of the Budweiser Irish Derby. The occasion, however, was somewhat overshadowed by the Soccer World Cup Italia '90 and in particular by the return on that very day to Dublin of Jack Charlton's heroes, where they received a reception unequalled in Irish sporting history. Though narrowly beaten at the quarter-final stage by the host nation, Italy, the Irish team — on their first entry on to the world stage — had both absorbed and thrilled an entire nation for a fortnight with their passionate and committed perform-ances. Certainly the almost surreal sense of national identity engendered by Ireland's marvellous contribution to Italia '90 will linger long in the memories of all those who participated, even if only as passive spectators, in the glorious voyage.

Notwithstanding the glamour of Ireland's World Cup involvement, the Budweiser Derby of 1990 turned out to be a race which also merited an entry in the sporting stories of the year and the reasons why will become apparent as the tale unfolds. Nine runners only went to post, but the race had a very competitive look to it. Only three of the contenders were Irish trained and in truth their chances of figuring at the business end of the race seemed remote. The remaining six runners all came from England and each, in varying degrees, could be fancied to take the first prize of over £366,000.

The Curragh race had received a late and unexpected boost with the decision by Sheikh Hamdan Al Maktoum to declare Salsibil, his dual classic heroine, in a bid to become the first filly for ninety years to win the Irish Derby. It should be pointed out of course that comparatively few fillies had taken part in the Irish Derby. In the period since the inaugura-tion of sponsorship the only members of the fair sex to have competed in the premier classic were Cervinia in 1963, All Saved in 1964 and Triptych in 1985. Although none of the three had succeeded in reaching a place, all had run respectably, All Saved and Triptych both finishing fifth, with Cervinia ninth in her year.

Salsibil had been a top-class juvenile and had ended her two-year-old campaign with a splendid success in the Group 1 Prix Marcel Boussac at Longchamp. After an impressive victory in the Fred Darling Stakes at Newbury on her reappearance, Salsibil had had to work a bit to get the better of Heart of Joy by three-quarters of a length in the 1,000 Guineas at Newmarket.

The daughter of Sadler's Wells had shown such speed in her career to that point that many doubted if she would have the stamina for the mile and a half distance of the Oaks. These doubts were reinforced when Epsom suffered three days of rain in the lead-up to the Oaks, but in the event Salsibil allayed any fears about her stamina with a comprehensive five length defeat of Game Plan.

Salsibil had done everything asked of her, but the Curragh represented the acid test. Was she as good as the colts? Had she really beaten anything of note? These questions would most certainly be answered, for among the opposition at the Curragh was the Epsom Derby winner, Quest For Fame. In the first ever clash of the winners of the Epsom Derby and Oaks in an Irish classic, the preponderance of opinion favoured the colt over the filly.

By the Arc winner and 1984 Sweeps Derby runner-up, Rainbow Quest, out of Aryenne, a winner of the French 1,000 Guineas, Quest For Fame was a quite lightly raced colt whose Curragh run would be only

the fifth of his career. In his only outing as a two-year-old, Quest For Fame had been second to Tyburn Tree in a maiden at Newbury in October. The Khalid Abdulla-owned colt returned to Newbury for his three-year-old début and registered a one and a half length victory over Dress Parade over one mile and three furlongs.

Quest For Fame announced his arrival in the big time with a one length second to Belmez in the Chester Vase over a mile and a half. It was a three-horse race and the value of the form seemed questionable at the time, but subsequent events proved otherwise. At Epsom on his fourth ever run, Quest For Fame showed the worth of the Chester form by winning the Derby by three lengths from Blue Stag, with Kaheel four lengths back in fourth place. Both Blue Stag and Kaheel were in opposition again, but there seemed no good reason why the Epsom form should be overturned.

The mount of Pat Eddery, Quest For Fame was bidding to win an unprecedented third Derby for his first-season trainer, 40-year-old Roger Charlton. Besides Quest For Fame's Epsom win, Charlton and Eddery had also combined to win the French Derby at Chantilly with Sanglamore. There was some debate as to whether Quest For Fame or Sanglamore was the better of the Derby winners, but that question would have to wait for another day.

The partnership of trainer Barry Hills and owner Robert Sangster had had a number of placed efforts in previous attempts to win the Irish Derby (Hills had of course trained the 1987 winner, Sir Harry Lewis). Hawaiian Sound in 1978, Glacial Storm in 1988 and

Observation Post in 1989 had all come close but not close enough, and Blue Stag, with Michael Kinane on board, was their representative on this occasion. Another likely raced colt, Blue Stag, would, like Quest For Fame, be having only his fifth ever outing at the Curragh.

Fifth on his initial two-year-old outing, Blue Stag next appeared at Nottingham where he beat Snurge by no less than twelve and a half lengths. Snurge, it should be noted, went on as a three-year-old to win the Doncaster St Leger and also finished a very good third in the Prix de l'Arc de Triomphe. Blue Stag, who like Salsibil was also by Sadler's Wells, was successful on his three-year-old début, beating Saumarez by three-quarters of a length in the Dee Stakes over an extended ten furlongs at Chester. It appeared to be a good recommendation for future success to be beaten by Blue Stag, for Saumarez of course went on to win the Arc later in the season! Following his Chester victory, Blue Stag came up against Quest For Fame at Epsom. His Derby second appeared to represent a step up in form, but further improvement was obviously needed if Blue Stag was to reverse placings with Quest For Fame at the Curragh.

The maiden Kaheel, who started at 33/1, had surprised by finishing fourth behind Quest For Fame at Epsom. His previous outings — second to Shavian as a two-year-old, and third to Lord Florey at Kempton as a three-year-old — were no more than promising. Alec Stewart's colt was clearly improving, but history suggested that Michael Roberts's mount had a lot to do at the Curragh.

A more interesting challenger from Newmarket was Henry Cecil's Belmez, a colt by El Gran Senor. With a victory over Quest For Fame to his credit, on paper Belmez's chances appeared second to none. However, the one-time Epsom Derby favourite had suffered a setback and had been forced to miss the English classic. Reports from the gallops were a little discouraging: there were suggestions that Belmez had yet to recapture his best form. None the less, having tasted Irish classic success the previous year with Old Vic, Henry Cecil would scarcely have saddled Belmez unless he was satisfied that his unbeaten colt was fit enough to do himself justice.

The other English runner was Deploy who, like Quest For Fame, was trained by Roger Charlton and owned by Khalid Abdulla. Deploy was expected to make the running for his stablemate, but his chances could not be entirely discounted. The forecast cut in the ground would suit the colt by the 1978 dual Derby winner, Shirley Heights, and his victory when giving 6 lb and a half-length beating to Down The Flag over twelve furlongs at Leicester certainly suggested that Deploy would have no trouble with the trip. As mentioned earlier, there were three Irish-trained runners — Alterezza, Emperor Chang and Super Flame — but only a super optimist could have fancied their chances.

On ground that was officially described as yielding, the betting on the race was quite intriguing. Even though connections had suggested that Quest For Fame was at his best with ground conditions on top, Roger Charlton's colt was heavily supported from

6/4 to a very tight 5/4. In the face of this support, Salsibil, put in at 7/4, eased out to 3/1 before firming slightly to 11/4 at the off. The pre-race rumours about Belmez's fitness certainly did not deter his backers, for he was the subject of sustained support from 6/1 down to 4/1. Blue Stag was in demand at 5/1, but there was little interest in the remainder. Deploy was sent off a 16/1 shot, while Kaheel was a 20/1 chance. The Irish trio were on offer at fancy prices.

The early pattern of the race followed expected lines. Walter Swinburn took Deploy straight into the lead. The rest of the field were tightly grouped in behind the front runner, with all the fancied runners close to the pace. Deploy's stable companion, the favourite Quest For Fame, moved into second place after about half a mile, with Blue Stag, Salsibil and Belmez all very much in touch. There was little enough change in the order as the field galloped on towards the straight.

Turning into the straight it was anybody's race. The order was Deploy, Quest For Fame, Blue Stag, Salsibil and Belmez. A little surprisingly, Deploy continued to put it up to his rivals, and even more surprisingly, the front runner's stable companion, the hot favourite Quest For Fame, was under severe pressure from Pat Eddery early on in the straight and was not looking anything like a winner.

Meantime the jockeys on both Blue Stag and Belmez were hard at work, and it was Willie Carson on Salsibil who appeared at the two furlong marker to have the most horse under him. Deploy still led, but with about a furlong and a half remaining, Carson asked Salsibil to go for her race. The filly quickly closed the gap between herself and Deploy, and racing on the outside of Walter Swinburn's mount, took the lead with about a furlong to go.

Although Deploy kept on very gamely, Carson was able to keep his filly going with hands and heels, and throughout the final furlong Salsibil never looked like surrendering her lead. At the line John Dunlop's filly had three-quarters of a length to spare over Deploy, who had surpassed all expectations in finishing second. Belmez, who was third, a further four lengths back, ran a fine race, but the pre-race rumours about his lack of match fitness seemed to have been borne out by his performance. Blue Stag finished a half-length further back in fourth place having had every chance, and Quest For Fame was a disappointing fifth, a neck behind Blue Stag, never threatening to take a hand in the final furlong. The Irish runners were, as expected, outclassed.

Although it had been ninety years since Gallinaria had won for her sex in the Irish Derby, Salsibil stamped her authority on the top colts of her year in unforgettable fashion. Praise was unstinting for the daughter of Sadler's Wells in the wake of her triumph. Although reluctant to make comparisons with his 1989 Epsom Derby winner, Nashwan, Willie Carson was adamant that Salsibil was the best filly he had ever ridden, and he added that she had more class than Troy, the impressive dual Derby winner of 1979. John Dunlop, who had saddled Shirley Heights to dual Derby success in 1978, was quite forthright in his assessment of Salsibil: 'She is the best animal I have ever trained and is quite outstanding.'

If Salsibil's victory was a triumph for the connections, it was no less so for her sire, the astonishingly successful Sadler's Wells. Brief details of the Northern Dancer colt's racing career were set out in the chapter on the 1984 race. Salsibil's success meant that the former Vincent O'Brien-trained colt had sired the winners of successive Irish Derbies from his first and second crops, a truly remarkable achievement.

Salsibil was well bred on the distaff side, for her dam was Flame Of Tara, who herself had been a top-class racehorse. Bred by Ms Pat O'Kelly at the Kilcarn Stud in County Meath (the same stud was also responsible for the 1966 Irish Derby winner, Sodium), Salsibil was Flame of Tara's second foal. Her first foal was Nearctic Flame, who had finished third in the 1989 running of the Ribblesdale Stakes at Royal Ascot. Flame Of Tara was by Artaius, and numbered among her successes the Coronation Stakes at Royal Ascot and the Pretty Polly Stakes at the Curragh.

This is an appropriate point to take a closer look at the tremendous success story of the Coolmore-based stallion, Sadler's Wells. At the time of writing (January 1995), horses sired by Sadler's Wells have won no less than thirty Group 1 or Grade 1 races in just seven seasons. For the record, the winners and races were as follows:

Brashee (Prix Royal Oak)
French Glory (Rothmans International)
In The Wings (Coronation Cup, Breeders Cup Turf, Grand Prix de Saint-Cloud)
Old Vic (French Derby, Irish Derby)
Prince of Dance (Dewhurst Stakes)
Scenic (Dewhurst Stakes)

Salsibil (Prix Marcel Boussac, 1,000 Guineas, Epsom Oaks, Irish Derby, Prix Vermeille)
Saddler's Hall (Coronation Cup)
El Prado (National Stakes)
Johann Quartz (Prix Lupin)
Masad (Gran Premio d'Italia)
Fatherland (National Stakes)
Barathea (Irish 2,000 Guineas, Breeder's Cup Mile)
Opera House (Coronation Cup, Eclipse Stakes, King George VI and Queen Elizabeth Diamond Stakes)
Intrepidity (Prix Saint Alary, Epsom Oaks, Prix Vermeille)
King's Theatre (Racing Post Trophy, King George VI and Queen Elizabeth Diamond Stakes)
Carnegie (Prix de l'Arc de Triomphe)

An even more remarkable feature of this list is that eighteen of the thirty successes were in races over a mile and a half — remarkable, because Sadler's Wells himself never won over a mile and a half. As is abundantly clear, when the progeny of Sadler's Wells are blended with the right type of female staying blood, stamina is all but guaranteed. From the above list, of course, it will be noted that Salsibil won more Group 1 contests than any other of Sadler's Wells' immensely successful offspring.

A brief word about Deploy, runner-up to Salsibil in the Irish Derby. His breeding is worth a closer look. By Shirley Heights out of Slightly Dangerous, breeder Khalid Abdulla so nearly got it right with his mix of Derby winner and Epsom Oaks runner-up. (Slightly Dangerous finished second to Time Charter in 1982.) After Deploy's near miss, the Prince tried again with Slightly Dangerous and sent the mare to a colt who was probably the best horse since the war not to win a Derby. This time he hit the jackpot. More of that in a later chapter.

If Salsibil had lived up to her owner's highest expectations, the Epsom Derby winner Quest For Fame was, by contrast, a sad disappointment at the Curragh. According to Pat Eddery, his horse was never moving well and was struggling to go the pace after only two furlongs. This seems a slight exaggeration and the probability was that Quest For Fame simply didn't like the softish ground. Subsequent events also tended to suggest that Quest For Fame had won a distinctly substandard Epsom Derby. Khalid Abdulla's colt didn't run again as a three-year-old after his Curragh flop. He returned to action as a four-year-old, but didn't enjoy conspicuous success. Probably his best effort was to finish third in the Breeder's Cup Turf over one and a half miles to the French filly Miss Alleged at Churchill Downs in 1991.

After her early season heroics, Salsibil was given a rest with the objective of proving her worth against all-aged opposition in the Prix de l'Arc de Triomphe. The Prix Vermeille at Longchamp over one and a half miles was chosen for Salsibil's Arc preparatory race. In quite a tight finish Salsibil came out on top, but she had only a neck and a half-length to spare over the aforementioned Miss Alleged and the English-trained In The Groove. Connections professed themselves satisfied with Salsibil's performance, although some observers felt that the filly didn't have a lot in reserve at the end of the race. Suspicions that perhaps Salsibil had gone over the top were proved correct when Hamdan Al Maktoum's exceptional filly could finish only tenth of twenty-one to Saumarez in the Arc. Interestingly, one of her Curragh victims, Belmez, finished five places in front of Salsibil at Longchamp in fifth place. Prior to her Arc disappointment Salsibil had run eight times and had won seven of these, finishing second in the other race.

Belmez, prior to his Arc run, had himself added considerable lustre to Salsibil's Curragh triumph with a battling success in the King George VI and Queen Elizabeth Diamond Stakes. As mentioned in the previous chapter, Belmez narrowly got the better of his front-running stable companion, Old Vic, by a neck in a driving finish. The going at Ascot undoubtedly favoured Belmez more than Old Vic, but it was none the less a top-class performance by the winner and one that tended to support the view that had Sheikh Mohammed's colt not got injured and instead been able to line up at Epsom, he would probably have beaten Quest For Fame. Indeed, it is arguable that a fully fit Belmez might have made Salsibil work a lot harder at the Curragh to claim the Budweiser Derby.

All that is speculation. What is fact is that at her mid-summer peak Salsibil was a marvellous filly, one of the best of her sex to appear on a racecourse over the past several decades. Good enough at her best to be ranked with those great French racehorses of the 1970s, Dahlia and Allez France, her history-making performance at the Curragh on 1 July 1990 will ensure that Salsibil long retains a permanent place in racing's hall of fame.

1M 4F

SUNDAY 1 JULY 1990

GOING: YIELDING

WINNER: Hamdan Al Maktoum's Salsibil by Sadler's
Wells out of Flame Of Tara
W. Carson

SECOND: Deploy by Shirley Heights out of Slightly
Dangerous
W. R. Swinburn

THIRD: Belmez by El Gran Senor out of Grace Note
S. Cauthen

S.P. 11/4   16/1   4/1
Winner trained by J. L. Dunlop

ALSO: Blue Stag 4th, Quest For Fame 5th, Super
Flame 6th, Emperor Chang 7th, Kaheel 8th,
Alterezza 9th & last

Quest For Fame 5/4 fav
Winner: 2nd favourite
Distances: ¾ length, 4 lengths
Value to winner: £309,500
Time: 2 m 33 s
Timeform rating of winner: 130.

BUDWEISER IRISH DERBY

Only six runners went to post for the 1991 renewal of the Budweiser Irish Derby. However, what the field lacked in quantity was more than made up for in quality. Bringing together the winners of the English and French Derbies, the Irish Derby could in 1991 justifiably claim to be the true championship test of the season for the classic generation.

The almost certain favourite was the Epsom Derby winner, Generous. To say that Generous was impressive at Epsom is to understate the tremendous ease of his victory. Taking over from the front-running Mystiko early in the straight, Generous strode away from the opposition and at the finish was five lengths clear of Marju, with a further seven lengths back to the third horse home, Star of Gdansk, whose connections had boldly decided to take on the winner again at the Curragh.

Prior to his Epsom triumph, Generous had run only once as a three-year-old and that was in the 2,000 Guineas at Newmarket. There, ridden by Richard Quinn, Generous had performed with great credit in finishing fourth to Mystiko, beaten about nine lengths. It was expected that he would improve for his first outing of the season, but few expected the improvement to be quite so dramatic.

It was shortly after the Newmarket 2,000 Guineas that Prince Fahd Salman, owner of Generous and principal patron of the Paul Cole stable, dispensed with the services of Richard Quinn and engaged 24-year-old Alan Munro to ride all his horses. The new partnership got off to the perfect start with Generous's Epsom victory, although many obervers felt that Quinn had been hard done by.

As a juvenile Generous had been campaigned with commendable openness. Bucking the trend of the late 1980s, Generous had been on the go from early in the season and in fact ran six times as a two-year-old. His early season form was good, if not exceptional. He ran at Royal Ascot and finished a good second to Mac's Imp in the Coventry Stakes. After a disappointing third in the Lanson Champagne Stakes at Goodwood, it was said that the heat and the flies had upset the colt in the preliminaries.

Generous was next sent to Deauville to contest the prestigious Prix Morny. Once again he disappointed, finishing a thirteen and a half length tenth to the precocious colt, Hector Protector, and though excuses were made for him, it was beginning to look as if the son of Caerleon would not fulfil his early season promise. Paul Cole, however, never lost faith in his charge and Generous began his rehabilitation in the Reference Point Stakes over a mile at Sandown with a comfortable win over the débutante, Rahdari.

It was in the final race of the season, however, that Generous showed that his trainer's high opinion of him was thoroughly justified. His overall form ensured that he was sent off a 50/1 outsider for the Dewhurst Stakes at Newmarket, but showing himself to be a very game and genuine colt Generous outstayed the opposition and won by three-quarters of a length from Bog Trotter. In the process he punctured quite a few lofty reputations. Generous incidentally was the longest-priced winner ever in the 115-year history of the Dewhurst Stakes.

The popular opinion after Generous's shock win was that it was a substandard Dewhurst, unlikely to shed much light on the classic picture for the following year. Not for the first time were racing fans to find cause to regret the error of ignoring racecourse form.

The principal opponent for Generous at the Curragh was the French Derby winner Suave Dancer. Unlike Generous, Suave Dancer was lightly raced as a juvenile and showed little enough on his only run, finishing a moderate third in a poor race. As a three-year-old, though, Suave Dancer blossomed.

After winning his maiden, Suave Dancer next contested the Group 2 Prix Greffulhe at Longchamp. For the first time Suave Dancer demonstrated in the Greffulhe that impressive turn of foot that was to become his trademark, and over the extended ten furlong trip he beat Beau Sultan and Toulon by four lengths and three-quarters of a length. Toulon, it is worth noting, went on to win the Doncaster St Leger. In his next race Suave Dancer was surprisingly beaten by three-quarters of a length by Cudas in the Group 1 Prix Lupin, again over ten furlongs at Longchamp.

Jockey Cash Asmussen accepted the blame for that defeat, believing that he gave his inexperienced mount too much to do in the closing stages. That theory was emphatically vindicated when Suave Dancer went on to take his revenge on Cudas in the French Derby (the Prix du Jockey-Club) over one and a half miles at Chantilly. Displaying a quite astonishing turn of foot, Suave Dancer simply brushed the opposition aside and won easing up by four lengths and one and a half lengths from Subotica and Cudas. Bearing in mind Subotica's subsequent career, the value of the form cannot be underestimated.

There were those who pointed out that the time for the French Derby — 2 minutes 27.4 seconds — on ground described as good to firm, was quite slow and this they suggested put a question mark against the form. Time experts, however, retorted by pointing out that the last three furlongs were covered in a very fast 34.4 seconds. None the less, because of the manner in which the French Derby was run, some pundits questioned Suave Dancer's ability to get the Curragh mile and a half on ground that would be softer than at Chantilly.

Suave Dancer's sire was Green Dancer, who was a high-class colt but a non-stayer. Green Dancer won the French 2,000 Guineas and the Prix Lupin in 1975, but he failed famously to stay the Derby trip at Epsom. Suave Dancer's dam was Sauvite, who was by Alleged, usually an influence for stamina, and because of this there appeared to be every chance that her son could stay a true run mile and a half race.

Unfortunately for Cash Asmussen, a broken collar bone prevented him from riding Suave Dancer at the Curragh. However, a better substitute than Walter Swinburn, with two Irish Derby successes to his credit (Shareef Dancer in 1983 and Shahrastani in 1986), could not have been imagined.

The big two appeared to dominate the race, but a couple of other runners could be given some chance of upsetting the two Derby winners. Vincent O'Brien's Sportsworld, running in the Classic Thoroughbred plc colours, was an unbeaten Alleged colt whose true worth was hard to gauge. Unraced as a juvenile, Sportsworld won his maiden over seven furlongs at the Curragh on yielding ground at the end of March. He next won a listed race over ten furlongs again at the Curragh, beating

Zivania by one and a half lengths, without impressing all observers.

His performance, however, in the Group 2 Windfields Farm Gallinule Stakes over ten furlongs was far more authoritative. A four length and six length victory over Runyon and Blue Daisy suggested that Sportsworld was improving with his racing, and he had to be given a realistic chance in the Derby. It was noted by some that Blue Daisy, beaten ten lengths by Sportsworld, had previously been just five lengths behind that very good filly, Kooyonga, in the Irish 1,000 Guineas, adding some lustre to the form. With Lester Piggott renewing his classic acquaintance with Vincent O'Brien, there would have been no more popular winning combination.

The fourth member of the field to rate serious mention was the aforementioned Star of Gdansk. All of twelve lengths behind Generous at Epsom, Star of Gdansk had a lot of ground to make up on the Epsom winner, but it was anticipated that the Curragh track would suit him better than Epsom. Certainly the Jim Bolger-trained colt had run very well over the course in the Irish 2,000 Guineas when just failing to hold on against the US-trained Fourstars Allstar, going down by a head.

The two remaining members of the field were rank outsiders with no realistic prospect of winning. However, with prize money of £18,000 for the fifth home and £12,000 for the sixth to finish, the connections of Nordic Admirer, in the race presumably to act as pacemaker for his stable companion Star of Gdansk, and Barry's Run, a maiden and strong favourite to finish last, were set to be handsomely rewarded for their enterprise in competing.

The going at the Curragh was officially yielding and this may have significantly influenced the betting market. In the week preceding the race there had been some speculation as to whether Generous or Suave Dancer would start favourite, but with the going placing the emphasis firmly on stamina, punters plumped solidly for the Alan Munro-partnered Generous. See-sawing between even money and 4/5, Generous was returned at the longer price. Suave Dancer eased by fractions from 7/4 and was returned at 9/4 at the off. There was very good support for the Irish hope, Sportsworld, and after touching 3's from opening offers of 4's, he settled at 100/30. Star of Gdansk eased to 12/1 from 10's, and the other two were running for the bookmakers.

The six runners were installed without any mishaps and the field was dispatched promptly. The early pace was made by the outsider Barry's Run, with Kevin Manning up. Generous was close up, together with Nordic Admirer and Sportsworld, while Star of Gdansk and Suave Dancer were held up in rear. The decisive moment in the race arrived as early as the mile marker when Alan Munro on Generous, sensing that the pace was too slow and not designed to bring out the best in his charge, sent the Caerleon colt into the lead.

Quickening the pace, Generous was soon two lengths ahead of the early pacemaker, Barry's Run, with Nordic Admirer and Sportsworld close behind, tracked by Star of Gdansk and Suave Dancer. Generous and Munro continued to pile on the pace and the partnership was three lengths to the good

over Sportsworld as the field made its way downhill to the straight.

Generous led into the straight, with Sportsworld and Lester Piggott still travelling easily in second place and Suave Dancer now third, having made smooth progress from the rear. Early in the straight Sportsworld's stamina suddenly gave way and Lester Piggott's mount was passed by Walter Swinburn on Suave Dancer who set off in pursuit of Alan Munro and Generous. Suave Dancer closed the gap on Generous, and a furlong and a half out almost drew level with the leader. A roar of anticipation from the packed enclosures greeted the move, and for a few strides it looked as if the French champion would go past Generous. But the gallant Irish-bred Epsom winner dug deep and courageously fought off Suave Dancer's challenge. In the final furlong Generous went away from his rival and at the post had a convincing three lengths to spare.

Star of Gdansk ran on under pressure to finish in third place, repeating his Epsom effort, and on this occasion getting fractionally closer to Generous. Sportsworld, who plainly didn't stay, was a further two lengths back fourth, and the other two runners completed in their own good time. It had been a fine race and there was generous applause (no pun intended) from the Curragh crowd as the high-class winner and gallant runner-up returned to the unsaddling area. On the day there was no doubting which of the two horses was the best and Walter Swinburn made no excuses for Suave Dancer, pointing out simply that he had been outstayed by the winner.

For trainer Paul Cole and indeed owner Fahd Salman, Generous's success more than made up for their bad luck with Insan in 1988. In fact both owner and trainer must by now have a soft spot for the headquarters of Irish racing. Their first classic successes were in the year preceding Generous's triumphs, with Knight's Baroness in the Irish Oaks and Ibn Bey in the Irish St Leger.

Generous was bred at the Barronstown Stud quite near to the Curragh and is easily the best colt sired to date by the French Derby winner and Irish Derby runner-up Caerleon. Generous's dam was Doff The Derby by the Preakness Stakes winner Master Derby and her son was sold as a foal for 80,000 guineas and later on as a yearling at Goff's Cartier Million sales for 200,000 guineas. Generous is from the same family as Triptych, that most durable high-class mare of the mid-1980s, and he certainly inherited the same strain of toughness that she possessed. By today's standards Generous was an absolute snip at his price and it will be interesting to see how his progeny fare on the racecourse.

After the Curragh set-to, different plans of campaign were mapped out for the two principals. Generous was aimed at the traditional mid-summer high point, the King George VI and Queen Elizabeth Diamond Stakes, while Suave Dancer was given a rest with the object of coming back to contest the Prix de l'Arc de Triomphe. Explaining his decision, trainer John Hammond said that Suave Dancer was still immature and inexperienced and he had had to be rushed a bit to take his place at the Curragh. Hammond was of the view that Suave Dancer had more improvement in him.

Generous meantime embellished his reputation further with a tremendously impressive performance in the Ascot feature. He dismissed his rivals with contemptuous ease as he strode to a seven length victory over the 1990 French Derby winner Sanglamore. He was put aside then, the intention being to prepare him for the October show-piece at Longchamp. After his Ascot victory many racing scribes could not envisage defeat for Generous in the Arc and he was a warm favourite with English bookmakers to round off his three-year-old campaign in style in Paris.

After his summer break Suave Dancer returned to action and the Leopardstown Champion Stakes was chosen as his preparatory race for the Arc. Run over ten furlongs Suave Dancer, now reunited with Cash Asmussen, did not appear to have a lot to beat, although the Eclipse winner Environment Friend was in the field. As odds-on shots go, 4/6 was a good price about Suave Dancer and he absolutely hacked up showing a quite devastating turn of foot to put the issue beyond doubt in a matter of strides half-way up the straight.

The stage was set then for a second clash between Generous and Suave Dancer, this time at Longchamp, and the debate between supporters of the two colts gathered momentum as the big day drew near. The story of the Prix de l'Arc de Triomphe is easily enough told. Though fourteen went to post, all eyes were on the big two. Generous was always to the fore and took up the running some way out. Suave Dancer as usual was held up by Asmussen and his supporters must have been more than a little anxious as his jockey made no move to improve his position even as the horses began the long sweep towards home.

The writing was on the wall for the dual Derby winner early in the straight as Generous, to the dismay of his backers, dropped tamely away. Meantime Suave Dancer, kept to the outside by Asmussen to avoid trouble, produced a superb burst of acceleration to power past his rivals in a matter of strides. A supremely impressive winner, Suave Dancer had vindicated his trainer's mid-summer opinion that he needed more time to reach his full potential. In winning at Longchamp, Suave Dancer incidentally became the first horse since Mill Reef to win both a Derby and an Arc in the same season. For the record, Generous finished eighth at Longchamp, beaten nine lengths in all by Suave Dancer.

The result at Longchamp intensified the debate as to which of the two, Generous or Suave Dancer, was the better three-year-old. Supporters of Generous pointed to his magnificent trio of successes in mid-summer at Epsom, the Curragh and Ascot, and wouldn't countenance the suggestion that he could be inferior to the John Hammond-trained colt. However, Suave Dancer's overall form was very impressive. His French Derby form stood up to the closest examination and his Arc victory was a performance of the highest class.

The official handicappers put Generous 1 lb ahead of Suave Dancer in the international classifications, although other form students saw things differently. A difficulty in assessing the merits of the two champions was that they had very different styles of running. Generous was a strong-running colt who at his best galloped the opposition into the ground, whereas Suave Dancer possessed a classic turn of foot which was quite as devastating as any seen in recent years.

Perhaps the fairest assessment is that 1991 was a vintage year, throwing up two colts who stood head and shoulders above their contemporaries. In Ireland, patrons at the Curragh were privileged to see both these top-class colts in action on the last Sunday in June. It was fitting too that for the first time in the history of the Irish Derby the English and French Derby winners finished first and second. Generous was superior to his rival on that day at the Curragh, but few could convincingly argue that Suave Dancer at his best was not his match.

1M 4F
SUNDAY 30 JUNE 1991
GOING: YIELDING

WINNER: Fahd Salman's Generous by Caerleon out of Doff The Derby
A. Munro

SECOND: Suave Dancer by Green Dancer out of Suavite
W. R. Swinburn

THIRD: Star of Gdansk by Danzig Connection out of Star Empress
C. Roche

S.P. Evens f   9/4   12/1
Winner trained by P. F. I. Cole

ALSO: Sportsworld 4th, Nordic Admirer 5th, Barry's Run 6th & last

Winner: favourite
Distances: 3 lengths, 8 lengths
Value to winner: £361,500
Time: 2 m 33.3 s
Timeform rating of winner: 139.

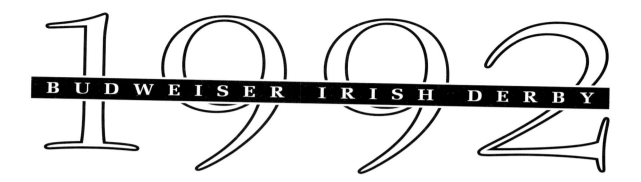

1992

B U D W E I S E R   I R I S H   D E R B Y

THE CURRAGH 28 JUNE 1992

Dr Devious was the outsider of trainer Peter Chapple-Hyam's two runners in the Epsom Derby of 1992. Rodrigo de Triano, partnered by Lester Piggott, had triumphed in memorable fashion in the Newmarket 2,000 Guineas and once declared to run by Robert Sangster in the Epsom Derby it was always likely that the partnership would start a sentimental favourite. As a result, the focus of public attention tended to shift away from stable companion Dr Devious and he started an 8/1 chance for the Epsom spectacular.

A consistent two-year-old, Dr Devious had sprung a bit of a surprise with a game win in the Dewhurst Stakes at Newmarket, but the conventional wisdom was that the 1991 race was a substandard affair. Race fans tend to have short memories, for much the same verdict was handed down about the 1990 Dewhurst winner, Generous.

At any rate Dr Devious returned to action as a three-year-old and on his first outing finished a meritorious runner-up to Alnasar Alwasheek in the Craven Stakes at Newmarket. Eschewing the usual European classic trail, the American-owned Dr Devious was then dispatched to the United States in an ambitious attempt to win the Kentucky Derby. The brave venture ended in failure: Dr Devious was a somewhat disappointing seventh in the American classic and returned from Churchill Downs with a lung full of dirt as a souvenir.

Apart from his unorthodox preparation, many pundits ruled Dr Devious out of consideration for Epsom on the grounds that his sire was the sprinter Ahonoora. The Doctor's critics were to be proved spectacularly wrong. Clearly deriving his stamina from his maternal grandsire, the dual Arc winner Alleged, Dr Devious credited his young second-season trainer with a splendid and most convincing victory in the Epsom Derby. In the process he foiled a massive and misplaced public gamble on stable companion Rodrigo de Triano, who patently failed to stay the Derby trip.

In winning at Epsom by two lengths from the Irish-trained St Jovite, the Ahonoora colt had proved that he was as tough as old boots. There seemed little doubt but that the Curragh, his next port of call, would suit Peter Chapple-Hyam's colt ideally.

Connections of the Epsom runner-up, St Jovite, were however looking forward keenly to renewing rivalry with the Derby winner. Trainer Jim Bolger was adamant that his colt had not been 100 per cent at Epsom (he had suffered a minor setback prior to the race) and apart from that he believed that his American-bred colt had been unsuited to Epsom's undulations. In addition, there was a theory that St Jovite was more at home on a right-handed track and so the Curragh would suit him better than Epsom. Another factor was the going. It had been good to soft at Epsom. The ground was certain to be faster at the Curragh and St Jovite's connections were understood to believe that this would favour their colt.

The formbook, however, made out a less convincing case for the Epsom runner-up. He was the champion two-year-old in Ireland, sure enough, but the strength of the 1991 Irish two-year-old crop was not adjudged to be of vintage quality. However, St Jovite had posted notice of considerable potential when on his final outing of the season he had finished a respectable fourth to 'wonder horse' Arazi in the Grand Criterium at Longchamp.

St Jovite's first outing as a three-year-old was a disaster. In heavy ground at the Curragh and over a trip (seven furlongs) far

short of his best, St Jovite had finished a well-beaten fourth to the Con Collins-trained Bezelle in the Gladness Stakes. He subsequently won the ten furlong Derrinstown Stud Derby Trial Stakes at Leopardstown, but had to be fairly energetically ridden by Christy Roche to dispose of some modest opponents.

The Jim Bolger-trained colt's next outing was at Epsom and his starting price of 14/1 seemed accurately to reflect his chances. While St Jovite had performed splendidly at Epsom, it must be recorded that he had been under strong pressure from some way out in the race and on the face of it there seemed little reason to suppose that he could turn the tables on his Epsom conqueror.

Besides the two principals, nine other colts lined up for the Budweiser Derby. In all there were four Irish contenders, four also from England and three from France. Of the three French-trained colts, Marignan and Contested Bid had met in the French Derby (the Prix du Jockey-Club), in which they had finished in second and third places respectively to Polytain. At Chantilly, Marignan, trained by André Fabre, had finished three-quarters of a length in front of the Maurice Zilber-trained Contested Bid, but the latter was fancied by some to reverse placings with Marignan at the Curragh. By Alleged, Contested Bid had, prior to his Chantilly run, been a good second to Johann Quartz in the Prix Lupin and both the track and the trip were thought likely to suit him.

The other French runner was Dive For Cover trained by John Hammond who had saddled Suave Dancer to finish second to Generous in the 1991 Budweiser Derby.

In fact, Hammond had only taken over the colt after his juvenile campaign from Mrs Jenny Ramsden, for whom Dive For Cover had won his only race by six lengths at Ayr. Three outings in France as a three-year-old had failed to produce a win and he looked to have no more than an outsider's chance.

Of the English runners, the two who merited closest attention were the John Gosden-trained Landowner and Michael Stoute's Ezzoud. The former, owned by Sheikh Mohammed, must have been showing something special on the gallops, for he was a late supplementary entry for the Derby at a cost of £75,000. If the Sheikh was to recoup his outlay, Landowner would have to finish no worse than second at the Curragh. His form had a progressive look to it. After successes in Windsor and Goodwood handicaps, Landowner had stepped up in class to run away with the Group 3 Queen's Vase at Royal Ascot. Although out of the miler, Kris, like Dr Devious his dam was by Alleged and so stamina was not an issue. Had he got the requisite class, though? Only the race would tell.

Michael Stoute, always a man to be respected at the Curragh, was represented by Ezzoud, the mount of Walter Swinburn. Ezzoud had run well in the St James's Palace Stakes at Royal Ascot, finishing a close-up third to Dermot Weld's top miler, Brief Truce. Although by the sprinter Last Tycoon, Ezzoud too was stoutly bred on the distaff side and the trip was not thought likely to pose a problem.

Sunday 28 June 1992 was a glorious day. Very warm, it was no doubt providential that a balmy breeze brought relief to the crowds who thronged the Curragh from early in the day. The warm sun and drying breeze ensured that the ground for the running of the Budweiser Irish Derby was good, fast ground. No excuse could be entertained for any of the runners on account of the going.

Betting on the Derby centred on the two principals. Although rumours had circulated about Dr Devious's well-being in the week preceding the race, on the day the big punters got stuck in. Anything better than 5/4 on was always availed of, and indeed the Doctor touched 8/11 at times before settling at the first-named price. St Jovite, who was put in at 3's, eased fractionally to 7/2.

Many had expected that St Jovite would be stronger in the betting market than turned out to be the case. What the pundits had overlooked was the evidence of recent history. Irish racing followers, who had not seen an Irish-trained winner of the country's premier classic since Law Society's victory in 1985, had long since ceased to be inspired by purely patriotic sentiments when putting down their cash.

Despite the strength of the first and second favourites, there was significant money in the ring for Sheikh Mohammed's Landowner. Backed from 12/1 down to 7's, clearly some punters believed that the Sheikh was going to draw a substantial dividend on his £75,000 supplementary fee. Ezzoud, despite some support, eased out to 10's from opening offers of 7/1. Of the two French challengers, both returned at 11/1, Contested Bid was the stronger, touching 10's from 12's, while Marignan drifted out from 8's. It was 20/1 bar these six.

Mention should be made at this point of the curious prelude to the Derby involving St Jovite's jockey, Christy Roche. Best remembered internationally as the man who, on Secreto, had so sensationally inflicted defeat on hot favourite El Gran Senor in the 1984 Epsom Derby, Roche became embroiled in a long drawn out feud with the Irish racing authorities in the period leading up to the Budweiser Derby. Suspended as a result of an incident in a race at Naas, Roche fought his suspension in the Irish High Court and whilst not ultimately successful, the hearing of his appeal against his suspension was postponed until after the running of the Derby, thus allowing him to ride in the classic. Both St Jovite's owner Mrs Virginia Kraft Payson and trainer Jim Bolger had threatened to withdraw the horse unless Roche was permitted to ride him at the Curragh, but happily recourse to such drastic action was not found to be necessary.

The Derby was the fourth race on a seven-race card. The day had started very well indeed for the Jim Bolger-Christy Roche team. They had won two of the first three races and must have regarded this as a good omen when saddling up the powerful US-bred St Jovite in the parade ring prior to the Derby.

The eleven runners proceeded to the start and were loaded without any fuss. In the splendid sunshine the starter effected a good clean break. Right from the outset it was clear that St Jovite's trainer had hatched a predetermined plan designed to give his charge the best possible chance of winning.

Besides the second favourite, the Coolcullen-based trainer had two other runners in the race. Neither Appealing Bubbles nor Mining Tycoon had any realistic chance of winning, but their participation enabled the Coolcullen contingent to dictate a very fast pace, thus giving the stoutly bred St Jovite every chance to bring his stamina into play, whilst at the same time hoping to expose any weakness in the sprint-bred Dr Devious.

Apprentice Conor Everard, riding in his first Budweiser Derby, set a blistering gallop on Appealing Bubbles, closely attended by both Mining Tycoon and St Jovite. John Reid on Dr Devious was in touch, however, and backers of the favourite had no cause for concern as the race entered its decisive phase. As his front-running stable companions gave way, conveniently allowing St Jovite to make his ground on the inside, Dr Devious had to be pushed around the weakening Bolger-trained horses to keep in touch with the second favourite.

Into the straight the two principals had sorted themselves out from the rest. Initially it was unclear which horse was going the best, but to the dismay of favourite backers, it was John Reid on Dr Devious who was first to go for his whip over two furlongs from home. St Jovite and Christy Roche meantime were galloping on resolutely, and soon the gap between the American-bred and the Irish-bred Epsom Derby winner began to widen appreciably.

With over a furlong to run St Jovite had gone at least four lengths clear of the hard-ridden favourite. Nothing else mattered, although the French horse, Contested Bid, was making some late headway under pressure from Pat Eddery. It was to be a futile effort. By now the success-starved Irish racing public had got the message. After seven long years an Irish-trained winner of Ireland's most prestigious race was at last about to become a reality. Following upon years of English domination, the outpouring of national pride and fervour couldn't be contained. The cheering commenced with a full two furlongs to run and gathered in momentum all the way to the finish as St Jovite and Roche stretched the distance back to his pursuers with each stride taken. It was certainly the most prolonged and emotional response to a Derby winner since Willie Burke's famous success on Santa Claus nearly thirty years earlier.

Six lengths, eight lengths, ten lengths and, incredibly, twelve lengths — St Jovite powered clear of the opposition. The official winning distance of twelve lengths — Dr Devious was a distant second — was the widest in the history of post-war classics. Shergar won the Epsom Derby by ten lengths, Noblesse and Jet Ski Lady the Epsom Oaks by the same margin, and Tudor Minstrel triumphed in the 1947 Newmarket 2,000 Guineas also by ten lengths. In fact one has to go back to 1895 to Portmarnock's Irish Derby win for a margin of victory equal to that achieved by St Jovite. (Records are made to be broken — in 1994 Turtle Island won the Irish 2,000 Guineas by no less than fifteen lengths. It has to be recorded that the ground was desperate and the winner was the only horse able to act on it.)

For the record, the French colt Contested Bid was third, a length behind Dr Devious, the 66/1 French-trained outsider Dive For Cover finished fourth three lengths further

back, with Ezzoud fifth and Marignan sixth. Landowner, who was apparently hampered in running, was a most disappointing ninth of the eleven runners. Mining Tycoon finished tenth and Appealing Bubbles last, but their role in fashioning St Jovite's victory should not be underestimated.

Even though the crowd didn't appreciate it at the time, St Jovite's performance (in the words of race commentator Des Scahill 'he annihilated them') not only broke all contemporary records for the winning distance, but smashed the track record in the process. The official time for the race was recorded at 2 minutes 25.6 seconds, shattering not only Tambourine II's 30-year-old Derby time, but also the best time ever posted previously at the Curragh (by Princess Patti in the 1984 Irish Oaks).

It must be pointed out that some time experts were unhappy with the official time set out above. On the Channel Four 'Morning Line' programme on the Saturday after the race, John Francome stated that a re-timing of the race based on an actual video recording threw up a time of 2 minutes 27 seconds exactly. That of course still ranks as an Irish Derby record time and, regardless of the time dispute, the truth is that St Jovite's performance stands as an outstanding and indeed spectacular display of sheer awesome power.

It is of interest to note that in response to a question that I put to Dr Vincent O'Brien about which Irish Derby winner, apart from his own horses, had impressed him the most, he unhesitatingly nominated St Jovite. Ladbroke's astute oddsman Mike Dillon was also fulsome in his praise of St Jovite, mentioning him in the same breath as Nijinsky. Incidentally, in winning at the Curragh St Jovite became the first Epsom runner-up to reverse placings with his conqueror in the Irish Derby.

The owner of St Jovite is the American horsewoman and breeding expert, Mrs Virginia Kraft Payson. Proprietress of a show-piece stud in Kentucky and a former regular contributor to the magazine *Sports Illustrated*, Mrs Payson clearly enjoyed one of the great achievements of her career in horse racing as she led in her champion racehorse to a fervent and enthusiastic reception from the Curragh crowd. She was entitled to, and doubtless did, feel a strong sense of pride at having been responsible for planning the precise breeding conjunction that had produced her outstanding Budweiser Irish Derby winner.

St Jovite (named after a ski resort in Mont Tremblante Park, Quebec) is by Pleasant Colony out of a mare called Northern Sunset. For many Europeans the name of the sire did not immediately ring any bells. Closer examination proved very much worthwhile. A grandson of the magnificent undefeated champion, Ribot, Pleasant Colony won both the Kentucky Derby and the Preakness Stakes (two legs of the American triple crown). Apart from St Jovite, Pleasant Colony also sired the 1993 Belmont Stakes winner, Colonial Affair. St Jovite's maternal grandsire, Northfields, was by the great Northern Dancer.

Northern Sunset, the dam of St Jovite, is a daughter of Moss Greine, who was herself sired by Vincent O'Brien's champion racehorse, Ballymoss. St Jovite's fourth dam

was the famous Carpet Slipper, dam of the unbeaten wartime Irish Derby winner, Windsor Slipper, probably the greatest racehorse ever owned by Joe McGrath. As Michael O'Farrell so succinctly put it in his report in *The Irish Times* of St Jovite's Budweiser Derby win: 'What more could one wish for in the pedigree of a middle distance colt than Ribot, Northern Dancer and Ballymoss!' What more indeed!

For trainer Jim Bolger, St Jovite's success at the Curragh marked the high point of a career that had been gathering impressive momentum for over a decade. Increasingly successful on his international raids, numbering Epsom Derby placings in consecutive years with Star of Gdansk, St Jovite and Blue Judge, and an Epsom Oaks victory with Jet Ski Lady among his triumphs, Bolger has now established himself, along with Dermot Weld, as the natural successors to the late Paddy Prendergast and the recently retired Vincent O'Brien as the leading lights of the newer generation of Irish trainers.

Brief mention should be made of two other matters pertaining to the 1992 Budweiser Derby. The first is Peter Chapple-Hyam's uncharacteristically ungracious remarks in the wake of Dr Devious's defeat. It was reported after the race that Chapple-Hyam had commented that the man who 'really runs Irish racing has won the Derby'. One fears that Peter allowed emotion to colour judgment here: the truth is that it was the horse who won the race, not the trainer.

The second matter is the rather sad souring of the partnership between trainer Jim Bolger and owner Mrs Kraft Payson, which culminated in the American owner removing her remaining horses from the Coolcullen yard before the start of the 1993 flat season. Comment is superfluous; what is without question is that Mrs Kraft Payson's decision is a blow to Irish racing.

After his Budweiser win, St Jovite went on to prove his champion status by beating older horses most impressively in the King George VI and Queen Elizabeth Diamond Stakes at Ascot. He had no less than six lengths to spare over Saddler's Hall when romping home in the mid-summer show-piece. St Jovite was subsequently controversially beaten by a short head in the ten furlong Kerry Group Irish Champion Stakes at Leopardstown by Dr Devious, the result of a jockey error. In his only other run as a three-year-old he finished fourth in the Prix de l'Arc de Triomphe on ground that was much too soft for him. At Longchamp St Jovite finished just in front of Dr Devious.

There was some surprise expressed in certain racing quarters when the end of season international classifications rated St Jovite fully 10 lb ahead of Dr Devious in the assessment of the relative merits of the 1992 classic generation. (Incidentally, St Jovite became the first Irish-trained horse to top the international ratings since El Gran Senor in 1984.) Anyone, however, who was at the Curragh on 28 June 1992 and who saw the superbly bred St Jovite, with his powerful galloping stride, shatter the pretensions of the Epsom Derby winner, and indeed all comers, could not possibly quibble with the findings of the panel of international racing judges.

BUDWEISER IRISH DERBY

1M 4F

SUNDAY 28 JUNE 1992

GOING: GOOD

WINNER: Mrs V. Kraft Payson's St Jovite by Pleasant
Colony out of Northern Sunset
C. Roche

SECOND: Dr Devious by Ahonoora out of Rose of
Jericho
J. Reid

THIRD: Contested Bid by Alleged out of Queens
Only
P. Eddery

S.P. 7/2   4/5f   11/1
Winner trained by J. S. Bolger

ALSO: Dive For Cover 4th, Ezzoud 5th, Marignan
6th, Ormsby 7th, Boloardo 8th, Landowner
9th, Mining Tycoon 10th, Appealing Bubbles
11th & last

Winner: 2nd favourite
Distances: 12 lengths, 1 length
Value to winner: £354,500
Time: 2 m 25.6 s (course record)
Timeform rating of winner: 135.

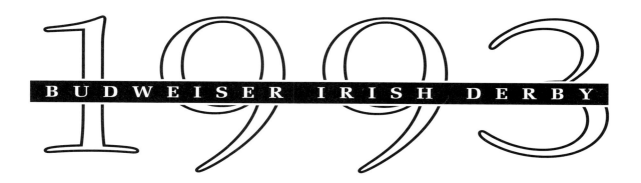

BUDWEISER IRISH DERBY

THE CURRAGH 27 JUNE 1993

The impression, gathering pace in the previous three years, that the Budweiser Irish Derby is now firmly established as the true championship test of the classic generation was further embellished by the 1993 renewal. In line with the pattern that had become the norm over a period of some fifteen years, the field was not especially large — eleven runners in all — but whatever about quantity, quality was very much to the fore.

For the second time in three runnings, the winners of the Epsom and French Derbies were in opposition and the clash between the unbeaten Henry Cecil-trained Commander In Chief and the French champion, Hernando, drew a tremendous crowd to the Curragh. For many racegoers the day started on a good note for, with the opening of the Newbridge bypass, the traffic delays which had become a feature of Derby days for Dublin-based motorists were banished for ever more into the collective

unconscious. In a summer which was in general quite dismal, mother nature chose to smile benignly on the Curragh on 27 June 1993 and the day was perhaps the hottest of the year (perhaps too much so for the comfort of many racegoers). The big race, too, turned out to be quite a hot one as well.

Principal attraction at the Curragh was the Epsom Derby winner Commander In Chief and the Dancing Brave colt was expected by many to start favourite and win. Commander In Chief was having only his fifth ever race at the Curragh, and all his public experience had been crammed into a ten-week period beginning in mid-April at Newmarket.

There, over a mile and two furlongs Commander In Chief, who started evens favourite, was an impressive six length winner from Silverdale. That Newmarket maiden success told us little enough, other than that Commander In Chief was a pretty useful prospect. Prince Khalid Abdulla's colt showed that he was going the right way when he followed up with a comfortable three and a half length and one and a half length victory over the subsequent Lingfield Oaks Trial winner, Oakmead, and Irish challenger, Blue Judge, over twelve furlongs at Newmarket on 2,000 Guineas day.

Less than two weeks later, the Henry Cecil-trained colt contested the Glasgow Stakes at York over an extended ten furlongs. On this, his third racecourse appearance, Commander In Chief had to be quite vigorously ridden by Pat Eddery to get the better of Needle Gun by a neck. This performance struck many observers as being less than convincing, and among those evidently unimpressed was jockey Pat Eddery who elected to partner Khalid Abdulla's other runner, Tenby, in the Epsom Derby, leaving Michael Kinane to pick up the spare ride on Commander In Chief.

In making his decision, Eddery was reflecting both professional opinion and the weight of statistical detail relating to Derby winners. Like Commander In Chief, Tenby was unbeaten, but unlike his stablemate, Tenby had winning form at Group 1 level as a juvenile and had followed up in the time-honoured fashion by winning a recognised Derby trial, the Group 2 Dante Stakes at York, as a three-year-old. It would have been quite extraordinary if Eddery had elected to ride a horse who had never won a listed race, never mind a Group race, in preference to one with Tenby's public form at Group level.

All of which was of little consolation to the Irish-born jockey when Commander In Chief with super sub Mick Kinane aboard romped home in the Epsom Derby, with a bitterly disappointing Tenby trailing home in a dismal tenth place. No explanation was forthcoming for Tenby's abysmal performance, the assumption of course being that he had run well below his best. Commander In Chief was followed home at Epsom by two 150/1 chances, Blue Judge and Blues Traveller, and there were those who questioned the value of the form.

Only three previous Epsom Derby winners had not been campaigned as two-year-olds. Commander In Chief thus joined the elite band of Bois Roussel (1938), Phil Drake (1955) and Morston (1973). Having notched up his membership of that exclusive club, Commander In Chief was aimed at the Budweiser Irish Derby in an attempt to add his name to the list of eleven previous Epsom Derby winners who had succeeded at the Curragh in making it a Derby double. This time of course he would be ridden by Pat Eddery, hoping to gain compensation for his ill-luck at Epsom.

One of the likely dangers to Commander In Chief at the Curragh was removed when the Epsom runner-up, Blue Judge, a son of Rainbow Quest, had the misfortune to fracture a cannon bone in a gallop a week before the Irish classic. Bearing in mind how much his trainer Jim Bolger had been able to improve the 1992 Epsom runner-up, St Jovite, between Epsom and the Curragh, it was regrettable that the horse who would undoubtedly have been the principal Irish hope was forced to miss the race.

The biggest danger on paper to Commander In Chief at the Curragh was the French Derby winner Hernando, who was trained by François Boutin, previously successful with Malacate in 1976. (Indeed Malacate was the last French-trained winner of the Irish Derby.) Coincidentally Hernando, like Commander In Chief, had not raced as a juvenile. His three-year-old campaign, however, gave every indication that his connections were intent on making up for lost time.

Hernando, who was by Nijinsky's son Niniski, first saw a racecourse on 25 March at Saint-Cloud where, in an extended ten furlong maiden and on soft ground, he was beaten a head by the more than useful Fort Wood. The value of this form was subsequently shown up in the best possible light when Fort Wood went on to win the Group 1 Grand Prix de Paris from subsequent Sussex Stakes hero, Bigstone. After a couple of subsequent victories, including a listed race on heavy ground again over an extended ten furlongs but this time at Longchamp, Hernando gave notice that he was a colt of considerable ability when he beat Commander In Chief's stable companion, Armiger, by a neck in the Group 1 Prix Lupin at Longchamp.

Armiger, who was also owned by Prince Khalid Abdulla, was ridden at Longchamp by Pat Eddery, and after his mount's defeat the jockey made the quite extraordinary statement that yet another of Abdulla's colts, the French-trained Regency, would have beaten the first and second in the Lupin by fifteen lengths! That particular opinion was put to the test a couple of weeks later, for both Hernando and Regency were among the contestants in the Prix du Jockey-Club (the French Derby) at Chantilly and, truth to tell, Eddery's rather sweeping assertion did not stand up.

On good to firm going Hernando cruised home at Chantilly by two and a half lengths from Dernier Empereur, with Regency back in fifth place, five and a quarter lengths adrift. There was a line of form indeed through the Barry Hills-trained Newton's Law, who had finished fourth at Chantilly, which suggested that Hernando was little, if at all, behind Commander In Chief. Certainly on all the available evidence the Stavros Niarchos-owned colt was a formidable opponent for the Epsom Derby winner at the Curragh.

Was Regency as good as Pat Eddery thought after the Prix Lupin? Well, in a move which surprised some, the Criquette Head-trained colt took his chance at the Curragh. Regency, like Commander In Chief, was a son of Dancing Brave and prior to his Chantilly run he had given an authoritative performance in the Group 2 Prix Hocquart. Run over a mile and a half at Longchamp on good to soft going, Regency had beaten Marchand de Sable by one and a half lengths. The official going at the Curragh was described as good to yielding and this was thought likely to favour Willie Carson's mount. It was reported, furthermore, that Regency was to run on his merits at the Curragh, but there was a suspicion in some quarters that his principal role was to set a strong pace for the stamina-endowed favourite Commander In Chief. Quite what would happen in the race only time would tell.

Of the eight Irish-trained runners, four at least were entitled to some consideration. John Oxx saddled two and both had possibilities. The more fancied of his twosome was the Aga Khan's Massyar, a colt by the 1988 dual Derby winner Khayasi.

Massyar had been competing in good-class company all season. After beating Fatherland by two lengths on his seasonal début over seven furlongs at Leopardstown, Massyar went on to finish a somewhat hampered third to Barathea in the Irish 2,000 Guineas, beaten a little over a length. The Aga Khan's colt's next outing was in the Group 2 Gallinule Stakes over ten furlongs at the Curragh which he won in workmanlike style. Massyar was difficult to rate accurately, but clearly his chances could not be ignored.

The same could be said about the other Oxx runner, Foresee. The Sheikh Mohammed-owned colt had encountered traffic problems at Royal Ascot when finishing a very close fourth in the King Edward VII Stakes, beaten less than a length. He appeared to be on the upgrade and was reported to have worked particularly well in his final preparatory gallop for the Derby.

The defection of Blue Judge had weakened trainer Jim Bolger's hand considerably. None the less the Coolcullen handler saddled no less than three runners in the Derby. While Lord Bentley and Via Parigi were long shots with little hope of ultimate success, the Blushing Groom colt, Desert Team, was not without prospects. His three-year-old campaign had been conducted exclusively in England and the best of his three runs there was a four length third to Tenby over ten furlongs at Newmarket. A disappointment in the Epsom Derby, where he had trailed home in eleventh place, it was noted by some that he had been by far the more fancied of Jim Bolger's two runners at Epsom, and if stable opinion was that he was a better colt than Blue Judge, then his chance most certainly had to be respected.

The only other Irish runner worth mentioning was Michael Kauntze's Shrewd Idea. The Alleged colt had put up quite a useful performance when a two and a half length second to the aforementioned Armiger in the Chester Vase, and subsequently had run third in a Group 2 race in Germany. If there was to be a shock, Shrewd Idea was the sort to provide it.

The feature of the betting on the race was the extraordinary strength of the favourite in the ring. In very early exchanges there were glimpses of 5/4 and 11/10 available about Commander In Chief, but in general business began with opening offers of even money. This hardly represented outstanding value, but it didn't deter the big punters from wading in, and the Commander was backed though all rates down to a quite ludicrous 4/7 at the off. It was reported afterwards that representatives of the English betting office multiples were very much to the fore in shortening up the price of the favourite.

In the face of sustained support for Commander In Chief, the French hope Hernando retreated by fractions from 7/4 to 9/4 despite some money for François Boutin's colt. Regency, put in at 7's, was quite weak and drifted out to 10's, where he was joined by Massyar, who attracted some interest after opening at 12's. The trio returned at 25/1 — Desert Team, Foresee and Shrewd Idea — had all opened at 20's. It was 100/1 bar these seven.

With every vantage point in the grandstands occupied, the attention of the crowd as the clock ticked around to 4.00 p.m. was firmly focused on the starting point for the Derby, directly across from the stands. Lord Bentley, partnered by Walter Swinburn, played up momentarily at the start, but soon all was well, the stalls opened, and the eleven-runner field set out on the classic trip.

Right from the outset Willie Carson took Regency, wearing the second colours of Khalid Abdulla, into the lead. Shrewd Idea and Warren O'Connor, followed by Desert Team and Christy Roche, moved into second and third places. Pat Eddery tucked Commander In Chief in just behind the leading trio and the second favourite Hernando, ridden by Cash Asmussen, was also kept quite close to the pace in fifth or sixth place.

The gallop dictated by Carson on Regency looked quite a good one: was it part of a pre-arranged plan hatched by the Abdulla team? The order didn't change much in the first half of the race, save that Commander In Chief moved into third place, racing on the outside and just ahead of Desert Team. Massyar made some headway at this point and was on the outside of Hernando going into the final five furlongs, the pair of them in fifth and sixth places. With about four furlongs to go then, the order was Regency, Shrewd Idea, Commander In Chief, Desert Team, Hernando and Massyar.

Regency still led turning into the straight, with Shrewd Idea holding on to his second place although under pressure. Straightening up, Pat Eddery set the favourite alight and racing on the outside, Commander In Chief quickly mastered both Shrewd Idea and Regency to take it up with over two furlongs to run. Neither Desert Team nor Massyar was

able to respond to the favourite's move, but Hernando still looked full of running.

When Cash Asmussen asked the question, Hernando quickly closed the gap so that with just under two furlongs to go he was within a length or so of Commander In Chief. It had come down to a battle between the big two as had been widely predicted. The Henry Cecil-trained colt was under maximum pressure from Eddery, but game and resolute as he was, Commander In Chief was responding tremendously to the pressure. Could Hernando find the turn of foot that he had exhibited at Chantilly?

For a time the issue hung in the balance. Eddery was hard at work on the favourite, while Hernando still appeared to have something left in the tank. With the favourite showing no sign of weakening, Asmussen called on his mount for the supreme effort. Hernando responded, but if he did, so too did the Commander. Galloping on with great heart, Commander In Chief held the persistent and game challenge of Hernando.

In fact the gap between the two horses remained remarkably constant throughout the final furlong and a half, at just over a length. It was only in the final seventy-five yards that Hernando succeeded in closing the gap slightly on Commander In Chief, and although he never looked like getting to the favourite, at the winning post the gallant French-trained colt was only three-quarters of a length adrift of the courageous and deserving winner. It had been a great race between two very good colts.

In third place three lengths further behind came Foresee, the best of the Irish, who, although behind early on and only seventh early in the straight, ran on to good effect through beaten horses. Regency, his donkey work done, was another five lengths away in fourth place. It was a further two lengths back to Massyar who plainly didn't stay, and he in turn was a head in front of Shrewd Idea who had run bravely despite being a little outclassed.

Commander In Chief thus became the twelfth horse to complete the Epsom-Curragh Derby double. For the record the others were Orby, Santa Claus, Nijinsky, Grundy, The Minstrel, Shirley Heights, Troy, Shergar, Shahrastani, Khayasi and Generous. Commander In Chief hardly seemed to be as good as most, if not all, of these, but a final verdict on him would have to await another day.

In the aftermath of the race it became clear that the Abdulla team had set out to blunt Hernando's finishing speed by employing a pacemaker of Regency's calibre. That horse's trainer, Criquette Head, did not appear to be enthused that her colt (who was certainly not far off Group 1 standard) had been delegated, or rather relegated, to the role of pacemaker in the search for classic gold. Be that as it may, there is no doubt that the tactics employed by the Abdulla camp were instrumental in fashioning Commander In Chief's victory.

On ground that had a bit of a cut in it, the time of the race at 2 minutes 31.2 seconds was fast, faster for instance by three-tenths of a second than El Gran Senor's time on firm ground in 1984. (It ought to be recorded that some race readers were sceptical as to the accuracy of the official state of the ground.) In an interview on RTE television after the race, Pat Eddery remarked how Regency had 'progressed the gallop all the way through the race', and of course this put the emphasis very much on stamina, which is a commodity that Commander In Chief possessed in abundance.

For Pat Eddery, the Commander's victory (his fourth Irish Derby success) was compensation for his misfortune in choosing the wrong horse at Epsom. For Henry Cecil, it was a second Irish Derby in the space of four years, following upon Old Vic's triumph in 1989. And for owner Prince Khalid Abdulla, it was his first Irish Derby success and more than made up for his near miss with Deploy in 1990. It also represented yet another classic success for Abdulla in 1993, for besides the Commander's dual Derby successes, he also owned Zafonic, impressive winner of the Newmarket 2,000 Guineas, and Weymss Bight, successful in the Kildangan Stud Irish Oaks.

Mention of Deploy brings one naturally to Commander In Chief's breeding. Like Deploy, the Commander is out of the Roberto mare Slightly Dangerous, the 1982 Epsom Oaks runner-up. While Deploy was by the dual Derby winner Shirley Heights, Commander In Chief's sire is Dancing Brave, arguably the best horse in living memory not to have won a Derby. Dancing Brave is of course a son of Lyphard, who himself was by Northern Dancer. Slightly Dangerous is out of the Oaks runner-up Where You Lead, whose dam was the great Noblesse, whom Paddy Prendergast trained to win the 1963 Epsom Oaks in spectacular style. The Commander's pedigree, besides being imbued with the requisite class, is full of staying power, and after his two Derby successes he was widely acclaimed as being by far the best colt yet sired by Dancing Brave.

As always, definitive judgment of the three-year-old generation has to be reserved until the best of that age group is pitted against the older horses. Commander In Chief was prepared for the traditional mid-summer clash of the generations, the King George VI and Queen Elizabeth Diamond Stakes. Although there were no French challengers, the race was a thoroughly intriguing affair. Best of the older horses was reckoned to be the 1992 Epsom Oaks and St Leger winner and Arc runner-up, User Friendly, but adding spice to the race was the presence of two three-year-olds, Epsom flop Tenby and the Peter Chapple-Hyam-trained Italian Derby winner, White Muzzle, yet another son of Dancing Brave.

In the event none of the above mentioned won. Victory went instead to the five-year-old Sadler's Wells colt, Opera House, who made it a hat trick of Group 1 wins, following upon the Coronation Cup and the Eclipse Stakes, with a one and a half length victory over White Muzzle, who got the better of Commander In Chief by a short head in a battle for the runner-up spot. Tenby proved that his Epsom form was just about right, for he was already beaten and on the retreat before the field turned into the straight. Like Arazi, and others before him.

he had packed all his best racing into his juvenile days.

In previews of the King George a number of racing journalists made the point that Commander in Chief, despite his record, had failed to capture the racing public's imagination. The inference was that the Henry Cecil-trained colt had to win the Ascot feature to prove himself in the highest class. Although an honourable failure, in truth Commander In Chief's King George defeat has to be classified as disappointing. In this connection it is worth bearing in mind that the ground at Ascot, which was on the soft side of good, was deemed more suitable for Commander In Chief, who had quite a pronounced knee action, than for White Muzzle.

At any rate after the King George, the Jockey Club handicapper Geoffrey Gibbs rated both Commander In Chief and White Muzzle at 127, with Opera House on 130. For purposes of comparison it is worth noting that the 1992 King George and Budweiser Irish Derby winner St Jovite was rated 136, with the 1991 hero of the same two races, Generous, given a rating of 138. These official assessments place the 1993 classic generation in cool perspective. All such considerations are of course relative. Whatever the merits of the crop, in 1993 Commander In Chief and Hernando gave us at the Curragh on Budweiser Irish Derby day the best three-year-old race of the season.

BUDWEISER IRISH DERBY

1M 4F

SUNDAY 27 JUNE 1993

GOING: GOOD TO YIELDING

WINNER: Khalid Abdulla's Commander In Chief by Dancing Brave out of Slightly Dangerous
P. Eddery

SECOND: Hernando by Niniski out of Whakilyric
C. Asmussen

THIRD: Foresee by Vision out of Sovereign Dona
J. Murtagh

S.P. 4/7f   9/4   25/1
Winner trained by H. R. A. Cecil

ALSO: Regency 4th, Massyar 5th, Shrewd Idea 6th,
Via Parigi 7th, Desert Team 8th,
Porterstown Boy 9th, Lord Bentley 10th,
Sirsan 11th & last

Winner: favourite
Distance: 3/4 length, 3 lengths
Value to winner: £342,500
Time: 2 m 31.2 s
Timeform rating of winner: 128.

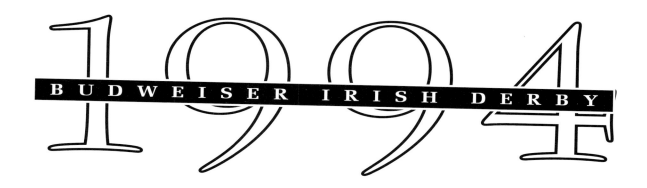

BUDWEISER IRISH DERBY

THE CURRAGH 26 JUNE 1994

The abiding memory for the majority of Curragh racegoers who attended the 1994 renewal of the Budweiser Irish Derby was, unfortunately, the weather. In marked contrast to 1993's glorious sunshine, Sunday 26 June 1994 was a dark gloomy day and a howling wind sweeping across the Curragh made it a distinctly chilly and uncomfortable experience, especially for those fashionably inclined. Hardened racegoers, however, used to the vagaries of the Irish weather, took the conditions in their stride and looked forward to an intriguing contest for the most coveted prize in Irish racing.

Clear favourite for the race was Henry Cecil's Epsom Derby runner-up, King's Theatre, who had looked all over a winner at Epsom Downs until collared close home by the fast finishing Erhaab. The winner had an awful lot to do rounding Tattenham Corner, and even straightening out for home, backers of the John Dunlop-trained American-bred colt could scarcely have fancied their

chances, so far back was the favourite. Willie Carson, however, got a dream run up the rails in the straight and, pulled to the outside well inside the final furlong, pounced on Michael Kinane's mount King's Theatre, who by this stage had got the better of an intense battle with the Peter Chapple-Hyam-trained Colonel Collins.

The official distances at Epsom were one and a quarter and one and a half lengths, and there was a body of opinion which suggested that Erhaab's triumph was as much down to stamina limitations in the placed horses as to the winner's innate brilliance. Erhaab bypassed the Irish Derby in favour of the Coral Eclipse, but Colonel Collins was sent on to the Curragh in an attempt to gain revenge over the Derby runner-up.

In all, nine horses went to post. Two of the Epsom also-rans, John Dunlop's Khamaseen, who had finished a respectable eight lengths fifth, and Clive Brittain's Ionio, who had been a further seven lengths adrift in eleventh place, renewed rivalry with the Epsom second and third at the Curragh. No doubt connections were encouraged by the fact that prize money was payable down to eleventh place.

The field was made up of the third and fourth placed horses in the Prix du Jockey-Club (the French Derby), Alriffa and Tikkanen, two Irish-trained contenders, Cajarian and Concept House, and probably the most interesting runner-up of all, the Epsom Oaks winner Balanchine, who had been a supplementary entry for the Budweiser sponsored classic at a cost of IR£60,000. Balanchine would need to finish third or better to justify the outlay.

Michael Kinane had established himself as just about the most sought after jockey in Europe over the previous five seasons or so, and yet, remarkably, the Irish champion had never tasted success in Ireland's principal classic race. The nearest he had come previously was when second on Dermot Weld's Theatrical in 1985. His best ever chance of filling this notable gap in his long list of big race triumphs was surely King's Theatre.

Henry Cecil's colt was yet another son of the brilliant Sadler's Wells and a half brother to the 1988 Royal Lodge winner High Estate. A promising fifth on his début behind Concordial at Newmarket, King's Theatre had notched up two comfortable successes in modest events at Yarmouth and Newbury in the month of September 1993. Stepped up in class, King's Theatre proved well up to the task when easily landing the Group 1 Racing Post Trophy at Doncaster over a mile on his final outing as a juvenile.

Reintroduced as a three-year-old in the Craven Stakes at Newmarket, King's Theatre got the better of Colonel Collins by a short head in a desperate finish. Run over a mile and on soft ground, the colt's connections were sufficiently encouraged by the display to dispatch their charge to contest the 2,000 Guineas over the selfsame course and distance. Sent off the 9/2 favourite in a field of twenty-three, King's Theatre led the stands side group for much of the trip, but on the fast ground was outpaced over the final couple of furlongs and finished a disappointing thirteenth behind the north of England-trained Mister Baileys.

King's Theatre next competed in the Group 2 Dante Stakes over an extended ten furlongs at York, but again encountered firm ground and was not at his best. He finished fourth, some six and a quarter lengths behind the winner Erhaab who, as related above, went on to confirm the Dante form at Epsom, although the margin of superiority over the full classic distance was significantly reduced. On all known form King's Theatre was a worthy favourite for the Budweiser Derby, and the forecast give in the ground would be very much in his favour.

A number of breeding experts were, however, sceptical about the colt's chances of winning a classic. King's Theatre's dam, Regal Beauty, had never won herself and came from a somewhat undistinguished family. The most forthright of the anti-King's Theatre brigade was James Underwood, editor of the *European Racing and Breeding Digest*, who had publicly promised to emigrate to Rwanda if King's

Theatre had won at Epsom, and repeated the promise (or threat) in the *Racing Post* on the eve of the Budweiser Derby.

Who, then, of the favourite's rivals was to come to Mr Underwood's aid at the Curragh? Clearly, Colonel Collins, who had finished only one and a half lengths behind King's Theatre when third at Epsom, had to be given the most serious consideration.

An El Gran Senor colt, out of a dam who was quite a smart winner at up to nine furlongs in France, Colonel Collins had shown consistent form in top-class company. In three outings as a juvenile, Colonel Collins had won a Newmarket maiden and a listed race at Newbury. After his strong finishing, short head second to King's Theatre in the Craven Stakes, he had been a good third in the Newmarket 2,000 Guineas behind Mister Baileys and Grand Lodge, finishing of course some way ahead of King's Theatre. On Epsom form, there seemed no reason why Colonel Collins should reverse placings with King's Theatre, but the Curragh was a different race and a different place, so who was to say?

If not Colonel Collins, what chance Balanchine becoming the second filly in five runnings to win the premier Irish classic, following Salsibil's triumph in 1990? A Storm Bird filly out of a mare by American Triple Crown winner Affirmed, Balanchine had been lightly campaigned as a juvenile. She had had just two outings in the month of September, and starting at odds-on in both, comfortably obliged in modest contests at Salisbury and Newbury.

Pitched in at the deep end on her three-year-old début, Balanchine failed by only a short head to the Tommy Stack-trained Las Meninas in a heart stopping finish to the Newmarket 1,000 Guineas, with the French filly Coup de Genie only a neck away third. A 20/1 shot at Newmarket, Balanchine was next prepared for the Epsom Oaks. On breeding, there appeared to be some grounds for reservations about her ability to get the twelve furlong trip, but the filly dispelled all stamina doubts with a game and convincing two and a half length victory over Wind In Her Hair on rain-softened ground at Epsom. Indeed, the most noteworthy feature of Balanchine's triumph was that she was, if anything, pulling clear of her rivals in the final furlong at Epsom. Her stamina therefore was not in doubt, but what was the value of the Epsom Oaks form? Pre-race opinion tended to place Balanchine somewhat below the class of the 1990 Budweiser Derby heroine, Salsibil.

As a two-year-old, Balanchine was trained by Peter Chapple-Hyam for Robert Sangster. Towards the end of the 1993 season, however, Balanchine was one of a batch of juveniles sold by his owner to Arab interests in Dubai. Sangster's famous colours of emerald green with royal blue sleeves were to be worn by John Reid aboard Colonel Collins at the Curragh, but no doubt the owner entertained mixed feelings as he awaited the start of the Budweiser sponsored classic.

After the French Derby (the Prix du Jockey Club) there was as usual a good deal of debate in the racing press as to which of the Derbies, the English or French, represented the better form. A definitive answer to that question was likely to be provided by the Irish Derby in that, besides the Epsom placed horses, the third and fourth placed horses at Chantilly, Alriffa and Tikkanen, were down to renew rivalry at the Curragh.

Alriffa was trained by Richard Hannon and had been unraced as a juvenile. On his second outing as a three-year-old he comfortably won a Kempton maiden, but improved significantly on that on his next run with a ten length victory over Darnay in a ten furlong listed event at Newmarket. From an unfavourable outside draw at Chantilly, Alriffa, on only his fourth ever outing, was a most creditable two and a quarter length third to Celtic Arms in the French Derby. There was understood to be considerable stable confidence behind the US-bred colt.

Another American bred, Tikkanen, had been only half a length behind Alriffa at Chantilly, and had finished well enough on that occasion to suggest that the stiffer Curragh track would suit him admirably. A three parts brother to the high-class stayer Turgeon, who had won the 1991 Irish St Leger, Tikkanen had displayed excellent form in the principal credential races in France prior to his performance at Chantilly. He had won the Group 2 Prix Greffulhe and had been third in the Group 1 Prix Lupin, both over an extended ten furlongs, and both at Longchamp. Among those behind him in the Greffulhe was Carnegie, who was to go on later in the season to land the Arc. The sole French challenger, Tikkanen, was far from being a forlorn hope.

A brief word about the two Irish-trained contenders is in order. The Aga Khan's

Cajarian, a son of the 1986 Irish Derby hero Shahrastani, had reasonable form to his name. A Group 3 winner as a juvenile, he was evens favourite for the Group 3 Derrinstown Stud Derby Trial at Leopardstown, but had disappointed when beaten a length by Antenna. He needed to improve, but was a considerable distance ahead of his other Irish-trained rival. Trained by Miss I. T. Oakes, Concept House had finally opened his account at the eighth time of asking in a twelve furlong Roscommon maiden a fortnight before the Derby when getting the better of Bubbly Prospect by a head in a photo finish. A follow up at the Curragh seemed unlikely.

The scene was set. Despite the fact that the rain held off, those far-sighted individuals who had remembered that most valuable of all racing tips — always bring a raincoat — had reason to feel smug as they were afforded some protection against the unseasonal chilly wind. The weather was less than auspicious, but at least in the betting ring things were hotting up.

As expected, King's Theatre held the call, and after opening at 5/4 he closed a firm even money favourite. Both Colonel Collins and Alriffa were put in at 9/2, but whereas the Epsom third proved weak in the market, easing out to 11/2, the French Derby third, Alriffa, was in demand and contracted a point down to 7/2. Oaks winner, Balanchine, was marked up initially at 5/1, and at first eased out to 6's, but then attracted good support and reverted to her opening price. Tikkanen was very weak drifting from 7's to 10's. It was 14/1 Khamaseen, and little was seen for the rest.

For the second year running the official going was good to yielding, and under an overcast sky the field was dispatched to a pretty good break. Right from the outset Willie Carson on Khamaseen set out to make the running. King's Theatre and Michael Kinane were a close up second, Alriffa and Pat Eddery were next, and the rest of the field were fairly closely grouped. There was little change for half a mile, where Balanchine and Frankie Dettori made a forward move on to the heels of the leading trio.

The John Dunlop-trained Khamaseen continued to cut out the running and at the half-way point injected some additional pace into the race. From the stands it was noticeable that King's Theatre was caught a little flat footed by the increase in pace. Balanchine, by contrast, was moving sweetly in behind the leader, Alriffa was holding his place, and Colonel Collins, who had been held up, was making some progress.

Some five furlongs out Balanchine moved up alongside Khamaseen and the pair raced alongside for the next furlong before the Oaks heroine took over at the head of affairs. With Khamaseen now weakening, King's Theatre regained second spot, while Alriffa was still third but was being pushed along to hold his place.

Turning into the straight the order was Balanchine, King's Theatre, Alriffa, Colonel Collins, a weakening Khamaseen, Tikkanen, Cajarian, Ionio, and Concept House who was never a factor. Over two furlongs out Dettori asked his filly to quicken, and the response was immediate. Balanchine quickly put daylight between herself and King's Theatre, and immediately the favourite and indeed

the rest of the field were struggling. Michael Kinane's mount made a short-lived effort to close the gap, but it was all in vain. Balanchine galloped on relentlessly and had stretched her advantage over Henry Cecil's colt to four and a half lengths at the line. By any standard, it was a most impressive winning performance.

The rest of the field was well strung out. Colonel Collins once again had to be content with the minor honours in a classic for the third time in a row, three and a half lengths adrift of King's Theatre. It was another five and a half lengths to Alriffa who was fourth, and Tikkanen was fifth, three-quarters of a length further back. Interestingly, Alriffa and Tikkanen had reproduced their Chantilly form almost to the pound.

Balanchine had won most convincingly, but the race had been rather uneventful. It was scarcely her fault, however, that the colts had been unable to give her a proper test. In fact, it is worth noting that the Storm Bird filly had beaten both King's Theatre and Colonel Collins far more decisively than Erhaab had done at Epsom. With her victory Balanchine had emulated the 1990 Budweiser Derby heroine Salsibil, and after a ninety-year gap two fillies had won Ireland's premier classic in the space of four years.

As mentioned previously, Balanchine had been sold by Robert Sangster as a two-year-old to the Maktoums. Running in the colours of Maktoum Al Maktoum, his younger brother Sheikh Mohammed also had a share in the filly. It was Sheikh Mohammed's idea to transport Balanchine and a few of his other horses to winter in the Dubai sunshine, and in the filly's case at least the plan had turned up trumps. It will be recalled of course that Vincent O'Brien had tried a similar experiment with conspicuous success back in 1967 when he sent Sir Ivor to winter in Pisa in Italy.

Balanchine was officially trained by Hilal Ibrahim and represented Godolphin Racing, the corporate name for the Maktoum racing empire. Those most closely associated with the European end of the operation were Simon Crisford and Jeremy Noseda, the latter a former assistant trainer to John Gosden. It was Noseda, in fact, who had supervised Balanchine's preparation after her return from Dubai in April. There was no disguising the delight on Sheikh Mohammed's face as he led in Balanchine at the Curragh. Few, if any, of his classic successes can have given him greater pleasure.

Balanchine was Storm Bird's twenty-sixth Group winner, and perhaps the best horse yet thrown by her sire. Best known previously as the sire of the brilliant and consistent mare, Indian Skimmer, other classic winners sired by Storm Bird were Summer Squall who won the Preakness Stakes, and Prince of Birds who was successful for Vincent O'Brien in the Irish 2,000 Guineas.

Of course, Storm Bird was himself a son of Northern Dancer, and a remarkable feature of the 1994 Budweiser Derby was the fact that the first four home were descended from Northern Dancer in tail male. 1994's classic results indeed provided further evidence of the absolute domination of the Northern Dancer bloodlines in European racing. Northern Dancer line horses finished in the first three places in

the Epsom Derby; first, second and fourth in both the Epsom Oaks and the 1,000 Guineas; and second, third and fourth in the 2,000 Guineas. A similar picture emerges in the corresponding Irish classics.

At the year end, all of the top ten sires in Great Britain and Ireland were directly descended from Northern Dancer. For the record, in descending order, the sires in question are Sadler's Wells, Chief's Clown, Green Desert, Caerleon, Last Tycoon, Storm Bird, Danzig, Alzao, Night Shift and Bluebird — a truly remarkable statistic.

It will be noted that Sadler's Wells (about whom I wrote at some length in the chapter on the 1990 race) was champion sire. 1994 was the third year in a row that the Coolmore-based stallion had been champion, making him the first since the great Hyperion to achieve such a distinction. In a documentary screened by RTE late in 1994 to mark the retirement from training of the incomparable Vincent O'Brien, the former master of Ballydoyle went to great pains to stress that Sadler's Wells' most significant contribution as the pre-eminent sire of his generation was to preserve the importance of stamina, as opposed to speed, in racehorses. (As mentioned elsewhere, eighteen of Sadler's Wells' thirty Group 1 winners were over a mile and a half.)

Coming from such a respected source, it is to be hoped that this salutary warning against the dangers of downgrading the importance of stamina in the breeding of thoroughbreds does not go unheeded. There is little doubt that if the day ever dawns when the classic European distance is reduced to a mile and a quarter from a mile and a half, the sport of horse racing will be a significantly poorer spectacle, certain to lose further ground as a spectator sport in the increasingly competitive sports and leisure industry.

Getting back to Storm Bird: as a sire he has never been noted as an influence for stamina. In Balanchine's case, therefore, it is to the distaff side of the pedigree that we must look to discover where the filly derived her undoubted staying ability.

Balanchine's dam, Morning Devotion, was a pretty useful sort, her best run for Michael Stoute being when she was third behind subsequent classic winners Oh So Sharp and Helen Street in the Group 1 Hoover Fillies Mile. Morning Devotion herself was out of a mare by Prince John, whose sons not only included the Belmont Stakes winner, Stage Door Johnny, but also the Irish St Leger winner, Transworld. For an American pedigree, this is as close as you're likely to get to an abundance of stamina. There is an interesting link, it should be added, between Balanchine and the winner of the first sponsored Irish Derby, in that the above mentioned Prince John was himself a son of Princequillo, who sired Tambourine II.

Before considering the wider significance of Balanchine's Curragh triumph, mention should be made of one of the big successes of the day. The Mitsubishi Diamond Big Screen, first used at the Lillehammer Winter Olympics, was situated in the Budweiser Green area and reproduced a clarity of picture that could scarcely have been improved upon in one's own sitting room.

No excuses were made on behalf of Balanchine's beaten rivals. Henry Cecil,

trainer of King's Theatre, summed up the race best when he told Damien McElroy of the *Irish Independent*: '. . . My horse gave all he had. He quickened a little, but Balanchine really accelerated and we have to accept she is top class.'

Balanchine provided popular young jockey Frankie Dettori with his first Irish classic victory. Son of the successful jockey Gianfranco Dettori, who rode as first jockey for Henry Cecil for a period in the 1970s, and who indeed won the Irish 2,000 Guineas for the late Stuart Murless in 1977 on Pampapaul, young Frankie established himself during 1994 as the natural successor to Lester Piggott in the affections of the legions of betting shop punters who follow racing on a daily basis.

Riding throughout the calendar year, taking in all-weather racing at Southwell and Lingfield as well as traditional racing on the turf, Dettori became champion jockey in 1994 with a final total of 233 winners. With his bubbly personality, he has endeared himself to racing fans everywhere and was seen at his most exuberant after he guided the Irish 2,000 Guineas winner Barathea to a tremendously popular success in the Breeders Cup Mile at Churchill Downs towards the end of 1994. Dettori will also be associated in the racing public's consciousness with the marvellously speedy sprinter, Lochsong, with whom he shared a string of brilliant victories, including successive triumphs in the Prix de l'Abbaye.

Although Balanchine had been a most emphatic winner of the Budweiser Derby, the perception that she had beaten a collection of non-stayers was one that was still aired in some racing circles in the immediate aftermath of her victory. As later events were to show, however, this viewpoint simply did not stand up, and Henry Cecil's dispassionate analysis was to be proved spot on. Certainly, ante-post bookmakers took the Budweiser Derby form at its face value, for Balanchine was instantly installed as ante-post favourite for the Prix de l'Arc de Triomphe.

After the Curragh, the racing world looked forward keenly to Balanchine taking on the colts of her own generation again and indeed older horses, the better to assess her standing. Less than a week after Balanchine's Budweiser Derby triumph, the Epsom hero Erhaab went down to a surprise defeat in the Coral Eclipse against the older horses, Ezzoud and Bob's Return. There seemed to be no valid excuse for the Epsom Derby winner, who if anything should have been suited both to the distance and the blistering pace set by the 1993 Doncaster St Leger winner, Bob's Return.

Not long after the Eclipse, however, there was very disappointing news about the Budweiser Derby heroine. Balanchine suffered a serious injury in the form of an obstruction to her small intestine. There was for a time genuine concern that the filly would have to be put down, but fortunately she recovered, although the setback was enough to bring her season to a premature conclusion. At the time of writing (January 1995), reports from Dubai are that Balanchine, who went there for the winter, is in very good form and present plans are to aim her at all the big mile and a half races during 1995. If this happens, and let's hope

that it does, Balanchine will be the first horse since Old Vic to be kept in training as a four-year-old after winning an Irish Derby.

With the Budweiser Derby heroine sadly *hors de combat*, the way seemed clear for Erhaab to re-establish his reputation after his Eclipse failure. He lined up as favourite for the King George VI and Queen Elizabeth Diamond Stakes against a pretty strong looking field.

In the event, the race had a sensational beginning when Walter Swinburn was unseated from the Coral Eclipse winner, Ezzoud, before the field had gone twenty-five yards. Ezzoud continued riderless and proceeded to interfere persistently with a number of the main protagonists throughout the race. Erhaab, about whom there had been rumours concerning his well-being in the run-up to the race, was one of those who was hampered by Ezzoud. However, that alone was insufficient excuse to account for another disappointing display by the Epsom Derby winner, who eventually finished a moderate seventh.

The winner was none other than King's Theatre, who gamely held off White Muzzle — runner-up for the second successive year — throughout the final furlong, in the process finally dispelling any doubts about his stamina. Even the aforementioned Mr Underwood acknowledged that he had been wrong about King's Theatre, who proved himself at Ascot a genuine Group 1 class colt, as well as gaining ample compensation for his two runner-up placings at Epsom and the Curragh.

Of course King's Theatre's success at Ascot was a tremendous boost to the

Budweiser Derby and to his easy conqueror at the Curragh, Balanchine. It was unarguable that on all known form, Balanchine was clearly better than the colts and the best three-year-old of her generation.

Further lustre was added to Balanchine's reputation later in the season when the Budweiser Derby fifth, Tikkanen, proceeded to mop up two Grade 1 contests in the United States, the Turf Classic at Belmont and the Breeder's Cup Turf at Churchill Downs.

At the year end, the international classification for 1994 merely served to confirm Balanchine's pre-eminence. In topping the ratings for three-year-olds and older horses, she became only the second of her age and sex — the 1979 Arc winner Three Troikas was the other — to achieve this notable distinction.

BUDWEISER IRISH DERBY

1M 4F

SUNDAY 26 JUNE 1994

GOING: GOOD TO YIELDING

WINNER: Maktoum Al Maktoum/Godolphin Racing's Balanchine by Storm Bird out of Morning Devotion
L. Dettori

SECOND: King's Theatre by Sadler's Wells out of Regal Beauty
M. J. Kinane

THIRD: Colonel Collins by El Gran Senor out of Kanmary
J. Reid

S P. 5/1 1/1f 11/2
Winner trained by H. Ibrahim

ALSO: Alriffa 4th, Tikkanen 5th, Ionio 6th, Cajarian 7th, Khamaseen 8th, Concept House 9th and last

Winner: 3rd favourite
Distances: 4½ lengths, 3½ lengths
Value to winner: £348,000
Time: 2 m 32.7 s
Timeform rating of winner: 131.

1995

BUDWEISER IRISH DERBY

1995 marked the tenth year in which the Irish Derby was run under the auspices of the Anheuser-Busch corporation. On a warm, pleasant midsummer's day, a record crowd turned up at the Curragh and were treated to a splendid race, with the outcome remaining in doubt until the very last stride.

The principal focus of interest for most of the record crowd was the hot favourite, the British-owned, bred and trained Celtic Swing. Even before the start of the 1995 flat season proper, there was intense speculation in racing circles as to the future prospects of Celtic Swing, the top-rated juvenile of 1994.

Rated 6 lb clear of his rivals in the official handicappers classifications, Celtic Swing had been unbelievably adjudged 15 lb superior to the next highest rated 2-y-o, Pennekamp, by the highly respected Timeform organisation. If Timeform were to be believed, Celtic Swing only had to turn up to make a clean sweep of 1995's top prizes.

As a juvenile, Celtic Swing had run three times and won three times. After a most impressive win in the Hyperion Stakes at Ascot on fast ground, Celtic Swing had demolished the opposition in the Group I Racing Post Trophy at Doncaster, finishing twelve lengths clear of Annus Mirabilis in second place. The going at Doncaster was good to soft, and the cut in the ground seemed to bring out the best in the colt by Damister.

Similar ground prevailed at Newbury when Celtic Swing reappeared as a 3-y-o. Ridden by his regular partner Kevin Darley, the combination landed the Greenham Stakes quite comfortably by one and a quarter lengths from Bahri. Was it the performance of a champion? Time alone would tell.

Owned by millionaire Peter Savill and trained in Sussex by the daughter of the Duke of Norfolk, Lady Herries, Celtic Swing had captured the imagination of the English racing fraternity as few horses have done in recent years. After his Newbury success,

Celtic Swing's supporters could not envisage defeat for the almost black colt in the Newmarket 2,000 Guineas, and he was a heavily backed 5/4 on favourite on the day.

The 2,000 Guineas was run on a blisteringly hot day, and the ground rode fast. When Celtic Swing took the lead entering the dip victory looked certain, but to the consternation of the colt's many backers, the André Fabre-trained second favourite, the aforementioned Pennekamp, displaying a blinding turn of foot, swept past Celtic Swing and won a shade cosily by a head from the rallying runner-up. Bahri was a good third.

The race had been thrilling, the best 2,000 Guineas for a number of years, and immediately afterwards talk of a return match at Epsom between the two high-class colts was on everyone's lips. Events, however, were to take quite a different turn.

To the consternation of sections of the English racing press, the connections of Celtic Swing opted for the French Derby (the Prix du Jockey-Club) in preference to Epsom. The prestige and standing of the Epsom Derby, a subject of considerable debate for a number of years, was deemed to have suffered a mortal blow.

The decision to go to France was, however, to be proved correct. Celtic Swing notched a priceless Derby success at Chantilly, beating the French-trained pair Poliglote and Winged Love by half a length and a short head in a race which developed into a six furlong sprint. The soft ground was in Celtic Swing's favour, but the slow early pace was not considered to have been suitable and the colt was not overly impressive in victory. Indeed, in the aftermath of the race there were some who questioned whether Celtic Swing's stamina would survive a true run mile and a half race.

Next stop for Celtic Swing after Chantilly was the Curragh. Whatever the views of others, quite plainly the connections of the French Derby winner had no stamina doubts about their colt, for they announced their intention of ensuring a strong pace at the Curragh by purchasing a pacemaker, Daraydan, to run in the second colours at the County Kildare venue.

Meanwhile, at Epsom, Pennekamp was expected by most professionals to prove himself a top-class racehorse in his Derby bid. Sadly, however, the son of Bering never got a chance to do so. Sustaining a hairline fracture to a fetlock joint in the course of the race, Pennekamp was not involved in the finish. The winner was the 14/1 shot, Lammtarra, who cut down his rivals in the final furlong with impressive ease, winning by a length and three-quarters of a length from Tamure and Presenting.

After proving to connections that he had recovered from his exertions at Epsom, the superbly bred Lammtarra was nominated to take his place in the Budweiser Irish Derby. The prospect of a Curragh showdown between the two Derby winners was a tantalising dish to set before racing *aficionados*, but as so often happens, fate intervened to dash hopes of such a meeting. Just days before the Irish Derby, Lammtarra wrenched a hind leg in training, and though the injury wasn't a serious one, the timing was such as to rule the Nijinsky colt out of the Curragh classic.

It was a bitter blow for all concerned, not least the Curragh management, and there was to be another shock for the race organisers on the day before the race. The Epsom third, Presenting, who had been second favourite for the classic, panicked as he was being loaded at Cambridge airport, banged himself about in the plane and, after being taken off, refused to go back on board.

Despite the defections, a competitive race took shape, the field of thirteen being the largest number to face the starter since Law Society beat twelve opponents ten years earlier. Apart from the favourite Celtic Swing, at least half a dozen of the contestants could be given a serious chance on all known form.

Among these were two colts who had finished behind Celtic Swing at Chantilly, Winged Love, who, as mentioned previously, had been a close third, and the Godolphin representative, Classic Cliche, who was substituting for the injured Lammtarra. A relatively inexperienced colt, Winged Love had been finishing to some effect at Chantilly, and as he had only just over half a length to make up on Celtic Swing on the book, his chance was there for all to see. As Sheikh Mohammed's first choice, doubtless the owner was hopeful that Winged Love would prove a worthy substitute for the sidelined Pennekamp.

Classic Cliche had been two lengths behind Winged Love in fourth place at Chantilly, and after the race jockey Walter Swinburn reported that his mount had been unlucky in running. Subsequently a slightly disappointing two and a half lengths second to Pentire in the King Edward VII Stakes at Royal

Ascot, Classic Cliche was one of the supplementary entries for the Budweiser Derby and could not be left out of calculations.

In the absence of both Lammtarra and Presenting, Epsom form was represented at the Curragh — perhaps a little precariously — by three of the also-rans, Court of Honour, Humbel and Munwar. The Peter Chapple-Hyam-trained Court of Honour had finished best of these in fifth place, just over three lengths behind Lammtarra, with Humbel a further three and a half lengths back in eighth place, and Munwar seven lengths adrift of Humbel in ninth position.

Court of Honour had started at 66/1 at Epsom, and his performance there must have both surprised and delighted connections. His proximity to Lammtarra was one reason, however, why form students placed a question mark against the Epsom form.

The Hamdan Al Maktoum-owned Munwar had been significantly backed at Epsom and wound up third favourite on the day. Munwar, however, was a big disappointment, but if one were prepared to overlook his Epsom run and look back to his Lingfield Derby Trial victory, the Kalaglow colt was definitely one for the short list.

Also from England came the Michael Stoute-trained Annus Mirabilis, who had undergone a somewhat unorthodox preparation for the classic. After a good second to rival Classic Cliche in the Dante Stakes over an extended ten furlongs at York, he had been literally nosed out of it by Torrential in the Group I Prix Jean Prat at Chantilly over nine furlongs. Brought back again in distance, Annus Mirabilis had contested the one mile St James's Palace

Stakes at Royal Ascot when he had been a respectable five and a half length fifth to Bahri. With his trainer's outstanding record at the Curragh, Annus Mirabilis's chances could not be ignored.

Perhaps the most interesting runner of all, though, was the principal home–trained hope, the unbeaten Definite Article. Like Classic Cliche and Winged Love, Definite Article was a supplementary entry for the Budweiser Derby. As it cost IR£60,000 for the privilege, it was clear that connections had a high opinion of their charge.

Definite Article was very inexperienced and had run only three times in all. On his second juvenile outing he had annexed the Group I National Stakes, although the form was not at the time rated very highly. On his seasonal reappearance, Definite Article had surprised many by the ease with which he gave weight and a two length beating to the Aga Khan's Shemaran in a listed race over ten furlongs at the Curragh. His trainer, Dermot Weld, was not at all surprised, however, and made it clear in post-race interviews that he regarded Definite Article as a high class colt.

The Weld stable had a second runner in the Derby, the Epsom also-ran, Humbel. On ground faster than he liked, Humbel had performed respectably at Epsom, but with Michael Kinane electing to partner Definite Article, the inference was that the Moyglare Stud-owned colt was superior to his stable companion. The major doubt entertained about Definite Article (and it was a serious one) was whether the Indian Ridge colt would see out the twelve furlong trip. If he were to do so, he represented Ireland's best chance of winning the prize since St Jovite three years earlier.

The fifth race on the card, the spectacle and sense of occasion was greatly enhanced when the runners for the Budweiser Irish Derby were paraded around on the course in front of the main grandstand before being mounted by their jockeys.

Weather conditions in Ireland in the ten days before the Derby had been untypically hot. Extensive watering had been undertaken by Brian Kavanagh and his team, and the results were clearly visible in the rich verdant green of the watered sections of the racecourse as opposed to the parched brown of the remainder. The going was officially good to firm, and a fast run race seemed in prospect.

Betting on the big race took quite a wide range. Put in initially at 5/4, Celtic Swing tightened to 11/10, but 5/4 was freely available again at the off. Definite Article, though quite well supported, eased from 4's to 5's, where he was joined by Winged Love, who hardened from 6's. Classic Cliche attracted support from 10/1 to 8/1, while Annus Mirabilis, though put in at 6's had few takers and drifted out to 9/1. Munwar, as at Epsom, had his backers and came in a couple of points to join Annus Mirabilis at 9/1. It was 16/1 Court of Honour and 25/1 and upwards bar those mentioned.

The loading process at the stalls went off smoothly, the last two to be loaded being the joint second favourites, Winged Love and Definite Article. From the outset the English-trained trio, Court of Honour, Classic Cliche and Double Eclipse were first to show. After about a furlong Celtic Swing's pacemaker, Daraydan, made his way to the head of affairs and took the field along at a good clip.

Daraydan was followed in the early stages by Munwar, whom Willie Carson had taken to the fore, Double Eclipse, Court of Honour and Classic Cliche. Winged Love was on the inside in sixth place going well, with Celtic Swing just outside the French-trained challenger in seventh place. Ireland's main hope, Definite Article, was tracking Winged Love.

At the half-way stage Daraydan had done enough and dropped back through the field very quickly. The order, then, as the field moved into the final six furlongs was Munwar, Double Eclipse, Court of Honour, Classic Cliche, Winged Love, Celtic Swing, Annus Mirabilis, Definite Article and Humbel, with the remainder closely bunched.

There was little change as the field descended towards the straight and all were in contention with the exception of the trailing Daraydan. Munwar relinquished his lead about four furlongs out as Double Eclipse took over. Turning into the straight Munwar dropped out quickly as Double Eclipse and Court of Honour duelled for the lead. Celtic Swing improved on the outside, as meantime Winged Love took advantage of a nice gap to go through on the rails. Definite Article nudged Annus Mirabilis slightly as the two horses simultaneously moved into a challenging position on the wide outside.

At the two furlong marker it was anybody's race. Six horses were spread across the track, with the winner impossible to call. Winged Love had got a dream run up the inside and just about led on the far rail from Double Eclipse, Court of Honour, Celtic Swing, who was already under the whip, and on the outside Definite Article and Annus Mirabilis.

With just under two furlongs to go, Celtic Swing dropped out beaten, and shortly afterwards Double Eclipse and Court of Honour had nothing left to give. Racing towards the final furlong Definite Article made ground on Winged Love and edged into a narrow lead with about a furlong to run. Annus Mirabilis was a close third, with the Irish-trained outsider Oscar Schindler, who had to be switched outside to make his challenge, running on well in fourth place.

Under Mick Kinane, Definite Article went half a length up well inside the final furlong and looked all over a winner. Irish cheers rose in anticipation of a home-trained success. But with the winning post in sight the French challenger, Winged Love, who had stayed on the fence all the way up the straight, could be seen gaining ground on Definite Article.

As the two horses raced together towards the line, Definite Article, feeling the strain, veered ever so slightly towards his French-trained rival, and perhaps that was his undoing. In the final dramatic strides, with the crowd in full voice, Winged Love, ridden by 22-year-old Olivier Peslier, got his head in front and at the line had a short head to spare over the gallant and luckless Definite Article.

A photo finish was called for, but few had any doubt that the André Fabre-trained colt had snatched it at the death, and the camera duly confirmed the fact. Annus Mirabilis ran a great race to finish third, three-quarters of a length back, and Kevin Prendergast's Oscar Schindler was a splendid fourth, a further three-quarters of a length adrift.

The big disappointment of the race was, of course, the short-priced favourite Celtic Swing, who finished a weary eighth of the thirteen starters, beaten about seven and a half lengths in all. The fast ground was cited by some as the reason for the favourite's failure, but owner Peter Savill refused to accept that as an excuse.

It was noteworthy that after the race, the legion of British journalists present were far more interested in listening to post-mortems on Celtic Swing's defeat than anything that the winning connections of Winged Love had to say. Despite endless lessons, it is always difficult to accept dreams turning to dust. Whether Celtic Swing will ever run again remains to be seen. What is certain is that the Damister colt's pretensions to greatness were finally laid to rest in the home straight in the Budweiser Irish Derby on 2 July 1995.

A few further details are worth noting about the race. The time — 2 minutes 30.1 seconds — was good, although considering the early pace and the state of the ground, not outstanding. The three Epsom also-rans who competed — Court of Honour, Humbel and Munwar — performed poorly, finishing ninth, eleventh and twelfth of the thirteen runners. And the value of the form of the race overall was open to question in that rank outsiders Damancher and I'm Supposin ran surprisingly well, finishing sixth and seventh respectively, the former just over four lengths off the winner. With similar doubts expressed about the Epsom form, a definitive view on the merits of the 1995 classic crop would have to await a later date.

Before going on to other things, it is worth sparing a thought for Michael Kinane.

On Definite Article, Ireland's champion jockey finished second for the third time in the only major race to have eluded him so far. A short head defeat made it all the more galling, but no blame whatever can attach to the jockey. As Kinane himself confirmed afterwards, it was clear that Definite Article just failed to see out the final gruelling 100 yards of the stamina-sapping trip.

None of the above comments should detract a whit from the winner's achievement. In victory Winged Love proved himself a rapidly improving 3-y-o, with the potential to improve even further. The first French-trained winner of Ireland's premier classic since Malacate in 1976, and the fifth in all, Winged Love is master trainer André Fabre's first Derby success anywhere. It seems unlikely that it will be his last.

From the first crop of In The Wings, a proven Group 1 performer, and himself a son of Sadler's Wells, Winged Love is the first foal of her dam, J'ai Deux Amours, who won a listed race over a mile at Deauville and was also Group 2 placed. Winged Love was also Sheikh Mohammed's second Irish Derby winner in his own right, following upon Old Vic in 1989, although Balanchine in 1994 almost counts as another.

The Sheikh's wonderful gesture in donating all of his Curragh winnings (almost £350,000) to local charities, including the St Vincent de Paul, is proof positive, if it were needed, that money alone has little to do with the supreme enjoyment and pleasure that he derives from his extensive world-wide involvement with the thoroughbred horse.

A final thought. What of Pennekamp whom André Fabre believed to be the jewel in his particular crown of classic hopefuls, before his Epsom mishap? What indeed?

Life is rarely neatly packaged and the unexpected lurks around every corner. But in sport it is easier to impose or detect an order on the ceaseless flow of thrills and excitement. This book opened with the first sponsored Irish Derby of 1962 and featured a pulsating clash between a French-trained contender and a home-grown hero. With a sense of symmetry that can only be applauded, the equine descendants of Tambourine II and Arctic Storm provided in 1995 another thrilling Hiberno-Gallic clash. And, as in 1962, so too did the victory go to France, and by the narrowest of margins. One can only echo what the French themselves would say — *C'est la vie.*

The 1995 renewal was in fact the thirty-fourth year of sponsorship of the Irish Derby. The original sponsors have since 1986 been replaced by Anheuser-Busch, and under its direction both the promotion and the staging of the premier Irish classic have been notably improved. Today the prestige of the Budweiser Irish Derby stands higher than ever before.

The splendid timing of the classic, and the essentially fair yet demanding nature of the Curragh racetrack seem guaranteed to ensure that the Budweiser Irish Derby will continue to remain both the glamorous showpiece of the Irish racing calendar, as well as occupying an honoured place in the select list of the world's great classic races.

BUDWEISER IRISH DERBY

1M 4F

SUNDAY 2 JULY 1995

GOING: GOOD TO FIRM

WINNER: Sheikh Mohammed's Winged Love by In The Wings out of J'ai Deux Amours
O. Peslier

SECOND: Definite Article by Indian Ridge out of Summer Fashion
M. J. Kinane

THIRD: Annus Mirabilis by Warning out of Anna Petrovna
W. R. Swinburn

S.P. 5/1 5/1 9/1
Winner trained by A. Fabre

ALSO: Oscar Schindler 4th, Classic Cliche 5th, Damancher 6th, I'm Supposin 7th, Celtic Swing 8th, Court of Honour 9th, Double Eclipse 10th, Humbel 11th, Munwar 12th, Daraydan 13th & last
Celtic Swing 5/4 fav.
Winner: Joint 2nd favourite
Distances: sh. hd, ¾ length
Value to winner: £338,350
Time: 2 m 30.1 s
Timeform rating of winner: N/A.

APPENDIX 1

SUMMARY OF RESULTS

	WINNER	S.P.	SECOND	THIRD
1962	Tambourine II	15/2	Arctic Storm	Sebring
1963	Ragusa	100/7	Vic Mo Chroi	Tiger
1964	Santa Claus	4/7f	Lionhearted	Sunseeker
1965	Meadow Court	11/10f	Convamore	Wedding Present
1966	Sodium	13/2	Charlottown	Paveh
1967	Ribocco	5/2f	Sucaryl	Dart Board
1968	Ribero	100/6	Sir Ivor	Val d'Aoste
1969	Prince Regent	7/2	Ribofilio	Reindeer
1970	Nijinsky	4/11f	Meadowville	Master Guy
1971	Irish Ball	7/2	Lombardo	Guillemot
1972	Steel Pulse	10/1	Scottish Rifle	Ballymore
1973	Weaver's Hall	33/1	Ragapan	Buoy
1974	English Prince	8/1	Imperial Prince	Sir Penfro
1975	Grundy	9/10f	King Pellinore	Anne's Pretender
1976	Malacate	5/1	Empery	Northern Treasure
1977	The Minstrel	11/10f	Lucky Sovereign	Classic Example
1978	Shirley Heights	5/4f	Exdirectory	Hawaiian Sound
1979	Troy	4/9f	Dickens Hill	Bohemian Grove
1980	Tyrnavos	25/1	Prince Bee	Ramian
1981	Shergar	1/3f	Cut Above	Dance Bid
1982	Assert	4/7f	Silver Hawk	Patcher
1983	Shareef Dancer	8/1	Caerleon	Teenoso
1984	El Gran Senor	2/7f	Rainbow Quest	Dahar
1985	Law Society	15/8f	Theatrical	Damister
1986	Shahrastani	1/1f	Bonhomie	Bakharoff
1987	Sir Harry Lewis	6/1	Naheez	Entitled
1988	Khayasi	4/5f	Insan	Glacial Storm
1989	Old Vic	4/11f	Observation Post	Ile de Nisky
1990	Salsabil	11/4	Deploy	Belmez
1991	Generous	1/1f	Suave Dancer	Star of Gdansk
1992	St Jovite	7/2	Dr Devious	Contested Bid
1993	Commander In Chief	4/7f	Hernando	Foresee
1994	Balanchine	5/1	King's Theatre	Colonel Collins
1995	Winged Love	5/1	Definite Article	Annus Mirabilis

(1 9 6 2 – 1 9 9 5)

WINNING JOCKEY	WINNING TRAINER	
R. Poincelet	E. Pollet (Fr)	1962
G. Bougoure	P. J. Prendergast (Irl)	1963
W. Burke	J. M. Rogers (Irl)	1964
L. Piggott	P. J. Prendergast (Irl)	1965
F. Durr	G. Todd (UK)	1966
L. Piggott	R. F. Johnson Houghton (UK)	1967
L. Piggott	R. F. Johnson Houghton (UK)	1968
G. Lewis	E. Pollet (Fr)	1969
L. Ward	M. V. O'Brien (Irl)	1970
A. Gilbert	P. Lallie (Fr)	1971
W. Williamson	A. E. Breasley (UK)	1972
G. McGrath	S. McGrath (Irl)	1973
Y. Saint-Martin	P. T. Walwyn (UK)	1974
P. Eddery	P. T. Walwyn (UK)	1975
P. Paquet	F. Boutin (Fr)	1976
L. Piggott	M. V. O'Brien (Irl)	1977
G. Starkey	J. L. Dunlop (UK)	1978
W. Carson	W. R. Hern (UK)	1979
A. Murray	B. Hobbs (UK)	1980
L. Piggott	M. R. Stoute (UK)	1981
C. Roche	D. V. O'Brien (Irl)	1982
W. R. Swinburn	M. R. Stoute (UK)	1983
P. Eddery	M. V. O'Brien (Irl)	1984
P. Eddery	M. V. O'Brien (Irl)	1985
W. R. Swinburn	M. R. Stoute	1986
J. Reid	B. W. Hills (UK)	1987
R. Cochrane	L. M. Cumani (UK)	1988
S. Cauthen	H. R. A. Cecil (UK)	1989
W. Carson	J. L. Dunlop (UK)	1990
A. Munro	P. F. I. Cole (UK)	1991
C. Roche	J. S. Bolger (Irl)	1992
P. Eddery	H. R. A. Cecil (UK)	1993
L. Dettori	H. Ibrahim (Dubai)	1994
O. Peslier	A. Fabre (Fr)	1995

APPENDIX 2

SUCCESSFUL JOCKEYS (1962–1995)

L. Piggott	5	W. Williamson	1
P. Eddery	4	G. McGrath	1
W. Carson	2	Y. Saint-Martin	1
C. Roche	2	P. Paquet	1
W. R. Swinburn	2	G. Starkey	1
R. Poincelet	1	A. Murray	1
G. Bougoure	1	J. Reid	1
W. Burke	1	R. Cochrane	1
F. Durr	1	S. Cauthen	1
G. Lewis	1	A. Munro	1
L. Ward	1	L. Dettori	1
A. Gilbert	1	O. Peslier	1

APPENDIX 3

SUCCESSFUL TRAINERS (1962–1995)

M. V. O'Brien	4	S. McGrath	1
M. R. Stoute	3	F. Boutin	1
E. Pollet	2	W. R. Hern	1
P. J. Prendergast	2	B. Hobbs	1
R. F. Johnson Houghton	2	D. V. O'Brien	1
P. T. Walwyn	2	B. W. Hills	1
J. L. Dunlop	2	L. M. Cumani	1
H. R. A. Cecil	2	P. F. I. Cole	1
J. M Rogers	1	J. S. Bolger	1
G. Todd	1	H. Ibrahim	1
P. Lallie	1	A. Fabre	1
A. E. Breasley	1		

APPENDIX 4

SUCCESSFUL SIRES (1962–1995)

Northern Dancer	4	Busted	1
Ribot	3	Lucky Debonnair	1
Petingo	2	Mill Reef	1
Great Nephew	2	Blakeney	1
Alleged	2	Be My Guest	1
Sadler's Wells	2	Nijinsky	1
Princequillo	1	Ile de Bourbon	1
Chamossaire	1	Caerleon	1
Court Harwell	1	Pleasant Colony	1
Psidium	1	Dancing Brave	1
Right Royal V	1	Storm Bird	1
Baldric II	1	In the Wings	1
Diatome	1		

SELECT BIBLIOGRAPHY

Baerlein, R., *Shergar and the Aga Khan's Thoroughbred Empire*, Michael Joseph, London 1984.

Braddock P., *Braddock's Big Race Guide*, Longman, London 1989.

Brie S. M., *Diamond Days — A History of the King George VI and Queen Elizabeth Diamond Stakes*, Hodder & Stoughton, London 1990.

Cauz, L. E., *The Plate — A Royal Tradition*, Daneau Publishers, Toronto 1984.

D'Arcy, F. A., *Horses, Lords & Racing Men — The Turf Club 1790–1990*, The Turf Club, The Curragh 1991.

Dossenbach, M. & H., *Irish Horses*, Gill & Macmillan, Dublin 1977.

Eddery, P., with Lee A., *Pat Eddery — To Be a Champion*, Hodder & Stoughton, London 1992.

Francis, D., *Lester — The Official Biography*, Michael Joseph, London 1986.

Herbert, I., & O'Brien J., *Vincent O'Brien's Great Horses*, Pelham Books, London 1984.

Hislop J., & Swannell D., *The Faber Book of the Turf*, Faber & Faber Ltd, London 1990.

Karter, J., *Lester — Return of a Legend*, Headline Book Publishing plc, London 1992.

Mortimer, R., with Neligan, T., *The Epsom Derby*, Michael Joseph, London 1984.

Mortimer, R., *The Encyclopaedia of Flat Racing*, Robert Hale & Co., London 1971.

Seth-Smith, M. (ed.), *A History of Flat Racing*, Times-Mirror, London 1978.

Smith, R., *Vincent O'Brien, The Master of Ballydoyle*, Virgin Books, London 1990.

Smith, R., *The High Rollers of the Turf*, Sporting Books Publishers, Dublin 1992.

Tanner, M. & Cranham, G., *The Guinness Book of Great Jockeys of the Flat*, Guinness Publishing, London 1992.

Tanner M., *Great Racing Partnerships*, The Sportsman's Press, London 1987.

Turner, C., *In Search of Shergar*, Sidgwick & Jackson, London 1984.

Welcome, J., *Irish Horse-Racing — An Illustrated History*, Gill & Macmillan, Dublin 1982.

Williams, G. St John & Hyland, F. P. M., *The Irish Derby 1866–1979*, J. A. Allen, London 1980.

Wilson, J., *Lester Piggott — The Pictorial Biography*, Queen Anne Press, Macdonald & Co., London 1985.

INDEX